Like, how does he find the time to read so widely and think so deeply? Following on the heels of his dynamite *Convergence*  tackles the huge issue of deliverance. I have r out the fifty years I have been in ministry, bu Bibli- cally and theologically thorough, and *erance*. This is exactly the kind of resource we be all Jesus wants us to be. Bible-book by ...ough the truth about the ministry of deliverance. ...u then step-by-step, Jon walks us into the nitty-gritty dynamics of such ministry in the local church. Would that this book had been available the last few decades. Thank God it is available now!

Darrell Johnson, Teaching Fellow for Regent College,
Scholar-in-Residence for The Way Church and Canadian Leaders Network,
Author of multiple books including *Discipleship on the Edge: An Expository
Journey Through Revelation* and *The Glory of Preaching*

Deliverance is a groundbreaking book in the field of Spiritual Warfare. I can't think of any other book like it. Jon uniquely blends excellent Biblical Theology, Church History, and extremely practical case studies that he's gathered throughout his vast ministry experience. This book has been personally helpful to me as I seek to equip people in my own context to minister to those in spiritual bondage. I highly recommended it.

Felipe Assis, Senior Pastor of Crossbridge Church
and Co-Director of City to City North American

This is an amazing resource around topics many would rather avoid but which is as real as anything else we face today in ministry. Jon has done a great job laying out the theological/biblical teachings on the demonic and spiritual realm and the practical/pragmatic realities from years of actual on-the-ground practical ministry. This book will serve you so well as a Christian, a leader, or just someone interested in this extremely important topic.

Mark Clark, Senior Pastor of Village Church
Author of *The Problem of God* and *The Problem of Jesus*

Deliverance is a game-changing book. It is guidance to those who want to be more strategic in spiritual warfare. It is a roadmap to those who don't know where to begin. Having watched some of this story unfold in real-time, I know that Jon's masterful telling of this deeply personal story will teach, encourage, and challenge you. I am thrilled for the Church that this book is here, now. The ministry that has grown out of what you're about to read is as wild, miraculous, beautiful and life-giving as you hope it is! Lives changed, people set free, churches learning to stand in their authority, spiritual gifts developed, sins confessed, chains broken, and oh my goodness is the love of God *there*. Rise up, Church. Buckle up, Reader. Let's see the captives set free in Jesus' Name.

Nathalie Wylie, Prayer Pastor at Sanctus Church

Deliverance is the new textbook for conservative AND charismatic pastors, churches and believers whose eyes are open to the spiritual and demonic realities around them. Jon combines accurate and comprehensive research alongside real life experiences, personal and ministry that bring a unique credibility to a controversial tension in the body of Christ. His exploration of current deliverance positions and models is extremely helpful—you will find yourself in one of them. Then, Jon explains the strengths Sanctus Church has synthesized into their model. This book will inspire you, challenge you and hopefully move you to register for Sanctus Church's additional training and network mentorship. I only wish I'd read it twenty years ago.

Ken Dyck, Founder and Executive Director of
Freedom Session International

DELIVERANCE

A Journey Toward the Unexpected

By

Jon Thompson

Author Photo by Matthew Robin, matthewrobin.com

Cover Design by Amanda Blake

ISBN: 978-1-950007-64-6

This book is dedicated to the 100's of volunteers and staff
at Sanctus Church who have courageously prayed
and worked to see people set free in Jesus' Name.

TABLE OF CONTENTS

FOREWORD

For over thirty years my wife lived with chronic illness. We saw every type of doctor you could imagine, lost count of how many treatments and therapies we tried, spent thousands of dollars, gave up all hope of her getting better, and started making plans for an early death. I was in my mid-thirties making plans to be a single father.

Then we discovered a generational curse. Four generations ago, a shaman in Mexico City had been hired to curse the firstborn daughters of her family line. We knew there was a lot of sickness and death in her extended family, but had never connected the dots. We immediately did the genogram math and realized, every single firstborn daughter for four generations had either died young or been struck with chronic, debilitating illness. All the way down to my wife T.

What the heck? It sounded like something out of a movie or fantasy novel, not my living room in Portland, OR, a "secular" city. While I had a theological category for a generational curse (curses show up all through the Old Testament), I had zero experiential knowledge of how to proceed. So, I called Jon. Jon Thompson has, for an increasing number of us, become a leading voice on deliverance ministry, especially those of us facing a rise in demonic manifestations in secular cities. Jon was beyond helpful – wise, experienced, thoughtful, biblical, and deeply prophetic. He gave us an advance copy of the book you're about to read, which became our working framework (Spoiler alert: it's excellent). Under Jon's tutelage we arranged for a deliverance session, fasted and prayed, and came expectant.

I'd never seen anything like it. Part of my wife's illness involved facial spasms due to a movement disorder. During the prayer to break the generational curse, T's entire body began to spasm and shake, worse than we've ever seen. (I should clarify, she is a very calm, down to earth personality, not remotely given to emotional expressiveness of this sort). The moment she prayed to break the curse, her entire body stopped shaking. Her eyes (which were spasming so bad they could not open), opened wide. It was like watching a fog lift off her entire body. Her back straightened. Her facial muscles were perfectly still. She started to laugh with joy.

Of course we tested the healing. "Wait and see," I said.

But she was completely healed. All symptoms gone. Decades of chronic health issues, ended in an instant.

Her healing and deliverance have since ushered in a whole new era in our spiritual formation, and opened up a whole new dimension to our view of the spiritual life.

How many T's are in our churches and lives? Men and women and even children who deeply love Jesus and follow him, but are living under demonic pressure?

What would it look like to live in deliverance?

John Mark Comer
Pastor of Teaching and Vision
Bridgetown Church

INTRODUCTION

Within much of the church, the conversation about the influence of demons has been dismissed, ignored, and exaggerated but rarely understood. Many Christians and non-Christians experience the presence of evil but do not have the categories to evaluate the experience, let alone be set free from their presence. No longer can these situations be located only overseas or reduced to certain ethnic groups with certain religious experiences. The truth is, this has always been around us but now, because of massive paradigm shifts, these experiences can be more easily talked about and engaged with. They are seemingly found in all areas of life regardless of education, ethnicity, or geographical location.

We live in a post-Christian, de-Christian, postsocial, postmodern (yet modern), multicultural, radically globalized, fully mobile, highly personal world. One of the great paradoxes of life today is an ever-increasing level of connectedness, paralleled by increasing levels of fracturing. Social media offers the hope of bringing us all together but is often the instrument for tearing us apart. The long held assumption that an increased awareness of diversity would easily lead to understanding and unity now seems to be morphing culture into something reminiscent of the ominous situation described at the end of the book of Judges: *"In those days Israel had no king; everyone did as they saw fit"* (Judges 21:25).

I happen to live just outside of Toronto, Canada—one of the most global cities on earth. The fourth largest city in North America, it's rated as one of the top five most multicultural cities in the world, with over 150-300 languages spoken every day. It's an amazing place to live. Our city can be seen as a microcosm of the world and we are trying to grow the church right in the middle of it.

Here in Canada, as in much of the West, Christians find themselves more and more at the edge of society, not the center. Along with marginalization, we now experience increased hostility and intolerance toward expressions of a Christian worldview. And more, with all the nations of the world here, Toronto is deeply religious, deeply spiritual, and deeply secular all at once. The need to deal with the kingdom of darkness in all directions is now a must. As you read this, you will hear from our journey of trying to deal with evil with the good news of Jesus to many people in multiple directions.

This book will provide the background and outline of the hybrid matrix of deliverance we use at Sanctus Church, which has assisted the pastoral leadership and our people in dealing with this growing and/or rediscovered phenomenon. This process has not only helped people come to faith in Jesus Christ, but to also be set free as they journey with Christ. Simply put, this is a snapshot of where we are today in our journey. Do we have all the answers? No, but these chapters outline who we were, where we are, and where we are going. In addition, this is a systematic explanation for this type of ministry. Our current practices are outlined biblically, historically, logically, and from experience.

If you are a pastor or church leader, it's important you understand that we don't consider our experience unique and unrepeatable or the exact template of how God must work in deliverance. We are convinced the biblical principles found here will apply anywhere, but local and time factors will shape your expressions. I believe you will find much of what we have done helpful, even our mistakes will show you what not to do. But there are significant time and faithfulness factors that you can't ignore without generating problems. We've been at this now for almost two decades. If we had known everything we know today back then and expected to "plug and play" a deliverance ministry into an unsuspecting local church, things would have blown up. These things take time. Sometimes, mistakes are actually necessary tools God uses to shape us. Faithfulness is not a spiritual sprint; it's a marathon.

I would be very glad if you come to the end of this book with a clearer picture of where to start and a vision for where you want to eventually get to, rather than expecting to implement a full-blown deliverance ministry right out of the gate with followers of Jesus for whom this may well be a whole new experience. I can almost guarantee chaos.

Here's my prayer for all of us:

Lord, deliver us from easy answers, packaged programs, and systems that minimize our desperate need for You to be involved every step of the way—even when (and especially when) we are actually doing it right! Jesus, You have promised to build Your church Your way. Help us do whatever we must do to let You do that! In Your name I pray, Amen!

CHAPTER 1
REDISCOVERING THE OBVIOUS

In the church context I serve in, we have seen many come to faith in the last decade and half from various backgrounds and cultures, and through this, a new common issue has emerged. Within their newfound faith, many are recognizing spiritual activity within themselves—and in their environment—which is evil. Much of it is connected to personal activities from their previous life or ones they are still indulging in that hadn't been previously identified as evidence of influence from the other side. Being in a somewhat conservative church, we had never acknowledged nor wanted to acknowledge or understand this part of the faith and yet we could not ignore the realities of what we were facing. Spiritual tragedies and necessities became the driving force behind ongoing decision-making. Working with the pastor of family care, a clinical psychologist, and a group of prayer people, the elders endorsed a team to deal with any case in which the demonic was suspect, making sure that all aspects (physiological, spiritual, and psychological) were looked at. As you can tell from the make-up of our original team, we were stepping into the unknown primarily armed with prayer—always a good first and ongoing step. We were like the disciples in Luke 11:1, asking Jesus, *"Lord, teach us to pray."* He has, and continues to teach us. Now, 19 years later, with two staff and 120 volunteers, not much has changed. This is one of the most important parts we want to share with you. Not just the theology, history, or best practices, but how we have had to deal with systems and churchwide understanding in order to do this well in a growing, multi-site church.

My chief objective in writing this book is to see people set free—not just those needing deliverance, but also those called to participate in this form of prayer ministry. As I continue to meet with people as a pastor, I am very concerned for those who have supernatural experiences that contradict, confuse, and distort a faith in Jesus, which they are trying to pursue or already have. Within the 900+ cases in which we have been involved, almost all have told us these experiences had been going on for years and they felt that the local church in its multiple expressions and backgrounds did not seem open to the conversation or able to help them discover answers. If there was openness, it was not seen or expressed. In other words, there was little public evidence that church leaders recognized the raging river of spiritual experiences (both good and evil) happening among the people in their congregations each week. Prayers for healing were generic and neither personal nor powerful. People were left feeling helplessly captive.

The other side of the coin is that many churchgoers are living in a syncretistic state, believing it is okay and even godly to mix different spiritual activities. The unstated objective seems to be to prove spiritual maturity by passing for pagans. I should note that we as a church are still in the early stages of being open about the real living conditions found in most churches in the West. Thus, as we have confronted this issue, we have come to realize that without a spiritual, power-based ministry, we will never be able to truly address what is at work among us.

We are certainly not new in discovering the reality of how much the spiritual realm impacts and undermines a lot of lives. The last few decades have produced a number of models in the church that seek to address the whole life of a believer, but as we will see, these models have, for the most part, overlooked a significant biblical and historical component that we are intentionally working to keep in mind and rely on in the ministry of deliverance. But I'm getting ahead of myself.

Given the polar opposites of orthodox theology and frequently unfaithful living, our leadership team and church have worked over the last two decades to build a theology for this local church ministry and in particular a deliverance emphasis with ongoing evaluations of our ministry so we can continue to operate in the environment in which we find ourselves. Much of this book is a review and updating of years of trial, error, and—by God's amazing grace—real progress in seeing remarkable evidence of God at work, consistent with a biblical and historical mandate. We are convinced that in doing so, there will at least be a door to walk through to continue to minister to this diverse group of people.

Using the term *biblical mandate*, as I just did, reminds me that while reading this book, you should keep in mind the difference between pattern and mold, guidelines and law, norms and regulations. The first term in each of those pairs is something that points in the right direction; the second refers to required actions. This distinction is crucial when it comes to handling the Bible as Bible-believing persons. Our high view of Scripture emphasizes that the Bible is the ultimate source for our faith, life, and practice; it tells us what to do and what not to do. This doctrine is summarized in 2 Timothy 3:16-17,

All Scripture is God-breathed and is useful for teaching, rebuking, correcting and training in righteousness, so that the servant of God may be thoroughly equipped for every good work.

When we take our high view of Scripture and exercise it in life situations, we discover that there are many choices to be made. Often, God's Word can be wholeheartedly obeyed in more than one way and no one way is effective in every case. Now, lest you think I'm undercutting an orthodox view of Scripture, let me give you a practical example that I'm sure you have experienced.

As historic, confessional Christians, all of us would say we want our worship to be thoroughly biblical. We don't want anything going on in our gatherings that violates Scripture. And yet, how many of us can point to a Scripture that precisely describes the way we actually do worship? We assume that because our pattern is familiar, comfortable, and even helps us to meet God on a weekly basis that it is uniquely biblical. Other believers, however, are conducting worship in very different ways, but having the same results.

Order, elements, participants, style—all the details of worship as you know it yet few, if any, of them, are actually regulated by Scripture. They do, however, meet biblical norms. They seek to apply principles in a situation.

So, the Bible mandates tithing and encourages giving, but gives few specifics on how it is to be collected. Is it with plates or bags? How much of our church budget is shaped by specific biblical texts? At some point in the past, everything you do in a worship service was brand new and untried; now it feels like there really couldn't be any other way to worship. At one time in history, organ music was the ultimate in secular encroachment on the Church. But before long, it was considered to be the exact pattern of worship in heaven. Some of us are old enough to remember when guitar music was synonymous with heresy. Now we have a generation who can't identify any use for all those funny looking pipes standing against the wall at the front of the sanctuary behind the drum kit.

What we refer to as deliverance ministry in our church has developed from years of God's guidance in spite of our reluctance, fears, and mistakes. We are merely a sample of what God can do among His people. We are not the standard, nor have we in any way achieved perfection. But we are pressing on into more of what God has called us to do, where He has called us to do it, as well as how we can do it. And along the way, real people are discovering deliverance.

A PERSONAL NOTE

I also need to clarify my own experiences. From the early days of my walk with Christ, long before I found myself becoming the lead pastor in a church,

I've had encounters that did not fit any of the categories I had learned to that point. My first intentional efforts to read the Scriptures were so frustrating that I pulled my pastor aside and asked, "Where's all the good stuff?"

He had no idea what I was talking about. Eventually I was able to tell him that I was upset after reading the Gospels and Acts because I didn't find anything vaguely familiar in my church. Where were the miracles and healings? Where was all the good stuff that filled the Bible pages? My pastor did the best he could, telling me that now that we had God's written Word, the need for such obvious displays of God's power were no longer necessary. I was never really convinced.

Since this ministry began, my personal experiences with gifts in discernment and words of knowledge have stretched me. During times of prayer, the sudden ability to see demons, hear what they were saying, or know things about the person we were praying for have been very unusual, unexpected, and not easily acknowledged. After prayer and oversight with our elders, I was affirmed in these giftings and called upon to use them. Yet, I did not have the biblical or theological categories to identify, understand, guard, and grow within these giftings. My doctoral dissertation and the eventual writing of this book have been key in my personal journey as I have defined and clarified a new passion within ministry.

In our church we have increasingly blended the ancient Christian world, traditional expressions, and contemporary experiments, especially in the area of worship. I believe this same integration is needed within deliverance ministries and other aspects of Christian living. There are strengths to be found within the liturgical, charismatic, evangelical, and social justice traditions. Within each tradition there are rites connected to deliverance, which tend to focus in different ways. Efforts to faithfully apply biblical teaching have led to various practices. Since we are dealing with such a diversity of people and backgrounds, a blended matrix is proving to be the door to dealing with many people who are coming from different starting points. I am passionate about the "both/and," not the "either/or" in considering practices that have been in place among followers of Jesus for centuries.

Lastly, I am fervent about this frontier of biblical ministry because I live in a very secular and, at the same time, spiritual environment. The nations of the earth are now in Toronto, bringing with them their spiritual worldviews and overtones. Immigrants that have lived in Canada for many years are reintegrating this into their lives. It is this post-Christian world that is demanding the church address and deal with spiritual power. I am finding many people wondering if the church can deliver the freedom it claims to have. This, in the future of my country, is going to be one of the most important questions and ministry realities. As Charles Kraft put it, "How do we call for allegiance, build people up in knowledge and use power to support and/or introduce people to Jesus?"[1] This is critical for me as a pastor and as a Christian in Toronto who longs to see the body of Christ healthy and growing throughout the world.

ASSUMPTIONS

Before I begin our story, let me clarify several assumptions I am intentionally making as I experiment with and experience deliverance ministry. You don't have to share these assumptions as you read the book, but realize that what we've experienced will cause you to question and maybe even change your own assumptions. I want to make sure we're on the same page, even if we don't currently think alike.

1. I am assuming not only that the Bible is God's Word, but that it accurately describes common spiritual phenomena in historical settings that are not limited to the past. This point is a crucial specific in a larger issue that comes up constantly when Christians are handling the Scriptures. People often take two pathways when it comes to the application of biblical truth. We might call these the *regulative* pathway and the *normative* pathway. Here is how I described the differences in these pathways in my previous book, *Convergence.*[2]

> By *normative* I mean a robust, orthodox doctrine of the Bible alongside a significant level of freedom in application. In other words, if we find it in Scripture, we should do it; if we don't find it, but it doesn't violate the letter or spirit of the Scriptures, we can do it too. Contrast this with the *regulative* position, which says, "If you find something in the Bible to do, you must do it; if you don't find it in Scripture, you shouldn't do it." One way to clarify this is to ask: Does God's Word tell us everything we as the church should do and not do? Does the Bible present a restrictive collection of directives that we must obey in detail without falling short or going beyond in any way? Or does God's Word give us reliable frameworks, limits, direction, and examples that provide ultimate guidance but don't necessarily prescribe every specific step to be taken?
>
> For many committed Christians, the assumption is that faithfulness and obedience are determined by how closely we see the Bible as regulative. Evangelicals in particular have often tried to make this the cornerstone of their self-descriptions. In practice, however, all of us handle the Word of God in more or less a normative way, though

we often hesitate to admit it or don't even realize we're doing it. This becomes obvious when we come up against a church practice or experience that is unfamiliar to us and which doesn't immediately bring a Bible passage or verse to mind. When we say, "I don't see that in Scripture," we reveal a regulative view. This objection is not saying, "If I can't see it, it isn't there," rather, "My internal review of the Bible has yielded no instances where something like that is either mentioned specifically or commanded, so it shouldn't be done." This is all well and good until we actually examine our own practices and apply the same standard.

Regardless of our church tradition, we conduct our spiritual lives almost entirely in ways that rise from previous normative uses of Scripture that now seem regulative because they have become part of our tradition. We treat the familiar as an exact replication of biblical instruction even though we may not be able to put our finger on where and how our practices relate to any specific texts. When encountering someone who insists on the "If I don't see it in Scripture, it can't be accepted" approach, I usually respond with, "Show me in the New Testament a church worship service that sets out the pattern your church uses every Sunday? How many items, including the bulletin, would remain in the service or in their current form if the criteria for inclusion were a specific biblical command? Please show me small groups, drama, worship teams, children's ministry, church architecture, and a mind-boggling assortment of other "must have" and "must do" parts of church life that actually can't be found in Scripture." There's nothing necessarily wrong with any of these; but we shouldn't present them as "Thus says the Lord" parts of our church life. The answer, "But this is what we've always done" is not the same as "This is what the Bible tells us to do."

I think Jesus Himself handled the Bible like this. His continual conflict particularly with the Pharisees of His day was not over the divine nature of the Scriptures. Both Jesus and the Pharisees believed the Old Testament canon to be God's Word. But each side interpreted and applied the Scriptures in very different ways. For example, note the running argument during Jesus' last week that is reported in the Gospels (Matthew 21:23-22:46; Mark 11:27-12:37; Luke 20:1-44). The bulk of these passages describe the religious leaders trying to formulate "gotcha" questions for Jesus that would trick Him into a statement they could use to condemn Him. Both sides in this confrontation used Scripture. But the climax comes in a telling statement

6

in Mark 12:32, made by the one Pharisee who asked an honest and personal question, *"Of all the commandments, which is the most important?"* (v.28). When he heard Jesus' answer he said, *"Well said, teacher . . . You are right . . ."* (v.32). They were in agreement.

Jesus understood and applied the regulatory aspects of the Scriptures, but he also frequently used them normatively. He ended that meeting of the minds with that Pharisee by making His haunting observation, *"You are not far from the kingdom of God"* (Mark 12:34). In other words, knowing what you should do is not the same as doing it. It doesn't address what you should do when you discover that you're unable to do what you should do. By "not far from the kingdom of God" did Jesus mean the proximity of the Pharisee to correct belief, or the proximity of the Pharisee to the Kingdom embodied in the King who was standing before him, or both? Jesus invited further conversation and understanding.

Meanwhile, His other primary human opposition, the Sadducees, reduced the Word of God primarily to the Torah (Moses' first five books) and were adept at sidestepping the spirit of the law while insisting everyone else stand squarely on their self-exempting applications of the law to the minutiae of life. In the hostile press conference mentioned above, Jesus made very clear what the Sadducees' problem was: *"Is not this the reason you are wrong, because you know neither the Scriptures nor the power of God?"* (Mark 12:25). He shattered their shallow dilemma over which of seven brothers would be married in heaven to the woman who had outlived all their marriages. They had taken a regulative view of God's instructions regarding levirate marriages (Deuteronomy 25:5), but expanded it in unwise normative ways to the point where they undermined the truth and practicality of God's Word with a silly argument based on an error of interpretation and a failure to appreciate the wisdom and power of God. Then their narrow, normative applications had taken the place of what God had actually said. Jesus' appeal to both the Scriptures and the power of God are highly significant and will come up again and again in our discussion of deliverance ministry.

Again, where the Scriptures are specific, we want to be specifically obedient. In many cases, God's Word is clear. By accepting the broader normative role of Scripture, we actually allow it to speak more clearly into our practices, not only by honoring the letter of the Law, but also by freely pursuing matters not specified that are part of our response to God's leading and general direction. This understand-

Jon Thompson

ing is critical and foundational to our approach in deliverance ministry, just as it is in all aspects of the Christian life.

For many in the evangelical world, the general subject of deliverance has been almost taboo. We have isolated the numerous Scripture passages that deal with confrontation of evil and the demonic and often failed to even ask: Are these passages regulative or normative? Our denial of or discomfort with evil has actually made us more vulnerable spiritually, and we are reaping the harvest of several centuries of inattention to the full teaching of God's Word.

2. Based on Scripture, I am assuming the reality of demons and their ability to harm and indwell human beings. In this, I am taking the example of Jesus and His followers within Scripture as my ministry model and approaching human problems by including the demonic in my list of possible causes.

3. I am assuming the act of deliverance is not an ancient myth or physiological manifestation only. The specifics of the biblical witness about deliverance as well as the witness of twenty centuries of at least some believers who were convinced this was part of the task of the church give us many examples, but don't eliminate the trial-and-error aspects of practicing this spiritual discipline today. Some of our best lessons and moments of seeing God's glory have come through the missteps we have made along the way. The normative freedom we have to attempt great things for God comes into play when we take passages that affirm speaking in tongues or prophesying in church with very little instruction related to the logistics. Or Jesus casting out a demon and then saying, *"This kind can come out only by prayer"* (Mark 9:29)—with no further direction (although fasting is mentioned in another Gospel). We are left to feel our way along, trusting in God's guidance. But nothing in Jesus' statement should be construed to mean, "So don't do it!" Every church conflict over ministry philosophy has its roots in this tension between normative and regulative uses of Scripture. The regulative view takes Mark 9:29 and decides: *When we suspect the demonic, we pray and fast—it's all we can do.* The normative view says: *Jesus indicates there's more than one kind of demonic influence, plus there's a variety of approaches to prayer and fasting—let's work on a process that confronts the demonic and includes individual and corporate prayer and fasting as the situation unfolds.* Out of this tension comes the answer to the question: Can you set up spiritual processes that are not specifically spelled out in Scripture, but don't violate Scripture while accomplishing Scriptural principles? We say "Yes."

4. I am assuming that since Jesus and the early church were involved in setting people free from the presence and destructive influence of fallen angels, the

8

local church should continue to do so out of obedience to Him, affirming that it is still Jesus doing the work by His Spirit.

5. I also make a significant assumption about all experiences in the context of Scripture as we have been discussing the last few pages. This assumption is sometimes pictured as a diamond, a triangle with an added center point, or a square (also known as the Wesleyan quadrilateral[3]). The four components of this assumption are Scripture, Reason, Experience, and Tradition. The error we as Evangelicals (yes, I'm one) have made is not thinking through what we mean when we hold up Scripture as central. When Luther and others proclaimed "sola Scriptura," they were not saying there's no other source of authority or direction; they were saying the Bible is the Supreme Court, the ultimate authority before which all other sources must remain submitted.[4] But they did still recognize the role of reason, experience, and tradition in reading, understanding, and applying Scripture. Our forefathers and foremothers in the faith discovered over and over again that Scripture can only be rightly understood and applied if we keep these three other "voices" in the discussion.

When we open our Bibles, we don't turn off our minds. We expect God's Word to stretch, heal, shape, and renew our minds even as we are using our minds to interact with what God has said. We don't close our eyes to our own experiences or the accumulated experiences of other believers (tradition) as we seek to rightly understand and obey God's Word. As Evangelicals, we may treat tradition like a four letter word, but this overlooks the obvious fact that we have our own (not that old) traditions and that cutting ourselves off from the unbroken flow of God's work in His church over the centuries doesn't really give us the right to say, "We're not like those people any more" (after all, we are their spiritual offspring). It also leaves us clueless about many important decisions and practices that believers have made since the close of the New Testament that do impact our lives every day. Many of the doctrines we are most passionate about: the nature of Christ, the Trinity, and others stated in the creeds were hammered out from Scripture in the centuries following the days of the original church. They got some things wrong, but they also got a lot of things right that we can't afford to ignore. Most of the theological errors and heresies we deal with today are simply updated versions of mistakes made in centuries past. Our spiritual ancestors answered those challenges with biblical wisdom; why not at least consider their solutions instead of assuming we know more and better today? Reason, tradition, and experience anchored and guided by Scripture still provide us with answers for whatever we face in these days.

Every time my church and I are confronted with experiential problems of a clearly spiritual nature or with theological questions, we respond by first asking, "What does Scripture say?" and then we intentionally ask: "How have other believers dealt with this problem? What does history (both ours and ancient) tell us? What are the logical and reasonable aspects of this issue?" We have come to realize that the default answer among many believers, "Just read your Bible and everything will be OK" is neither a practical nor even a biblical response to real challenges. Although He was often confronted by both honest and devious questions throughout His ministry, Jesus never responded by saying, "Just go back and read the Bible." He even told the Sadducees they were diligently misreading the Bible! He brought reason, experience, and tradition to bear to silence opposition. But again, He also used Scripture to reasonably point out where tradition had gone off the rails. He understood that some things are beyond reason, *"With man this is impossible, but not with God; all things are possible with God"* (Mark 10:27). And in His experience of extreme hunger and temptation by Satan, He did not let His self-awareness or physical need overrule the truth of Scripture: *"Jesus answered, 'It is written: "Man shall not live on bread alone, but on every word that comes from the mouth of God."'"* (Matthew 4:4). He remains our model for obeying Scripture while keeping reason, experience, and tradition in the conversation. The power of Jesus' parables can be partly traced to the way He used common experiences and traditions to build amazing lessons that could entertain the crowds while deeply touching His targets.

This whole discussion comes back to the fact that we must have a way to evaluate and respond to genuine spiritual experiences in the Church today that, surprisingly, often closely parallel what the Bible actually describes. But if we are dedicated readers of church history, we discover that dealing with evil has been a consistent hallmark of God's people. The gates of hell have not prevailed against the Church, but they haven't stopped trying. The long view that history gives us allows us to appreciate the theology we gained from Luther and his associates in the Reformation, but when it comes to dealing with the way things are today, the Church Fathers are much more helpful. You see, the Reformers lived in a world where everyone was at least nominally Christian but just the wrong type. The Church Fathers lived in a world eerily similar to the world I see around me in Toronto, where Christianity is sidelined at best and considered dangerously out of step at worst. The conditions we face today are much more comparable to Rome and Corinth in the first century than to Wittenburg and Geneva in the sixteenth. We are so post-Christian, so de-Christian; we are becoming pre-Christian.

It is time we stop ignoring experience in our theological discussions and ask ourselves regularly just how many of the experiences in our lives each day are spiritual. Since experiences are not self-authenticating and can be both good and evil, it's great that we have Scripture, reason, and tradition to evaluate what is happening to us. But we can't do that if we fail to acknowledge these experiences to begin with. It's interesting that in the Old Testament language, the word *know* refers to experience as much as to rational thought. To know one's wife in the ancient times referred to the most intimate aspects of that relationship.

We tend to equate *knowing* with facts; when it's just as much about experience. When I look out over my congregation each week I am struck by the thought that they have experienced a torrent of spiritual events throughout the past days—some from God; many from the other side. If our picture of church life is limited to a pastor having an encounter with God each week that he then shares on Sunday with everyone else who has lived a normal, world-oriented life, we are severely limiting God and crippling other believers. Life in the Body of Christ flows through everyone, not just the chosen few. The descriptions of corporate worship in the New Testament assume every believer will have something to share (Colossians 3:15-17). This level of participation and acknowledgement of each person's real spiritual life following Jesus and resisting the devil ignites worship!

As a church we don't deny or ignore experiences, but we do spend a lot of time evaluating the sources and meanings of the experiences. Are they from God, the devil, clinical issues, or last night's pizza? Our discoveries shape how we respond to those experiences. Sometimes an antacid tablet will do the trick; other times, counseling with a trained professional can resolve the weight of unhealthy thinking patterns or mental health issues; and sometimes direct spiritual confrontation of the demonic is necessary. All of which leads me to ask: "How often do you monitor the flow of experience in your own life? If God was speaking, would you hear? If the devil was affecting you, would you recognize his influence?"

6. Another major assumption has to do with how the dynamics of spiritual life are maintained in balance. This principle shows up in many ways and I owe a debt to Charles H. Kraft for pointing me in this direction.[5] If we use a three-legged stool, we can picture how principles often function in groups of three to create a balance that is missing if any of the items is taken away. In this case, I'm assuming that allegiance, truth, and power act as a trio in which each is essential in maintaining spiritual balance. They are each critical as one of the three legs of the stool—if any one is removed, the stool collapses.

When it comes to Jesus Christ, allegiance (commitment, faith, and trust), is either present or absent. Our allegiance is no longer to ourselves or a different worldview when we put our faith in Jesus Christ. I was a Buddhist, now I'm a follower of Jesus; I was a Muslim, now I follow Jesus; I was an atheist, now I follow Jesus. Right allegiance replaces wrong allegiance.

Truth—the second leg of the stool—represents a reality that displaces and counteracts lies I once treated as truth. The truth, as Jesus said, sets us free—free from falsehood and from enslavement to the father of lies. Truth is God's Word understood and applied.

Power—the third leg of the stool—is the presence of God's holy power used to unseat and remove unholy power. When God is at work, there is power involved; when the devil is present, there is a different sort of power involved. God's power confronts and overcomes Satan's power.

In some churches today, they will emphasize one of these "legs" over the other two and practically ignore another. For example, some churches are all about allegiance, all the time. Their main message is "Come to Jesus and trust in Him." The gospel is central, but sometimes seems to be the only message. Every service is an evangelistic appeal to unbelievers. But inevitably, though it is exciting to see many putting their faith in Christ, even some of these new believers will say, "Now I need to be taught; I want to grow." The hunger for truth and teaching challenges the centrality of the gospel as the one thing we talk about.

Not surprisingly, the church down the street specializes in teaching. The pastor is a gifted communicator and people flock to hear him, many coming from the environment where the focus is allegiance every week. They appear to be growing, but few people seem compelled to impact the world, feeling they need more teaching before they can step out. Eventually they feel as if they're in a vacuum when it comes to experiencing God's direct presence, despite their increase in knowledge. Knowing more about God doesn't necessarily equate to knowing Him better.

Then they hear about another church that promises direct, powerful experiences with God on a weekly basis. This church is all about speaking in tongues, healing services, being slain in the Spirit, and any number of other apparently strange occurrences. So all these profound experiences happen but is anyone really meeting the true Jesus? What is the true source of the experiences and are any growing deep in their faith?

Your own church probably fits one or two of the profiles above in some way. Yet when we turn to Jesus, who is our model, what did He emphasize among the allegiance, truth, and power priorities? He emphasized all three. He didn't overlook any of them. He called people into allegiance to

Him; He taught truth to individuals, small groups, and multitudes; and, by the power of the Spirit, He defeated the powers of evil in decisive confrontations. An effective imitation of Christ on the part of both the Church and individual believers requires that we keep all three of these things—allegiance, truth, and power—on our radar every moment. This is almost impossible to do alone— it must be a corporate effort on the part of the Church with each of us doing our individual part.

How you respond to all of this in this moment says a lot about where you stand when it comes to spiritual conflict. You may have been taught that once you came to Jesus everything was OK. Your allegiance is sorted out, so the devil can't touch you. Or you may have been told, "Well, Satan can bother you some, but if you read your Bible and participate in Bible studies, you'll sail right through. The truth will protect you." Or maybe you were taught, "Trusting Jesus and reading your Bible are good, but what you really have to do is strap on your spiritual armour and do battle with the enemy." The problem is, none of these (allegiance, truth, or power) is optional or unimportant. We need to maximize each of them—trusting in Jesus, feeding on the Word, and engaging the enemy—without overlooking any of it.

All of this is necessary because of the following reality that brings us to the core of what we have discovered about prioritizing allegiance, truth, and power: Unholy power doesn't leave just because there is truth in the room; unholy power leaves when there is applied power in the room. Lies and falsehood can remain in the company of genuine allegiance, but crumble under the weight of truth. And God's power and truth have little effect when there is no allegiance to Him. This is why we see Jesus say, *"Daughter, your faith (allegiance) has healed you"* (Mark 5:34), yet also read in verse 30 that *"Jesus realized power had gone out from him."* Before she reached to touch His tassels, while hidden in the crowd, she had believed the truth about Him to the point of acting on it. Allegiance, truth, and power were all present, as they always were during Jesus' ministry here on earth.

Let me quickly add a note of fair warning as you dive into this book. As occurs every summer during my seminary classes, the exposure to all aspects of spiritual warfare and godly versus evil power generates unexpected experiences for many people. If you are reading this merely as an academic study, realize it will tend to leak or rupture into other areas, particularly your personal life. The breadth and depth of your connection with God through Jesus Christ will be exposed as you think about the reality of the spiritual realm and its impact on daily living. I'm recording here a prayer of protection over your heart, mind, and soul as you trust God, seek His wisdom, and encounter His power in ways you may not previously been fully aware of. May

God receive glory from what happens in your life and throughout your sphere of influence and ministry.

7. As a final assumption, let me add the importance of a biblical worldview in relation to the universe. I've hinted at this already, but I need to clarify that I'm writing to orthodox Christians, those who are united with me in being able to say and affirm the Apostles' Creed. Let me pose this question: Would you say the lens you and those closest to you use to look at the world is biblical, or something else? Because I've noted that even in some conservative Christian church settings, where there is assumed biblical faithfulness, the participants do not, in fact, apply the Bible to their lives. They trust the Bible generally, but actually doubt it when it comes to specifics and the direction it gives. So, if your view of the universe is that it is a closed, mechanistic system governed by the latest "laws" of science, you need to realize your view is not biblical, whatever you claim about the Bible. Too many of us who claim to be Christ-followers describe ourselves as orthodox, but live like we're atheists. Do we believe God can and does intervene in His Creation? Or did God create, but then recuse Himself from interrupting history in any way? The Bible describes the world as physical and spiritual—one reality. We are not dualists, Buddhists, or gnostics. We believe, according to Scripture, that all Creation (both spiritual and physical) is good—though it has been marred by sin. Part of the reason we reject dualism (spirit=good; physical=evil) is because we believe God became flesh. The incarnation was the visible joining of the physical and spiritual in the single person of Jesus. His body, cross scars and all, is now glorified and will be visible to us who spend eternity with Him. Or think about the end of time when all of creation is restored; we won't float up into the heavens. The end of the story is the restoration of the new heavens and the new earth—physical and spiritual making up "capital 'R' reality."

You are a complex human being, made up of body and soul, yet one person. This is the biblical worldview: First, that you and I are physical and spiritual all at once, and second, that the universe is populated with sentient beings who interact with each other, not just laws that run the place. The Bible declares there is a God, the ultimate sentient being, who is the Author and Creator of all, and who continually sustains the universe and interferes with it according to His will. The Bible further depicts the world as full of angels, demons, and human beings who regularly interact with each other within the universe God has created. As Paul Heibert puts it, we live in an "organic universe."[6] When I verbalize this picture for groups, people often think I'm talking about something like Star Trek with different life-forms elsewhere, but I'm not. I'm describing existence here and now. What amazes me is that as Evangelicals who have fought long and hard for the authority of Scripture, we often reject so much of the actual biblical witness about these aspects of reality and the supernatural. We consign it to the past and are shocked when it confronts us in the present. Why do we do this? Is it because we have overlaid a psychological filter or a materialistic grid on Scripture and lost our capacity to hear it speak directly? Have you over-spiritualized your view and isolated it from everyday life? What would happen if you began to think of God as an interventionist who is active all the time and everywhere in His world? How would your view of circumstances change if you suddenly began to include in the picture a significant amount of interaction and even conflict between demonic and angelic forces, as well as human beings like yourself? If your family, educational, and even church background has in some way ripped Jesus' worldview out of your thinking, then you will not only have a persistent problem with the rest of what you read here but also need to have a conversation with Jesus Himself. It doesn't really make sense to say, "I want to become like Jesus" if in practice that means, "But I don't want to think like Him, act like Him, or obey Him in any way other than the most superficial recognition." Taking Jesus seriously as Lord, Savior, and Model must include the way you approach every aspect of life, including—and especially—the spiritual. Have you asked Him what He thinks of your personal worldview?

DEFINITIONS

Alongside my primary assumptions, please note the following terms I will be using along with their definitions. One of the discoveries we have made as a church is that, in all areas of our life together, time spent clarifying and agreeing on definitions has prevented many needless misunderstandings and saved a lot of time later during significant discussions because we're speaking the same language. As you're reading through these, ask yourself: How would this language work in my church? What words would immediately be misunderstood? How aware are we of the terms we use when we are talking to one another about anything?

Unfortunately, as Christians, we frequently find ourselves talking about the same experiences, but using such different language that we are bound to confuse one another. My favorite illustration happens to me all the time. On any given Sunday, it's not unusual to find in our church a charismatic, a liturgical believer, and a more traditional Christian. At the close of the message I hear the following responses by people who just listened to the same teaching. The charismatic hugs me and says, "O yes, Pastor, anointed preaching today. The fire came down!" The Baptist shakes my hand formally and says, "Pastor, that was a good word this morning." A little later, the liturgical guy smiles as he passes and says, "I heard echoes of Augustine, St. John of the Cross, and C. S. Lewis—food for contemplation the rest of the day." They wouldn't understand each other but they are describing the same experience.

There's an existing lexicon in every church to talk about the subject matter we're about to explore. But in all likelihood, not everyone knows it. One of the first and greatest challenges in developing a shared biblical worldview in a church is the time-consuming and strenuous task of identifying an agreed upon language you will use to communicate. If you are in ministry, you must learn to monitor your own language for clarity and take the time to ask others to explain what they mean—not because they aren't being clear, but because you want to make sure you are hearing what they are saying. I very often find the disagreements are more a matter of language than they are of meaning. And we Christians need one another too much to settle for misunderstanding each other.

Here is a sample of the language we use that you will read throughout this book:

1. Spiritual Warfare/Spiritual Conflict, Exorcism, Releasing Prayer, Deliverance: Identifying and expelling fallen angels from a human being by applying the power of the Holy Spirit and the name of Jesus of Nazareth, the second Person of the Trinity.

2. Restoration Prayer: The process and practice of deliverance—research, confession, prayer, church support, and spiritual authoritative commands.

3. Hybrid Matrix: The combination of different models from history and current parallel practices creates the model we use (called Restoration Prayer).

4. The Church: Can refer to Roman Catholic, Orthodox, and Protestant traditions. These are the various groups that trace their origin to the New Testament and Jesus Christ: Lord, Savior, and Founder.

5. Charismatic: Those who believe all the spiritual gifts are for use today and are given to people as the Holy Spirit sees fit. This is not a denominational label, so we often call ourselves "small 'c' charismatic Christians."

6. Evangelical: Those who hold to the Bible as their authority for faith, life, and practice. They also hold to the idea of personal conversion, evangelism, and the cross as the full act of God on behalf of humanity.[7]

7. Cessationism: The theological view that all overtly supernatural gifts, such as tongues and prophecy, ceased at the death of John or by the canonization of Scripture.

BATTLE LINES

Before we step into the Old Testament to begin our survey, let's look briefly at the conflict we face today. Spiritual warfare is simultaneously carried out on three fronts. Scripture is clear that there is a holy Trinity as well as an unholy trinity. According to Scripture (Ephesians 2:1-3; 1 John 2:16), the latter of these is made up of the world, the flesh, and the devil. When this evil triad is mentioned in the Bible, the term *world* refers to human systems that function in an ungodly way, *flesh* refers to our sin-infected human nature, and the *devil* is the chief fallen angel, a sentient being who fell/corrupted himself before the beginning of time. Now, when people think about spiritual conflict, they almost always focus on the devil despite the fact that Romans 6 is clear about the pervasive influence of the flesh, and John 17 is clear about the threats from the world.

Further, spiritual conflict is actually an attack from three fronts in two areas: doctrine and experience. The basis of our thinking and the reality of our experiences are continually under assault. Spiritual warfare is as much an intellectual/spiritual fight as it is a feeling/ emotional/ experiential fight. Both of these areas of vulnerability must be guarded in order to ensure victories. For example, in the intellectual or thinking area, 1 Timothy 4:1 warns that there will be evil spirits teaching demonic doctrine. That means there are demonic beings manipulating and directing the influence of evil philosophies that may affect millions of people. There are worldviews dominant in many places and over many lives that are actually demonic. To summarize, you always have the world and its ungodly system, the flesh expressed in individual or corporate wrestling with sin in its internal and external manifestations, and then the kingdom of darkness adding its own push to destroy all that God has made.[8]

There are somewhere around 300 references to the demonic in Scripture. A variety of terms are used: the devil, Satan, demons, evil spirits, god of this age, spiritual forces, etc. The Bible exposes us to a view where human beings experience both the kingdom of evil and the kingdom of God. We begin with the biblical reminder that all human beings are made in the image of God. This is the basis for persistent respect of life in the womb as well as in the final stages of aging. The Bible is also clear that each human being is owned either by God or by Satan. Each of us is either possessed by Satan or possessed by the Spirit of Jesus. We are citizens of one kingdom or the other. Think of the implications of 2 Corinthians 4:4, *"The god of this age has blinded the minds of unbelievers, so that they <u>cannot</u> see the light of the gospel that displays the glory of Christ, who is the image of God"* (NIV2011). I added the underline. Do we believe this? That the bulk of humanity at any moment is incapable of seeing the truth of the gospel? If we did believe it, would we not be diligent to pray before we preached or shared our faith—that God would open blind eyes and hard hearts to respond to the gospel?

When you read the word "possessed" in the last paragraph, you may have assumed some kind of weird influence, but I'm using the term to indicate ownership. Possession is always positional and sometimes presence. You are either owned by Christ or still owned by the other side. There are only two kingdoms; there's no in-between place. Note how Ephesians 2:1 confirms this view: *"As for you, you were dead in your transgressions and sins, in which you used to live when you followed the ways of this world and of the ruler of the kingdom of the air, the spirit who is now at work in those who are disobedient"* (NIV2011). He was talking to believers about their previous position and describing where most people live today. Every non-Christian you've ever met is owned by the devil. Do you believe that hard reality? If you don't, you are not demonstrating a biblical worldview. If you do believe this, does it actually affect your life?

What this means is that when you become a Christian, you switch allegiances. Ownership changes hands. At this very juncture, one of the critical things modern Christianity in the West has lost is the affirmation of Jesus' ownership of our lives and living based on it. To put this in biblical language, when you stopped being a slave to sin, you became a slave of Jesus. You are always owned by someone. In Christ, you've been bought and paid for (see 1 Corinthians 6:20). Until that transaction has been realized in your life, you are still owned by the devil.

Paul and the Gospels are clear about these matters, but we tend to fudge on them. Frankly, we find it hard to believe nice people are owned by the devil. But the bottom line is the Scriptures only make room for two kingdoms, and every human is a citizen of one or the other. The fundamental question is not of behavior, sincerity, or personality, but of position. We can trace this reality all through the Bible. The two kingdoms are at war with one another. We're engaged in spiritual warfare; we can't be bystanders. The crucial battle has been won at the cross and the eventual victory is assured, but in the meantime, the battle is real. It has always been real, all the way back to the garden in Genesis. So that's where we'll go next as we seek a clearer understanding of the nature of our faith.

Jon Thompson

CHAPTER 2
AN OLD TESTAMENT AND BEYOND VIEW OF THE DEMONIC

At the heart of the deliverance worldview is the work (actions and sacrifice), person (character), and theological outlook (teaching) of Jesus the Christ. He who is God in flesh, the One who brought the kingdom in power, sent the Holy Spirit, birthed the Church, is both foundation and head of the Church, and whose work is now being done through the church, is the heart of where this study must begin and end. But starting with Jesus means a careful understanding of all that went into His worldview.

As John's Gospel makes clear in its opening verses, Jesus' worldview starts at the very beginning. Before we can examine the Gospel accounts of Jesus' life and teaching, their impact on church history, and eventually as models of deliverance or to our own practice, we need to understand the worldview of Jesus as well as the worldview of the early church, which was firmly entrenched in the Old Testament and Intertestamental periods. This first section of our study is truly a summary. As God in the flesh, Jesus was also a first century Jew. With this in mind, and if we're paying attention, we can see that the encounters, the language, and the presuppositions of Jesus and His followers are rooted and developed in the often-overlooked, but great secondary theme found within the Old Testament—Spiritual Conflict.

The assumption by many that spiritual warfare is a New Testament phenomenon left largely untouched in the Old Testament is sadly mistaken. The basis for our understanding of the kingdom of darkness in conflict with the kingdom of light comes from throughout the Old Testament, starting at the very beginning. In fact, the second verse of Genesis (Genesis 1:2), following hard on the grand opening declaration of God's initial creative act, records the first case of spiritual conflict in Scripture. A literal translation of the verse goes something like, "and the Spirit of God was hovering over the chaotic, destructive waters of creation." In Hebrew, the tone conveys resistant hostility. Much in the way that God created "light" before He created the objects we connect with light (sun, moon, and stars), the introduction of "waters" shows up here before water as we know it appears in the order of Creation. There is an ominous presence of evil right from the start of Creation.

21

Gregory Boyd, in his book *God at War*, gives an outstanding summary of the roots and foundations of spiritual conflict found within the Old Covenant.[1] His five conclusions helped me understand more broadly the work of God, the mindset of Jesus and His early followers, and the early years of the movement called "The Way" years before it was called Christianity.

OLD TESTAMENT BACKGROUND

Boyd writes that within the Law, Wisdom, and Prophetic books, the sovereignty of Yahweh is central. One expression of that oversight is seen as He battles cosmic forces.[2] Near Eastern culture understood these battles to involve "hostile, proud, raging, destructive forces of chaos opposing God's will that threatened the very foundation of the earth, Yamm, Leviathan, Rahab and Behemoth."[3] Yamm, connected to the Sea, was worshipped by groups of Arabs before the coming of Islam. Further, as Bob Becking writes, "The personal names Ya'aqan (Numbers 33:31-32; Deuteronomy 10:6; 1 Chronicles 1:42) and Aqan (Genesis 36:27) have been interpreted as containing a reference to an animal deity worshipped by the Edomites."[4] Leviathan, in both Hebrew and Canaanite imagery, is a twisting serpent of the sea with seven heads. It is connected to Yamm and was seen as a hostile and strong cosmic creature that God struggles with and then subdues (Psalm 74).[5] Rahab is also connected to the sea and some suggest battled God Himself preceding the creation of the heavens and the earth.[6] Behemoth is best "understood as a mythological creature possessing supernatural characteristics."[7] These evil forces, when later seen in the Apocrypha and New Testament are fully understood as expressions of the kingdom of darkness, [8] but the ancient Hebrew and Canaanite literature makes it clear that these entities were worshipped as gods. They were also feared and opposed as forces that threatened the fabric of Creation and their dwelling place was described in language similar to what we found in Genesis 1:2—in chaotic, destructive waters.

In the beginning, when the uncreated was being created, there seems to be a foreboding darkness—a disorder, something not just out of place but dangerous, wrong, evil, rebellious. This darkness, this deep, this abyss, this water? Again, in Hebrew this reads that there was a dark, dangerous, hostile, raging out of control sea, described as the deep.

It becomes even more significant when we flip to the end of the Bible and read Revelation 21:1, *"Then I saw 'a new heaven and a new earth,' for the first heaven and the first earth had passed away, and there was no longer any sea"* (NIV2011). Our attention is immediately drawn to the new heaven and new earth and we may miss the last phrase, *"and there was no longer any sea."* Now the sea is gone? "But I like the sea," I told God, "Can't I sit by the ocean when all this is over?

Surely, Jesus, I can learn to surf with the new resurrection body I am getting, right?" So many of us love the water and the sea, but the point isn't the absence of oceans and beaches from the new Creation; it actually is that there will no longer be any chaotic, destructive waters or their inhabitants in our renewed environment. There's a connection here between the first beginning and this new beginning. Think for a moment of the interesting note from the ministry of Jesus that His defeat of the demonic gang called Legion at Gadara involved not only their infestation of the pigs but also their stampede into the waters of Galilee, but more on that later.

These revelations about spiritual warfare in the Old Testament come as somewhat of a shock to those of us raised to believe that terms like "Leviathan" and "Behemoth" were simply odd names for unusual animals, like crocodiles, whales, and perhaps dinosaurs. Equating these terms with the presence of strong demonic powers operating in the world and controlling entire cultures begins to explain why there was such a strong attraction to pagan religions. The idols themselves were not all that appealing, but the powers in the background of idolatry were enticing and real. Their true character is gradually revealed as Scripture unfolds.

Though God has absolute sovereignty, another secondary theme emerges within the Old Testament narrative related to the cosmic conflict. Though these forces are not equal to God in any way, they are allowed to continue to resist God's will and do appear to thwart His will for a time. This is why, for example, as someone living in the tension of the in-between we currently face in life, "the psalmist has to continually remind himself—in the face of evidence to the contrary—of Yahweh's primordial victory."[9] Here are two significant examples of the angst and hope expressed by the Psalmists. Two Psalms that reflect on God as Warrior, while dealing with Israel's past, are Psalm 77:16-20 and Psalm 114. In Daniel G. Reid's book, *God as Warrior*, an entire chapter deals with God as warrior against the forces of chaos.[10] Psalm 77:16-20 reads,

> *The waters saw you, God, the waters saw you and writhed; the very depths were convulsed. The clouds poured down water, the heavens resounded with thunder; your arrows flashed back and forth. Your thunder was heard in the whirlwind, your lightning lit up the world; the earth trembled and quaked. Your path led through the sea, your way through the mighty waters, though your footprints were not seen. You led your people like a flock by the hand of Moses and Aaron.*

This psalm is one of personal lament and has the three classic characteristics of this genre: address (Ps. 77:1-2), complaint (Ps. 77:3-4), and petition (Ps. 77:10-12).[11] Though the psalmist is not specific with the grievances or prob-

23

lems, they provoke a sense of overwhelming futility. In Psalm 77:10, he re-counts the acts of victory God as king and warrior had done on behalf of his people:

> The Psalm thus recalls a time when chaos (in the form of the Egyp-tian army) threatened God's people on the historical plane. It de-scribes the life-threatening situation, by using the imagery associated with sociological chaos (the sea). By comparing his present despair with Israel's trouble at the time of the Exodus, the psalmist experi-ences peace in the face of his personal chaos.[12]

It is also interesting that the biblical writers express the knowledge that the God of Israel is greater than all other gods (Ps. 77:13) and thus when recalling the Exodus, they acknowledge the supernatural element of battle behind such a great event.

The other example is in Psalm 114. Rich with imagery and perspec-tive, it also recounts the miracle of the Exodus and uses the Divine Warrior motif when God deals with nature or opposes other gods. The first stanza references the Exodus and the conquest of Canaan, for this symbolizes the building of God's house or sanctuary. It is a poetic description of the personi-fied reaction of nature that is significant. The references to "fleeing," "turning back," and the "earth trembling" all show that nature is subject and is meta-phorically frightened as the Divine-Warrior approaches.[13] This idea is high-lighted when the author reminds us of God's sovereignty over nature (Ps. 114:8) through the acts of Exodus 17 and Numbers 20:8. Yet there is a curi-ous phrase, which also deals with God as warrior. In Psalm 114:4, the phrase "the mountains leaped" is key because it relates to God overcoming the Ca-naanite gods. Some have argued that the phrase refers to the earthquake that accompanied the giving of the law at Sinai, yet

> ...the fact, however, that the only other predication of 'raqud' to 'leap' of mountains and hills in the verse are located in Canaan or Palestine, not in the Sinai Peninsula. The mountains of pre-Israel Palestine were the dwellings of Canaanite gods; well might they leap in fright at the approach of the awesome God of Israel.[14]

The second insight within the Old Testament is that there is little time spent talking of or defining the concept of evil spirits or demons, yet references to lesser or other gods are commonplace. These are often called the "gods of the nations," implying some kind of spiritual beings worshipped by those peoples. Though authors define the idea of only one true living or

Supreme God, they also assume the reality of others, what Boyd calls "creational monotheism." These gods have authority and geographical influence and much of the time are connected to nature (Deuteronomy 4:19-20; 32, Psalm 82, Job 5:20, Habakkuk 3:11). They have the choice to serve God or, if they choose to rebel, they will then die like humans (Daniel 10, Psalm 82:7).[15] In fact, these beings take on many of the same characteristics and behaviors we find in demons described in the New Testament. They are openly antagonistic to God and eager to hurt and destroy people made in His image.

When Moses appears before Pharaoh at God's direction to challenge the Egyptian ruler and demand the release of the Israelite people, Pharaoh is not impressed. He challenges the authority of Moses and the identity of the God he is claiming to represent. Moses shows Pharaoh a sign of God's sanction by casting down his staff, which turns into a snake. Mocking the demonstration of power, Pharaoh motions to his own sorcerers who proceed to do the same thing with their staffs. It appears Moses' sign has been outdone by the Egyptians until his snake proceeds to devour the other snakes. This is a conflict being acted out between the gods of the nations and the God who has chosen the insignificant Hebrew people as His own.

One of the biases hampering our understanding of the fierce spiritual conflict raging in the Old Testament is the assumption that idols are fake. We can point to texts that recognize the figures are made, molded, or carved with human hands (Leviticus 26:1; Judges 1:5; Psalm 97:7; Isaiah 45:16). Idols are objects of wood and metal. We conclude that since they are inanimate objects, their only "power" comes from that given to them by humans. And yet Paul reminds us in 1 Corinthians 10:20 that those who bow to idols are worshipping demons. If demons can inhabit people, they can make use of idols to accomplish their destructive purposes.

By the way, this misunderstanding has handicapped many Christian efforts historically when they have assumed the "spirit world" that controls people in various places before the Gospel arrives is little more than fairy tales with no real power. Too often the demonic has been met with attempts to educate and modernize so-called "primitive" peoples whose awareness of actual evil beings was much more accurate than those who came to evangelize them. In fact, their view has turned out to parallel the straightforward biblical view. Countless Christian leaders have learned the hard and humbling way that evil spiritual powers are a real and difficult resistance to the spread of the good news about Jesus. Today in the West, these lessons are being learned again and again.

Back in the Old Testament, there is a significant case study on demonic power found in the early chapters of 1 Samuel, when Eli and his wicked sons allow the Ark of the Covenant to be carried into battle with the Philistines without seeking God's direction for this action. Not only were the Israelites humiliated and defeated in battle, the Ark was captured and carried off by idol worshippers. The Philistines placed the Ark in the temple of their fish-god Dagon for safekeeping. Much to their surprise, they found their idol facedown before the Ark of the God of Israel the next morning. Thinking this was some kind of accident, they stood the idol up again. The next morning, the idol had resumed its humbled position, now with its head and hands removed and piled on the threshold of the temple. Then a plague of tumors broke out in the city and the Philistines quickly decided it was not in their best interests to keep the Ark. As this story unfolds, it becomes a clear accounting of an encounter between the God of Israel and the demonic powers at work among the Philistines. They might defeat the Israelites militarily, but the God of Israel proved Himself capable of vandalizing their gods and destroying their population. In terror, the Philistines sent the Ark back to Israel. The gods of the nations were not just idols; there were demonic powers active in those settings. But the God of Israel was greater and worthy of worship and obedience.

Third, the person, not just the idea of Satan, is found within the Old Testament. Unlike others, Boyd argues that the devil was never a being following God's commands but

> ...rather he is an adversary against God even more than he is an adversary against humans. His character is consistently seen as malicious. It is this malicious element in his character at this early stage of revelation that lays the foundation for the later perspective. Here, we shall find, the figure of Satan comes to absorb within the chaotic cosmic characteristics previously attributed to Leviathan and other anti-creation beasts.[16]

Fourth, the snake found in the story of post Creation is Satan. The serpent in Genesis 3 symbolizes and embodies this fallen angel, but the text does not refer explicitly to Satan. The tempter is simply called a "nahas," which is a common Hebrew word for serpent. A more directly sinister nuance may be seen in Hebrew, when "nahas" is seen in verb form, which means "to practice divination, observe signs" (Numbers 23:23; 24:1). For the most part, the terminology does not so much convey an ominous presence of evil but an acknowledgment of the pervasive effects of influencing evil powers and the behaviors related to engaging with the demonic that was just mentioned. Near Eastern divination formula frequently includes procedures involving a serpent.[17] Throughout the world even today, in various countries I've visited, the occult and evil spirits are most often depicted with serpent terminology. Charles Scobie's writings from a biblical theological perspective say:

> Historically what we see throughout the Bible as a whole is a growing awareness of the existence of a personal power of evil in the world. Canonically, it is legitimate and indeed necessary to read Gen. 3 in the light of the later, joined between the forces of good and the forces of evil.[18]

Many argue that Isaiah 14 and Ezekiel 28 both include references to Satan. We should note that there is a huge disagreement here. The Church Fathers connected both passages to the fall of Satan while the Reformation thinkers almost unanimously rejected the interpretation.[19] Calvin's response to those thinking Ezekiel 28 is about the fall of Satan is similar to how he responds to Isaiah 14.

> The exposition of this passage which some have given, as if it referred to Satan, has arisen from ignorance; for the context plainly shows that these statements must be understood in reference to the king of the Babylonians (Tyre in our sense). But when the passage of Scripture is taken up at random, and no attention is paid to the context, we need not wonder that mistakes of this kind frequently arise.[20]

Those in Calvin's camp would say both these passages are about Creator versus created, humans that refuse to submit to God, which is the "great folly of humanity."[21] Yet Boyd brings a needed balance. He rightly understands that hermeneutically, much of the time there are two meanings or reasons for a historical/scriptural narrative. Having explained this principle, Boyd then agrees with *both* the Reformation and Church Fathers, using the power of the "both/and" and rejecting an "either/or" position:

> Isaiah 14 and Ezekiel 28 can also be understood as referring not only to the fall of human kings but also to the fall of Satan. While we are not told virtually anything about the time and circumstances of this cosmic fall, we are told enough to infer that it should not have happened. These two passages are both spoken as lamentations for someone gone wrong. Drawing on familiar Near Eastern images, both passages depict someone created great who became prideful in his heart and rebellious in his spirit, and who then was cast down.[22]

Lastly, there are very specific references to Satan within the Jewish writings. Boyd, in his summary, focuses on Job, who gives the most revealing exposure to our enemy. Others agree, including Scobie, who outlines the view this way,

> He is a personal being, whose title and role is as adversary and accuser. He unjustly accuses Job with God's permission. He also is an agent of suffering and tempter which as one author says the traits which will develop into the kind of character which he possesses in New Testament time can already be dimly discerned.[23]

This personal being, who stands as an accuser to those called by God, is also seen in a heavenly court scene in Zechariah 3 and 2 Samuel 24. Yet it is in the prologue of Job 1-2 that we begin to truly understand that the universe God created is not just space, heavenly bodies, the animal kingdom, and those made in the image of the Creator. There is a world of the "in between."

> Almost all primordial peoples have realized, and as the New Testament makes even more explicit, there is also an incredibly vast, magnificent, complex and oftentimes a warring and hostile 'world in between' that we must factor in. The book of Job and the entire Bible also assumes that we know next to nothing about the going on of this 'world between.' For example in the whole of Scripture and in direct contrast to much other literature in the ancient world and throughout history, we are given the name of only two angels. It is only through direct revelation that one gains a perspective like Daniel's on the warring cosmic princes or the prophetic perspective Jeremiah speaks of as one who is privilege to listen in on the assembly of Yahweh's council of gods (Jeremiah 23:18, see 1 Kings 22:19-20, Isaiah 6:8, Psalm 82:1, 89:7, 103:20-21, 148:2, Job 1:6, 2:1). It is because of our near total ignorance—not on the basis of his sheer divine authority– that Yahweh instructs Job and his friends to remain silent in the face of evil. It is, in the end, neither God's fault nor Job's fault.[24]

Satan, this accuser with access to the very presence of the Creator God, is both a defined and living reality in the pages of the Old Testament. His appearance in Job occurs at God's summons; he is under authority and can do nothing without God's permission. Based on Job's experience, we are left chastened and humbled over our lack of true understanding when it comes to God's ways and the spiritual aspects of reality.

Yet it is in the coming 400 years of silence that this evil-driven creature and those loyal to him become more clearly identified, which builds the foundation for the worldview of Jesus and the early church. The same tempter

who convinced Adam and Eve to turn away in rebellion and shatter the amazing Creation that was God's gift to them shows up with the same tactics in the
temptation of Jesus. The denial of consequences ("you shall not die") and the
exaltation of self over God ("you will be like God") presented in the garden
were again presented to Jesus in the wilderness. The attack on the One born
to be our Savior was a real and consistent glimpse into the enemy that has
labored to destroy us from the beginning.

INTERTESTAMENTAL/APOCRYPHA BACKGROUND

As a teenager who was seriously (I thought) engaged in following Jesus and on
the lookout for a cause, I discovered that the official pulpit Bible in our
church had the Apocrypha in it. It was one of those massive volumes, too
heavy to lift, and too cumbersome to use that served as a visual symbol of our
commitment to the Word of God. Yet in my young mind, how could we allow this significant statement to be compromised with these non-canonical
additions?

Fortunately, cooler heads prevailed over my outrage and thanks to
God's work in my life, I have since come to see the inter-testamental writings
as significant sources of information without having to give them status as
divinely inspired. I now take the Wesleyan approach and, as John Wesley
urged, read them for beneficial instruction, not authoritative direction.[25] The
area of spiritual warfare we are exploring was shaped in many ways by the understanding developed during those post-prophetic centuries. It certainly had
a profound effect on the spiritual worldview present when Jesus came to
earth.

What we call the 400 years of silence between the Testaments were
not all that silent. God may not have been inspiring further Scriptures, but
history was in motion. The rise and fall of Alexander the Great took up a
great deal of the world stage, the Holy Land included. Israel remained under
the control of various foreign powers. One of these powers, the Seleucids,
displayed aggressive forms of anti-Semitism, including the obsene desecration
of the Temple with pig's blood. Rather than discouraging the Jews, this act
sparked a revolt under a family called the Maccabees that for a time restored
self-rule to the Jews. The Roman Empire would eventually put an end to that.

Between the Old and New Testament there were also huge developments in theological reflection and application that set up the worldview, theology, and practice of exorcism. The rabbis in Israel were busily interpreting
the Scriptures in light of current events. During this time, Jewish scholars in
Alexandria, Egypt produced a Greek version of the Old Testament we now
call the Septuagint. The theological view that emerged throughout these cen-

turies could be defined as "modified dualism." The highest angel within the council of Yahweh had misused God-given authority, rebelled, and thus became the god of this world. The role of guardian angels is foundational to this construct. Writers of this period expand on the idea of lesser gods or mediating angels that have authority over all aspects of God's creation.[26] The Book of Jubilees, 1 Enoch, and the Testament of Adam all point to groups of angels or lesser gods overseeing and controlling Yahweh's creation. And since some of them rebelled, God must now come again to rescue not just humanity, but all of creation, for to Jewish authors, creation had been swallowed up in the belly of Leviathan. So God, though seemingly having lost this battle, is now coming in full divine power to throw out these created beings that have abused the gift of authority over nature and all creation.[27]

> Fundamentally, it meant that the mediating angelic authority structure that Yahweh had set up at creation had gone bad from the very top. Hence everything underneath this highest authority, everything both in the heavens and the earth, had been adversely affected. Vast multitudes of powerful angels, having been given authority over various aspects of creation, could now wage war against God and against his people. Not all angels fell but in the minds of these writers, a great many did. Demons sometimes portrayed as mutant offspring of the Nephilim but other times portrayed as fallen angels themselves could now freely infest this satanically governed world and work all manner of evil in it. What was to have been a godly council of heaven and godly army for the Lord had turned on itself into a fierce rebel battalion that fought against God and did so in large part by terrorizing the earth and holding its inhabitants captive.[28]

There was also a significant theological development in the relational understanding between humanity, God, and the angels—both good and bad. The *Testament of Levi* outlines that angels brought prayers to God and functioned as intermediaries and that arch-angels are ones that worked on behalf of those called righteous. It set up a "bureaucratized theology of prayer."[29] Yet it is the book of *Tobit* that provides the most grounding to the New Testament worldview of spiritual conflict and the act of exorcism as a vehicle for release and relief. The angel, Raphael, seems in action to be an iconic forerunner to Jesus' actions and mission. In *Tobit* 12:17-22 it reads,

> They were both alarmed; and they fell upon their faces, for they were afraid. But he said to them, "Do not be afraid; you will be safe. But praise God forever. For I did not come as a favor on my part, but by

the will of our God. Therefore praise him forever. All these days I merely appeared to you and did not eat or drink, but you were seeing a vision. And now give thanks to God, for I am ascending to him who sent me. Write in a book everything that has happened." Then they stood up; but they saw him no more. So they confessed the great and wonderful works of God, and acknowledged that the angel of the Lord had appeared to them.

Here are the parallels for Jesus' mission, Jesus' return, and the act of ascension which, as we will see, all have spiritual warfare overtones. Yet more to the point at hand,

> The angelology reflected in Tobit continues to be manifested in even more developed form, throughout the New Testament. Demons are the source of affliction in an individual's thoughts, and in the Gospels and Acts, exorcism is the vehicle for relief. Angels act on behalf of individuals even to the point that each person is presumed to have his or her own angelic protector or representative in God's court (Matthew 18:10, Acts 12:15). Demons forces must be bound in order to be rendered ineffective (Tobit 8:3, Revelation 20:2). Tobit causes Asmodeus to flee, but Raphael overpowers and binds the demon (8:3).[30]

In two small verses from *Tobit*, we see the formation of the worldviews found within the Synoptic Gospels and Acts. *Tobit* reads,

> As he went he remembered the words of Raphael, and he took the live ashes of incense and put the heart and liver of the fish upon them and made a smoke. And when the demon smelled the odor he fled to the remotest parts of Egypt, and the angel bound him (Tobit 8:2-30).

This inferred theology of binding and causing the demon to flee is not only seen in every act of exorcism within the New Testament, but also becomes the grounding for post-apostolic writings such as the text *Testament of Solomon,* in which "the interview of Solomon with the demon Asmodeus, who plots against newlyweds and is defeated by precisely the same means as in Tobit (see *Testament of Solomon* 5:1-13)."[31]

All of the above and much more set the stage for the arrival of Jesus. He didn't enter a spiritual vacuum; His upbringing occurred in an environment fertile with spiritual thought and conversation. We get a glimpse of Jesus joining that conversation when He visited the Temple as a 12-year old (Luke 2), but it's important for us to see that His ministry launched before an audience that was very much active with spiritual activities and thinking. It's easy for us to think the gap in inspired Scripture between Malachi and Matthew was a kind of spiritual dead zone, but it would be more accurate to say that during this time, the Jewish community was working much out theologically and this understanding deeply informed Jesus and His original audience.

CHAPTER 3
THE SYNOPTIC GOSPELS AND DELIVERANCE

Before we explore the act of freeing (or deliverance), another foundational theological idea needs to be clarified. As the New Testament era dawns, Jesus' view of "kingdoms" is most important—both His view on the Satanic kingdom as well as the Kingdom He now brings, which not only causes the clash but also begins the gradual replacement of one kingdom for another. As a first century Jew, Jesus' view of the world naturally stems from the Old Testament as well as the thinking shaped by the events that occurred between the covenants.

When Jesus comes onto the scene, He is not just born into a community whose worldview is that of the Intertestamental period; He also embraces and sharpens that worldview. It's not so much that all of Jesus' teaching is new, since He built upon and assumed much of the thought present in His time. He spoke with authority and finality on things that were current concerns of His audiences. In other words, the blackboard on which Jesus was writing wasn't blank and the culture He was speaking into wasn't ignorant. It was filled with biblically (Tanakh-Old Testament) based ideas, pictures, and teaching that Jesus clarified and challenged while He lived the amazing life we find recorded in the Gospels.

Notice that throughout Jesus' ministry, the signs He performed, like casting out demons, were never greeted with shocked responses by His audiences as if they had never seen or heard of such things before. Even in John 9, when Jesus heals the man born blind, the surprise expressed by the disciples and others isn't so much about the healing as it is about the fact that people were healed of blindness from other causes, not from blindness as a birth defect. He also challenged their assumption that birth defects were evidence of someone's sin being punished.

Throughout His three-year ministry, Jesus' message was focused on the kingdom. He made this clear in three ways: He announced Himself as "I am," or king; He taught authoritatively about the kingdom; and He did deeds representative of the kingdom. In short, He not only proclaimed the kingdom, He also brought the kingdom and demonstrated His kingship.

Think for a moment about the significance of the healings that occurred during Jesus' ministry. How did they matter? They demonstrated His kingdom rule. A mark of the eternal kingdom is no more diseases. Jesus, under His Father's permission, was providing a foretaste of that future state and His ability to bring it about.

In John's Gospel, exorcisms are not recorded because they do not prove the divinity of Jesus nor is the kingdom of God a primary theme of his gospel. However, despite not including any direct acts of deliverance, John does theologically outline the world possessed by the dark kingdom. Satan is called the *"prince of this world"* (John 12:31; 4:30; 16:11) and the world is *"under the power of the evil one"* (1 John 3:8). The word "prince" is *"archon"* which is the "highest official in a city or a region in the Greco-Roman world."[1] Jesus enters into this kingdom to birth His Father's kingdom and thus replace the illegal one. John must be paired with the other three gospels. When brought together, they give us the upstairs and downstairs view of the whole conversation. As one of my professors[1a] once pointed out when reflecting on John 12:27-31, the judgment of the prince of this world is tied directly to Christ's death on the cross. The twofold "now" is significant. We have death, resurrection, and ascension all together as one act of triumph. The enthronement of Christ dethrones the enemy. In John, the battle is engaged at one major place: the cross. Jesus makes this clear in describing the ongoing work of the Holy Spirit as confirming the victory accomplished at Calvary: *"When he comes, he will prove the world to be in the wrong about sin and righteousness and judgment . . . and about judgment, because the prince of this world now stands condemned"* (John 16:8, 11, see also 1 John 3:8).

The imagery of D-Day and V-Day are appropriate here. D-Day was the invasion of the allied forces in Normandy in 1944. This was the decisive battle but the fighting was continued for months until Berlin was liberated in 1945. In the interim, although the outcome was not in doubt, the fighting was still intense and dangerous and lives were still lost. We find ourselves between D-Day and V-Day (See also John 14:30, Colossians 3:15). The battle is won upstairs but is being worked out down here.

The last sentence above is actually somewhat cautious given the entire witness of Scripture. Jesus did not just enter Satan's kingdom; He invaded. He freed captives. He reclaimed territory. He expected absolute allegiance from those invited to follow Him. While on earth, He was behind enemy lines—causing havoc and eventually sealing the fate of our enemy through His work on the cross.

Christmas, then, is an invasion. The Prince of Peace was born to challenge the Prince of the Air. In Revelation 12, we find an overarching panorama of history, including Heaven's view of the invasion. While the vivid picture of the pregnant woman in the opening verses of the chapter has informed much of the Roman Catholic iconography of Mary, the verses are actually depicting Israel as the people through whom the Son of God entered the territory of the enemy.

The red dragon pictured next is not intended to be seen as the next arrival in lineal history (as in Greek thinking), but is actually a picture of the longstanding spiritual opposition in a Hebrew framework, which anticipates the arrival of the child and pictures the rebellion in heaven led by Satan and drawing a third of the angelic "stars" to their fall to earth. Lucifer was by no means alone in his attempted coup of God's throne. A state of war broke out in heaven which expelled Satan and his forces and caused them to regroup on earth to continue their rebellion.

Also included in Revelation is the ominous scene in which the woman is about to give birth to a baby clearly identified (the iron scepter is the clue; see Psalm 2:9) as the Messiah, but which the dragon intends to kill at birth. This is the dark side of the Christmas story: The undercurrent of hostility seen in Herod and in the killing of the infants of Bethlehem points to the momentous spiritual conflict raging behind the scenes. Herod was not just an evil, paranoid leader. He was demonically driven to serve Satan's purposes. The kingdom of darkness knew it had been invaded and reacted to eliminate the invading force, centered on a child who would reclaim God's authority over creation.[1b]

The Gospels clearly include the parallel realities of the worldly realm alongside the spiritual realm throughout the earthly life of Jesus. But we miss this overlapping account because we're not looking for it, or in some cases, are studiously avoiding it, as when we downplay Jesus' frequent conflicts with demonic forces. Eventually the decisive battle at the cross will be waged, but before then there will be years of skirmishes as the kingdom of darkness is confronted and then defeated by the kingdom of God. Jesus made possible the salvation of humanity and the re-establishment of that perfect kingdom which was in place in Eden and will return as the new heaven and new earth.

Luke would later summarize all of Jesus' ministry in Acts 10:38. He *"went about doing good and healing all who were oppressed by the devil, for God was with him."* As Boyd explains, "When Jesus healed people, he saw himself as setting them free from the power, and the whippings of the devil."[2]

Before we get to Jesus' acts of freedom, it is important to clarify what kingdom He was bringing, which is the foundation to any act of Godly deliverance. George Ladd defines the kingdom this way: "The kingdom is primarily the dynamic reign or kingly rule of God, the sphere in which the rule is experienced."[3]

So, the kingdom of God is not a place yet, the kingdom of God is not the nation of Israel, the kingdom of God is not the church, the kingdom of God is not geography. The kingdom of God is any space or place where the reign and rule of God is welcomed, embraced and accepted! If you are a Christian, you are a member of the kingdom because you have welcomed Jesus to be your Savior and King! Without Jesus the kingdom is not found, you cannot separate the king's presence from His kingdom!

The preaching of the kingdom was the central theme of Jesus of Nazareth (Mark 1:15; Matthew 4:17), and today those that claim succession and relationship with Him continue to proclaim the message of this kingdom. From the sending of the twelve (Matthew 10:7) and the seventy-two (Luke 10:9,11), to the founding of the church in Acts, and through Revelation, the proclamation of this kingdom does in some way tie to the sovereignty and rule of its sovereign, Jesus of Nazareth. And it should be noted that a kingdom, by very definition, is seen and its dynamic is experienced primarily through acts of the kingdom, not just words of the kingdom. The kingdom doctrine is expressed through demonstration. Doctrine is understood, confirmed, and demonstrated through deed; it is word *and* deed in very essence.

> The New Testament fully shares the Old Testament belief in the sovereignty of God. Despite many appearances to the contrary, God is on the throne (Matt 5:34, Heb. 8:1). The persecuting Domitian may be on the throne of the Roman Empire, but John begins his vision by assuring his readers that 'there in heaven stood a throne, with one seated on the throne'.[4]

Yet this shared view fails to fully define the kingdom. Ladd, in *The Presence of the Future,* writes,

> The critical problem arises from the fact that Jesus nowhere defined the phrase. We must therefore assume either that the content of the phrase was so commonly understood by the people as to need no definition or that the meaning of Jesus' proclamation is to be interpreted in terms of his total mission and conduct.[5]

I think the answer is both. Jesus assumed a cultural/religious shared understanding, which explains much of the silence Ladd refers to here. But we are not left with this silence when we take the time to look at His claim through

His words and deeds. A compelling picture of the kingdom emerges from Jesus' ministry throughout the Synoptic Gospels (Matthew, Mark, and Luke).

THE KINGDOM IN THE SYNOPTIC GOSPELS

John the Baptist is the embodiment of the tension existing between the old and new ages. He is the dividing point between the two epochs, the older and newer covenant. He is the last prophet of the Old Testament who called out to the people of Israel to repent and reminded them that the Day of the Lord was not far off and was now about to dawn (Matthew 11:12-13; Luke 16:16).[6] But he made it clear he was not the one they were waiting for. "I've got water," he said, "but the One coming has fire!" As an aside, John the Baptist is my "patron saint" for ministry. He reminds me, as a pastor, that I can point to Jesus and then sleep at night. My responsibility is to proclaim, not to change people. If ministry means restlessness and sleeplessness, I've misplaced my responsibilities and need to take another look at John the Baptist.

Though the ministries of Jesus and His cousin John were similar, they parted ways when Jesus made an announcement in Nazareth that changed the world (Luke 4:14-29). On that occasion, He inaugurated a new era in the ongoing development of salvation history:

> At this point his preaching lost much of its earlier continuity with John's call for renewal. Jesus introduced an entirely new theme: the gospel was no longer a future hope but a present reality of eschatological significance. This served to heighten the expectation of the people.[7]

Jesus' announcement of the kingdom as recorded in Luke and throughout His entire three years of ministry was expressed in word (teaching) and deed (deliverance, healings, and so on). For those paying attention, He identifies Himself with "I am" passages (primarily in John's account), which both His friends as well as His enemies hear as claims to divinity. On several occasions, God the Father lends His own confirmation of Jesus' identity by announcing, *"This is my beloved Son, in whom I am well pleased"* (cf. Matthew 3:13-17, 17:1-13; Mark 1:9-11, 9:2-13; Luke 3:21-22, 9:28-36).

The central style of His teaching was articulated in parabolic form. When asked why He used parables as His central form of expression (Matt 13:2, 10), Jesus replied,

> *The knowledge of the secrets of the kingdom of heaven has been given to you but not to them. Whoever has will be given more, and he will have an abundance.*

Whoever does not have even what he has will be taken from him (Matt 13:12-13).

Through various parables dealing with growth (Matthew 13:1-9; Mark 4:1-9; Luke 8:4-8), the Banquet (Luke 14:16; Matthew 22), stewardship (Luke 19), and seeking (Matthew 6:25-33; 13:45-46), we begin to see the nature and purpose of this kingdom. Arthur Glasser writes, "God is a seeking God. Indeed, if the Kingdom means anything, it is that God is visiting his people to invite them to its eschatological feast."[8] We see the personal call, the present reality, and the expected future of such teaching. The parables together form a theology of kingdom, which is

> ...present though ongoing reality to be entered through the new birth (John 3:5) necessitating the conscious acceptance of God's sovereign rule over one's life. The parables point in various ways to the mission of the church and look forward to the final victory of God in history. The Kingdom is both presence and promise; both within and beyond history; both God's gift and (the believers) task; we work for it even as we wait for it.[9]

All of this brings us to the implications for spiritual warfare and gives proper context to the act of deliverance. What has been called "inaugurated eschatology" or the kingdom of "now" (Luke 10:9, 17:21; Matthew 12:28; Romans 14:17) and "not yet" (Matthew 25:34; 1 Corinthians 6:9-10; Luke 13:29, 22:18) has already emerged through the teaching of Christ.[10] The teaching and proclamations of Jesus were that people needed to have their eyes opened to their condition and thus see their need for this kingdom's message. This simple statement was new and a move away from the Jewish thought of the time (John 4:7).[11] His call to turn from darkness to light and be freed from the power of Satan and have one's sins forgiven was attested to by His miracles. Those miracles, however, should not only be viewed as proof of His Messiahship and personal authority, nor as acts of human compassion alone, for they were also done to show that the kingdom was indeed present.[12] In particular, the act of deliverance was viewed by Jesus as the first assault on the kingdom of darkness, and at the cross He would take the whole kingdom of darkness to defeat.[13] As Gustaf Wingren writes,

> When Jesus heals the sick and drives out evil spirits, Satan's dominion is departing and God's kingdom is coming (Matthew 12:22-29). All of Christ's activities are therefore a conflict with the Devil's (Acts 10:38). God's Son took flesh and became man that he might overthrow the

power of the Devil, and bring his works to naught (Hebrews 2:14ff, 1 John 3:8).[14]

So every time a sick person was healed or a demon-possessed person was delivered, something important was also occurring: Jesus was demonstrating His kingdom rule. These were momentary glimpses into the coming future when there would no longer be such destructive evidence of the kingdom of darkness. God's kingdom was challenging, defeating, and eventually eclipsing the kingdom that had dominated earth and would continue to have its way for a while. Every power of darkness, including death, was shown to be defeatable. Lazarus hopping out of the tomb (John 11:38-44) anticipated an age in which death would no longer be inevitable, even though Lazarus himself would eventually have to die again. Permanent resurrection would not be established as the norm until after Jesus' own resurrection following His work on the cross.

Now, every time there is a genuine obedience or imitation of Christ among Christians (loving the poor, welcoming sinners, forgiving others, etc.) we are seeing evidence of the kingdom of God. These are small acts of rebellion, resistance to the faltering kingdom of darkness and further extensions of the reality of God's kingdom here on earth. Many of these acts that the world declares impossible are, in fact, very possible because they are done with and through God's power. Living the "boring Christian life" can actually be a successful campaign against Satan's power because someone is regularly saying "yes" to the new kingdom and "no" to the old one. This is also why, throughout the history of the church, believers who have done their best to live faithfully under very difficult political and ethical situations have had to endure over-the-top persecution—because the dark kingdom reacts to even a gentle threat to its power.

While Jesus was on earth, establishing the beachhead of the kingdom of God, He was the original Spirit-led human, carrying out His Father's will. He willingly set aside his prerogatives and power and took on human form (Philippians 2:5-11). He was still fully God, but willfully limited His power and actions to what was supplied by the Holy Spirit. He was unique. Jesus was the embodiment of the kingdom, fully living willingly under the reign and rule of God the Father! But now that He has stepped away and sent the Holy Spirit to indwell believers, there are millions of Jesus-people running loose on the planet. The kingdom of darkness is under siege and not happy about it. And one of its ongoing strategies in countering what God is doing is to convince believers that they do not have the Spirit of Jesus and cannot see the Holy Spirit at work powerfully in their lives. The dark kingdom's success in this strategy is seen anywhere where the church is not having a significant impact on the world. Against this, we must remember Jesus' promise that His church—His people—will prevail over the gates of hell.

CASE STUDIES IN THE GOSPELS

During my years in the church, one of the persistent impressions I picked up was that the narrative content of the Gospels should never be used for theology. The accounts contained useful information, but only passages that were clearly teaching-based could be used for on the ground ministry. This shifted the focus of theological thought from scattered passages in the Gospels to the Pauline and other epistles in the New Testament. To put it succinctly, the record of the life of Jesus was to show us only our amazing Lord and Savior, but had little to show us about His role as our model—because we aren't God.

It took me a long time to realize that there is wisdom in the caution that narrative is not necessarily about what *should* happen but what *did* happen. It doesn't necessarily mean that what happened can happen again. But (and this is the point that gets lost) it also *doesn't* mean that it *can't* happen again. The application of teaching content is what should happen. Hearing a good story may or may not move me to action; hearing an instruction or teaching should move me to action. But I have become convinced that, particularly in the case of Jesus, both His actions and His teaching were crucial in developing healthy and correct theology. And the main reason for this conviction is that He tells us to do that. Yes, He does say, "If you love Me, do what I tell you to do," but He actually also says, "If you obey me, you will do even greater things than I have done." When He taught what we call the Lord's Prayer, He said, "Pray this way." After He washed the disciples' feet, He asked, *"Do you understand what I have done for you?"* (John 13:12b), then added, *"I have set you an example that you should do as I have done for you"* (John 13:15). The narrative of Jesus' life provides us with patterns that we dare not ignore if we are listening to what He taught. We are missing a major part of the reason Jesus came if we focus solely on His saving work and ignore His modeling work.

Since we are intent on laying a biblical foundation for deliverance ministry, it's important to connect the dots here regarding the discovery I just described. I did not grow up as a follower of Jesus or entered structured theological training with the idea that I would be participating in casting out demons, speaking in tongues, or seeing miracles happen. On the contrary, I was a somewhat confused Trinitarian cessationist. The Christian surroundings in my early days were dispensational and anti-charismatic. I was conservative and Baptist. I believed in the Holy Spirit, but thought He had stopped doing weird stuff once the New Testament was written. The strange goings on were for the church down the street; we were strictly by the book and not trying to replay the stuff that happened back in Bible times. Those things made me nervous because I had always been taught that anything unusual was a sign of disorder, and that God was a God of order. The problem that became more and more apparent (and I eventually realized was a problem I always had) was a pattern I could not avoid. Things came to a crisis when I was an eighteen-year old learning to minister at a Christian summer camp. The programming involved a lot of fun and light biblical teaching.

To my surprise, young people began to approach me with comments and questions that had nothing to do with the content of my speaking. For example, a young girl from a Plymouth Brethren church came to me with an admission that she had done something wrong. I thought I was prepared for anything a young person might confess, but was shocked to hear her say, "I was at a party and my friend, who is a Wiccan, introduced me to witchcraft and has been showing me how to do it and I started to do it. And I'm beginning to think it's not right."

All I could do is nod my head in agreement with her assessment—yes this *was* a problem and definitely not right.

She continued, "Now I'm feeling mixed up and confused; I don't know what to do."

I didn't say this, but my first thought was, "I don't know what to do either!" What I did say—moving into unfamiliar territory—was, "You're right; Jesus does say 'No!' to that behavior. And thanks for confessing it, like God tells us to do in James. So maybe it would be good for us to pray together right now. You could tell Jesus you're sorry." I found myself clueless about what to do next, but we prayed, and apart from the strangeness of the situation and maybe some hesitation on her part before she spoke, we experienced several minutes of simple confessing and surrendering prayer asking Jesus to free her. Afterwards, there was a sense of calm and a feeling that whatever that was, we had given it to the Lord and done the right thing. It was a memorable incident, but not earth shattering for me.

A year later I received a letter from her parents that began, "Thank you for delivering our daughter from Satan." That set me back. They continued to describe how their daughter's life had radically changed after that moment at camp. She was living for God and taking steps to become a missionary. Their words made me think, "What happened? I just prayed with her." I had no context to recognize what God had done or why and how He had done it.

The next summer, another girl approached me and said, "Jon, I don't know why I'm talking to you about this, but I feel I have to." I flashed back to the previous year and braced myself as she continued, "I'm a committed Christian who has been baptized, but I have recently been involved in playing a lot with Tarot cards with my friends, though I'm feeling more and more like it's wrong. But I'm not sure why."

I said, "Well, the Bible does talk about the dangers of witchcraft." Inside, I was struggling with the level of discomfort I was feeling. I sheepishly continued, "I don't know that much about this, but I did read a book by this Neil Anderson guy and he's got some instructions about how to pray in situations like this." I pulled out the book and frantically thumbed through the index looking for references to Tarot cards. Wanting to press forward, I invited her to pray as I walked her through what I thought she should say. After a few phrases of confession, I invited her to say, "I'm sorry, Jesus, for playing Tarot cards." Up to that point, she had been repeating my words exactly. Now she said, "I'm sorry, Jesus, for playing—." There was an awkward silence. Not sure what to do, I thought she had gotten distracted, so I said the phrase again. It took me a couple more tries before I realized she was actually unable to say the words "Tarot cards" in prayer. I was suddenly aware of the strong impression of negative, binding, spiritual power surrounding us. The theoretical reality of spiritual bondage was now becoming very real to me.

Out of a sense of desperation, I began to pray, "In Jesus' name—" and suddenly she yelled out, "TAROT CARDS!" Whatever was stopping her from speaking had been shattered.

I was stunned. Something very true and real had just happened and it didn't fit my categories or assumptions. That encounter with evil propelled me on a journey that has now lasted almost two decades. But I have to admit that the beginning phases of the journey were more a concerted attempt to avoid and ignore what had happened, while at the same time immersing myself in typical ministry activity and preparation. I became a youth pastor and went to seminary. I studied biblical theology, learned systematic theology and ethics, debated with many, and tried hard to steer clear of the dark side of spirituality.

But reality was never far away. Not long after I became a full-time youth pastor, a fourteen-year-old approached me and said, "Jon, something really weird is happening in my house. I know it's strange, but I'm sure something is following me everywhere I go."

My initial response was to doubt this girl. I knew she was prone to lie a lot. But it just so happened that a friend of hers had slept over at her house that weekend. She, I considered trustworthy. So I asked her, "What do you think about this?" She said, "I was there, it happened; I had the same experiences she is telling you about."

I had simply been trying to "do ministry" and yet these odd events kept confronting me along the way. I wasn't even sure who I could talk to about these things, since no one in our denomination was on record as having a public opinion about demonic activity. But I thought of a woman named Christel who scared me a little because she seemed to talk to Jesus in a way that I wanted to, but had not yet experienced. Then I realized there was another person in our church who also prayed with authority. I asked the two of them to join me with the girl at the church for prayer. We were miles from her home when we prayed.

This started as a classic example of Paul's phrase in Romans 8:26, *"we do not know what we ought to pray for."* But as we simply began to pray to Jesus, I opened my eyes and was suddenly able to see the thing. I was acutely aware, in my mind, of the evil spiritual presence in the house. (There was a small part of me inside repeating "I'm a Baptist" over and over.) This spirit and I were aware of one another. The two women continued to pray.

Without a plan in mind, I simply said, "In Jesus' name, you can't touch her in the living room anymore." The spirit I was addressing disappeared. Thrilled and relieved, I concluded we had done the right thing and solved the problem. We finished our prayer time and excused ourselves.

A week later the young woman approached me again and said, "Well, Jon, it works in the living room, but I'm still bothered everywhere else in the house."

My internal response was, "Oh no, I'm becoming one of *those* people!" But that moment actually represented a change of direction in my journey from avoiding the reality of spiritual influence to recognizing it everywhere. And almost from that moment, in our conservative, evangelical church, person after person, when allowed the freedom to report, volunteered experiences of evil spiritual encounters. We weren't promoting or preaching about the demonic, but its presence was being revealed among us. Personally, I wanted to run somewhere else. You could say that my early steps in the journey to understand deliverance ministry looked more like the marks in the road of someone being dragged along.

The ministry of deliverance has never been marketed among us. By the time I was allowed to pursue my doctorate, we had been learning and responding to the needs that had been revealed in our church for thirteen years. Much of it was trial and error, seeking direction from others who had experience in the area of spiritual deliverance. We made many mistakes, but also saw God do some amazing things to free people from demonic oppression. All of this was in the context of a growing church with ministry demands in every direction. I pursued a master's degree at a local seminary to increase my formal understanding of the Spirit's work. Eventually, I made this the focus of my doctoral thesis in an effort to evaluate whether what we were doing was right or wrong. We wanted to identify biblical boundaries and maintain an orthodox faithfulness in every area of our ministry.

One of the terms I use to summarize the development I just described is *organic*. We weren't following a plan; we were doing our best to keep in step with the Holy Spirit, guided by Scripture. There were two significant discoveries we realized along the way. First, the demonic behaved in ways that closely paralleled both the biblical descriptions and reports from believers across the centuries. And second, I saw a troubling pattern in the fact that most of the people who were reporting demonic oppression were not unbelievers, but people who seemed to be average followers of Jesus. According to my theology of freedom in Christ, this kind of thing wasn't supposed to happen!

By the time I began serious work on my doctorate I had decided I wasn't just going to read the Gospels as narrative confession. I was also going to read them through the lens of case studies. In particular, I wanted to take the time to look at every report of Jesus' interaction with the demonic to catalog what He did and didn't do as well as the other details and outcomes of His actions. I wanted to discover if there was a pattern in Scripture that might still be applicable today. Could I build both orthodoxy as well as orthopraxy from what Jesus said and did?

Meanwhile, my exposure to the odd and out-of-the-ordinary spiritual experiences was increasing exponentially. I now reflect about how on several occasions, in dealing with the demonic, I had demons laugh at me. I would get angry and they would mock me. Raising my voice and trying to increase my authoritative tone didn't seem to accomplish anything more than upset those I was trying to help. These disconcerting experiences challenged my understanding of the ways and means of using God's power in confronting evil. God's sovereignty, my own cultural presuppositions and limitations, and the circumstances presented a maze I didn't find easy to figure out. But I wanted to. So I came to God's Word, and particularly the Holy Spirit inspired biographies of Jesus, with the desire to let them speak and to pay attention to what the record was saying.

Next let's move into the Synoptic Gospels to see various acts of deliverance in their raw form and let the Scriptures speak for themselves. I hold the view that these encounters are not just recorded acts of history, but case studies. These deliverances allow us to build orthodox theology (right thinking) and good orthopraxy (right practices). Without this secondary step, God is reduced to history and the future with very little in the "in between."

CHAPTER 4
THE GOSPEL ACCORDING TO SAINT MARK

As we now journey into the Gospels, we remember to keep a balance between the record we find in Matthew, Mark, and Luke and the somewhat different approach taken by John. These two streams of witness give us the full view of Jesus' character, words, and works. We understand the first three Gospels as being Christology from below, presenting the unique human life of the God-man Jesus. John then provides the Christology from above, emphasizing the divine signs within the life of the God-man Jesus. Both these aspects of Jesus are crucial, and to miss either lands us quickly in heresy.

As we trace the ministry of Jesus through the Synoptics, I am focusing on the Gospel of Mark simply because he is the chief source for Matthew and Luke. Also, in looking at the different parallel passages, I will not cover every example since many are repeated with small variations between authors. Mark, rushing us to the cross, is quick to move Jesus into public ministry. He outlines the Gospel (1:1-13), calls His first disciples (1:14-20), and then launches His ministry in a way unlike what we see in the other Gospels, with a demonic encounter. As Jesus teaches, the reaction is from the kingdom of darkness. Mark, with great intention, maintains the theme that Jesus is a person with more power than John the Baptist (1:7), himself a teacher of great authority (1:22-23), leading up to one with greatest spiritual authority. The clash of kingdoms that will eventually lead to the cross is immediate.

> Only Mark makes the story of Jesus' confrontation with evil spirits the initial public act in Jesus' ministry (since the calling of the disciples has no witness apart from Zebedee and his hired men). The narrative has a clear Christological function. Jesus' identity, which was announced earlier by a voice from heaven, is now shouted out by a spirit. Transcendent forces recognize him for who he really is. However human Jesus appears throughout the subsequent narrative, he is also a figure of mystery and power.[1]

As Jesus begins to preach with power, the immediate result is not unity but disunity. His message causes strife, which manifests in the form of a demon within the congregation (Mark 1:23-25) recoiling from the presence, power, and purity of Jesus Himself. It also caused the people to note the mark of authority in Jesus' teaching that wasn't present in "the teachers of the law" (Mark 1:22). The amazement of the people has less to do with the demon being expelled than with the apparent ease with which Jesus exercised authority and power. But let's look closely at the setting.

One key observation made by Alan Cole has often been missed historically as well as in the present, yet is very important for pastoral reflection: "It is a strange commentary that a demonized person would worship in the synagogue with no sense of incongruity until confronted by Jesus and indeed apparently with no initial desire to be delivered from his affliction."[2] And yet the context clearly implies this man was an accepted member of the local synagogue and that others were not aware of his demonic oppression. He was nevertheless sitting "in church," listening regularly to the reading of God's Word, yet not unmasked until Jesus appeared on the scene.

Do you see it? This is so important—one can be in the presence of truth, but until the Author of truth comes, many that are afflicted by fallen spirits may not look for help or even have an awareness of the presence of evil within a person or persons. This first encounter gives us so much more insight to the act of deliverance. First, the phrase "evil spirit" or "unclean spirit" gives us a helpful understanding of their nature. Unclean or evil are not primarily moral or sexual terms, but shape phrases to point to the opposite of holiness (see Leviticus 11:44). What is unclean or evil is the reverse of wholeness, completeness—God's kind of shalom/peace itself. It is a phrase meaning "out of order."[3] All this implies that in their DNA, the unclean spirits are the reverse of holiness. It is their nature to be against God and His kingdom, which is characterized by right order, peace, and abundant life.

As we let the Scriptures speak, we very quickly see that what many pastors and teachers have taught on the clashing of kingdoms through this type of act is wrong. The demons are often presented in sermons as cowering before Jesus, crying out in fear with no ability or appearance of resistance.[4] This is not true at all. Verse 24 is merely the first of many passages showing a hostile, defiant, and offensive nature even towards God in flesh, their Creator. The phrase *"what do you want with us"* can also be translated "what is then between us and you," or "you do not have any business with us yet!" This is a phrase found throughout the Greek Old Testament (1 Kings 17:18; 2 Kings 3:13; Hosea 14), which "functions as a defensive formula denying communality with the person to who it is addressed."[5] It really is an aggressive act with spiritual ability and power. Not so much cowering as it is counter attacking the authority they perceive in Jesus. The hostility is also seen with the demoniac calling out "Jesus of Nazareth." It is better translated "you Nazarene" which really lets the reader feel and understand the hostile tone and intent.

Still, within the second part of verse 24, we see another layer in the interaction between the Son of Man and the kingdom of darkness. The question is, why this clash? Again, many devotionally and pastorally paint a picture of weak, feeble spirits with no ability to challenge. But, though they are weak in front of their Creator, demons still resist to the very end. They cry out Jesus' identity, *"the Holy One of God."* Accounting for this demonic behavior is one of the most important historical and pastoral insights to spiritual combat.

> The unclean spirit recognizes Jesus as the Holy One of God, the Bearer of the Holy Spirit, and between the Holy Spirit and an unclean spirit there exists a deadly antithesis that the demons know. This formula of recognition however does not stand all alone. It is part of a larger complex of material exhibiting a striking difference between the forms of address employed by the demoniacs and the titles used by ordinary sick individuals. This latter group appeal to Jesus as 'Lord' (7:8), 'Teacher' (9:17), 'Son of David' (10:47-48) or 'Master' (10:51) The demoniacs however address Jesus as 'the Holy One of God' (1:24), "the Son of God' (3:11) or 'the Son of the Most High God' (5:7), formulations which identify Jesus as the divine Son of God. The contrast in address is an important characteristic distinguishing ordinary sickness from demonic possession, and reflects the superior knowledge of the demons. The recognition-formula is not a confession, but a defensive attempt to gain control of Jesus in accordance with the common concept of that day, that the use of the precise name of an individual would secure mastery over him.[6]

Don't miss that point. Their accurate naming of Jesus is not an acknowledgement of His rightful divine status, but an attempt to co-opt Jesus by fearlessly identifying Him. In first century thinking, there was power in knowing names—the power of direct address or command. We might sense some of this difference in the two commands: "Hey you, stop that" and "Tom! Stop that." Their awareness of Jesus is motivating a vicious counterattack. They aren't giving up without a fight. They are willing to test whether or not they or Jesus have greater power. This becomes a crucial factor when we enter into the process of deliverance because we can't assume the battles or the victory will come easy just because we are on God's side. Jesus dealt with the demonic decisively, but never casually. And if the demonic openly mocked and resisted the second Person of the Trinity, they will treat us the same way. Those who participate in authentic deliverance ministry can expect to experience immediate as well as ongoing attacks from evil forces.

The way we respond to the phrase *"Holy One of God"* (v. 24) also reveals what I call a chronological snobbery problem in the church. This condescension basically says, "I know and understand better than ancient people did—they were ill-informed and stupid. We know so much more now than they did." We struggle with poor and negative assumptions about the past, thinking our technological advances make us improved human beings compared to our ancestors. Our "scientific age" deludes us into concluding the ancients really didn't get it. So when secularists (what many Christians today actually are) read passages like this one in Mark, what is their immediate response? Someone with experience in psychological training might conclude that the behavior recorded by Mark is not demonic but simply schizophrenia or some other mental disorder. They might even suggest that Jesus is actually hurting the person by improper diagnosis and treatment. Our default setting is naturalism with its conviction that everything can be explained by natural, scientific, rational means without resorting to something "unreal" like the spiritual. Our chronological snobbery causes us to miss the nuances that clearly indicate our forebearers were quite perceptive. The Scriptures reveal a diagnostic sensitivity in recording the cases Jesus dealt with that we dare not ignore when we're helping both sick people and the demonized.

As a brief aside, let's look at the demonic use of the name *Jesus of Nazareth*. Jesus' name was quite common, and like many names in His age, it was qualified by location of origin. Jesus was as frequent a name in the first century as it is in Mexico today. In Mark 1:24, the demon uses "Nazareth" to identify the name in a clear, specific, and hostile way toward Jesus.

The act of expulsion is seen in verse 25. When He rebukes them (note the demonic had used the phrase "what do you want with *us*" in verse 24), His statement uses a judicial term meaning to "lay a strong charge or penalty."[7] This is what the act of deliverance is in its purest sense, to subdue evil power (Zechariah 3:2; Psalm 68:31, 106:9). It comes from the Hebrew *"ga 'ar"* and always implies "a word with effective power."[8] In comparison to contemporary exorcists of the day, who always asserted to the kingdom of darkness their own name, relationship, and connection with the deity, Jesus speaks with direct authority and they respond, thus again showing His great power to be unlike any others at that time.[9] Again, the witnesses were stunned, not by the obvious presence of the demonic, or because they had never seen this act before but by the simple and powerful way Jesus confronted and defeated the power of evil.

Note also Jesus' call for the spirit to "be quiet," which comes from the idea "to be muzzled" and "tied shut." It infers power to overcome and is a strong, blunt phrase, which in modern English could be translated "shut up."[10] Another thematic reason for Jesus' demand for silence is what scholars now call "the Messianic Secret," which is central to Mark's theology and the reason for the muzzling of the demonic.

> Jesus wanted people to find out who he was but not from some ugly defensive spirit. Yet one must not miss the truth that 'to allow the defensive utterance for the demon to go un-rebuked would have been to compromise the purpose for which Jesus came into the world, to confront Satan and strip him of power. As such, this initial act of exorcism in the ministry of Jesus is programmatic of the sustained con-

flict with the demons which is a marked characteristic in the Marcan presentation of the gospel.[11]

The events in the first chapter serve as the pattern throughout Mark for such spiritual encounters. The process is fleshed out like this: a meeting between Jesus and the demons, their attempt to assault or resist Jesus, a commanding of submission and silence, the command to leave, the abrupt and sometimes violent exit of the evil presence, and then the community amazement, which results in huge public relations for Jesus and His ability.[12] From this first act to the healing of Peter's mother, Mark's storytelling quickly includes the whole community bringing "all sick and demon-possessed" (1:32), and Jesus delivering many from the kingdom of darkness.

At this point when I'm teaching students on the subject of deliverance, the question of demonic purpose often comes up. Why are demons so set on inhabiting human beings? With all of Creation to wander in, why do they regularly torment us? The answer comes when we remember the original fall of Satan. He was determined to usurp God's place on the throne of heaven. He decided he would demote the Creator to a lower position while assuming ultimate power. That plan was shattered. But in his fallen state, he discovered there was another place in Creation with a throne designed for God to inhabit—the human heart. Demonic possession is an affront to God. Even demonic harassment is a mockery of God's rightful place. Everything demons are about is against God. They hate beauty, color, Creation itself—and they hate us. We always remind them of their rejected Creator, since we are made in His image. Even humans who reject God and declare allegiance with Satan are hated by the demonic because they remain reminders as image bearers of God. And those of us who are inhabited by the Holy Spirit are especially toxic to the demonic. They reacted to Jesus; they will react to us. This is the reality Scripture teaches when it comes to the spiritual realm. We need to listen and allow God's Word to help us see the world around us more clearly.

The second reference to the demonic within Mark is more generalized and though there is not much new insight here, it does reflect one new facet of deliverance. Jesus commands silence within this context because He wants His followers to find out who He is (8:29) without the demonic interference, but it also shows that they must admit who He is.

> James 2:19 shows that such grudging acceptance of God by the demons as an unwelcome reality is far apart from true Christian faith: though demons may well admit, they do not trust, but only 'shudder; that is not the biblical 'fear of the Lord.'[13]

The summary of Jesus' ministry in Jewish Galilee found in Mark 1:38-39 involves word and deed—preaching and the driving out of the kingdom of darkness. William Lane points out that this summary is important.

In this connection, it may be significant that there is no reference to acts of healing in the summary statement. Healing is an aspect of the redemption but it demonstrates Jesus' confrontation with Satan less graphically than the restoration to wholeness of those who had been possessed by demons.[14]

The next example of an act of deliverance is in Mark 3:7-12, during the latter part of Jesus' ministry in the Galilee region. As the demons came into contact with Jesus, again they cried out, "You are the Son of God." As in chapter one, the demonic cry is not submissive, but resistive. When they called Him out by name, this was an attempt to disarm and overthrow Jesus, trying to overcome His ability to control them.

> These cries of recognition were designed to control him and strip him of his power, in accordance with the conception that knowledge of the precise name or quality of a person confers mastery over him. In this context 'Son of God' is not a messianic title but a recognition of the true status of their adversary.[15]

The greatest or most vivid encounter between Jesus and the demonic in the Synoptics is found among the tombs of Gerasenes in Mark 5:1-13. Jesus has now crossed into non-Jewish territory to do ministry and the encounter follows a pattern similar to Mark 1:21-28. In English, we often miss the power of the encounter. The man filled with evil did not just meet Him; it would be better translated "immediately accosted Him."[16] The story now outlines this man's terrible existence which:

> ...is a multi-colored tableau of the power of evil. The alternations between the plural voice of the demons and the singular voice of the demoniac, captures the havoc that such possession does to personal identity. Superhuman strength is coupled with manic self-destructiveness. The possessed person is alienated from family and friends.[17]

And yet this is also someone's son, brother, and a member of the community. Their treatment has escalated to chains and expulsion out of desperation to protect others as well as to provide the man some protection from himself and the spiritual forces afflicting him. There is no doubt about what is wrong with him, but they are ill-equipped to intervene on his behalf. So, he lives among the tombs.

As already seen, they (the demon speaks as one but declares in verse 9, *"we are many"*) cry out and call Him by name, *"Jesus, Son of the Most High God."* Again, this is the defensive tactic of trying to overcome Jesus by identifying Him, His power, and His name. The English NIV does not reflect the hostile nature of the encounter. What is conveyed in the original language is not a helpless person pleading for help, but an aggressive reaction against who the evil spirits perceive Jesus to be. The demonic cry out, "What have I and you in common?" or "Why do you interfere with me?"[18]

Yet this encounter does go further than the others recorded by Mark. In fact, it is common today to assume this kind of encounter is the standard demonic face-off. People think that unless there is this level of outlandish, over-the-top behavior, it's safe to bet there is no demonic involvement. But the unwillingness to admit that evil might be subtle and devious as well as obvious, depending on circumstances, leaves many vulnerable to destructive demonic harassment. Back to the encounter in Mark 5, as William Lane notes,

> It is surprising to find the demon addressing Jesus by his personal name, although it is possible that he had heard one of the disciples use this form of direct address. What is more noticeable is that the demon is fully aware of Jesus' divine origin and dignity. 'Son of the Most High God' is not a messianic designation but a divine one and in spite of the syncretistic associations that gather around the term 'Most High.' The full address is not a confession of Jesus' dignity but a desperate attempt to gain control over him or to render him harmless, in accordance with the common assumption of the period that the use of the precise name gave one mastery over him. The very strong adjuration 'by God' has a strange ironic ring in the mouth …He invokes God's protection but the adjuration is without force, for Jesus is the Son of God.[19]

In verse 7, the plea to not torture (*basanizein*) is usually used in connection to the last judgment (Matthew 18:34; Luke 16:23, 28; Revelation 18:7, 10, 15). The kingdom of darkness recognizes and fears the end.[20] The actions attributed to the man (rushing at Jesus and aggressively speaking to Him) are actually carried out by the spirits in awareness of their impending doom. This reality was true in Jesus' context and remains true in ministry today. The power of their future fate has a direct effect on the current state of the demonic and influences their behavior. As a pastoral side note, every time I deal with the demonic, I read to them Revelation 20 and point out that they chose the wrong side and have eternity in hell waiting for them. They know it, but they won't give up because in their DNA is hatred for their Creator and every part of Creation—particularly us.

Jesus commands the demon(s) to leave, but here it comes as an afterthought, an obvious result. "It is put in the form of a subordinate clause and Mark's historic imperfect may be translated 'For he had said to him, unclean spirit come forth out of the man'."[21] This means the demonic did not immediately obey Jesus. They resisted His command, perhaps an indication that since there were multiple demons involved, they may have each faked ignorance, "Who should leave? Me?"

Notice how the encounter unfolds in verses 8-13:

For Jesus had said to him, "Come out of this man, you evil spirit!" Then Jesus asked him, "What is your name?" "My name is Legion," he replied, "for we are many." And he begged Jesus again and again not to send them out of the area. A large herd of pigs was feeding on the nearby hillside. The demons begged Jesus, "Send us among the pigs; allow us to go into them." He gave them permission, and the evil spirits came out and went into the pigs. The herd, about two thousand in number, rushed down the steep bank into the lake and were drowned.

Here Jesus demonstrates the principle that knowing the name actually can gain mastery or power over an enemy. The demons had tried this against Jesus but failed because of His strength; He now reverses the same tactic against them with success. Their response to His demand for their name already establishes His authority. They declare they are "Legion," which referred to a Roman military force of 6000 soldiers, but many think this is more of a colloquial phrase indicating an overwhelming presence.[22] This does invite the question of how many demons could actually inhabit a person. The spiritual realm is not subject to spatial limitations as we might assume. The best answer to the question is: more than we think, but whether it's one or many, the results are havoc and destructiveness.

The demonic beg to stay in the area and Jesus allows this by sending them into a herd of pigs. This, of course, reinforces the non-Jewish and unclean background of this story, for like tax collecting, pig herding was banned, because no Jews were even allowed to keep pigs.[23] Yet this also gives insight to another key idea when dealing with this act of freedom. It would seem that in ancient understanding, the demonic were localized or had geographical assignment or preferences. This comes into play in Luke 11 and Matt 8:12, which we will look at later. Boyd provides helpful context when he writes,

The demons' desperate plea to remain in the area by entering a local herd of swine is also significant. Ancient people generally associated a particular region and this seems to be reflected in this passage. The desperation of their cry makes it appear that these degenerate spirits somehow needed to remain in this region, as though (perhaps) this was some sort of geographical assignment they had received from their chief and had to obey.[24]

Given that Jesus was invading territory held by demonic power, it is also significant to note that this is the first time in the Gospels that Jesus was sharing the gospel in a primarily non-Jewish region. Boyd mentions some kind of territorial responsibility issued to these demons, but it is also possible that the local population had invited the presence of the demonic and given them permission to exert power over people, thinking it could be controlled or beneficial. They learned that the short-term advantages of being allied to evil lead to long-term consequences. That herd of drowned pigs was a significant part of the region's economic wealth.

When God's Spirit is moving in this fallen world, the results are amazing and also disruptive. People who are transformed by their encounter with Jesus, as the man from Gadara clearly was, may discover that their entire social environment deeply resents what has happened to them. The expulsion of the demons, their destruction of the pig herd, the loss of their savings and the population's demand for Jesus to depart were all part of a complex sequence of events that show interrelationship between what is occurring at the natural level of things and what is occurring in the spiritual realm. A larger lesson from this event is that the cost of deliverance is often borne by the surrounding community, sometimes unwillingly. Another cautionary note from this passage as we approach deliverance ministry today is that the more the demonic is "legion," the more obvious and wide-ranging the struggle will be.

One last example from Mark is found in the transitional chapter, where the identity of Jesus is finally understood and the "Messianic secret" is starting to be shed. Mark records this encounter (9:17-29), which transpires within a communal setting. After the ministry-defining event of Jesus' transfiguration, Jesus, Peter, James, and John come down to find a man desperate to see his child free from evil while religious leaders were sitting in judgment. This encounter and deliverance is also a needed case study when letting the Gospels' witness influence our theology and practices. It offers additional significant details not included in the other accounts, but fleshes out certain undefined areas of demonic behavior.

First, we again see the terror and bizarre behavior of the demonized. "Not only does this account like the Mark 5 account show supernatural strength, but here the child convulses on the ground, becomes stiff and rigid and also causes self-harm and replicates disabilities like being deaf and mute."[25]

In the text, we don't see the effects of the demonic until the spirit sees Jesus. Until then, the discussion has been about the father's desire to get help for his suffering child. By the time Jesus arrives on the scene, the genuine longing for help has been set aside for an argument about the inability of the disciples to cast out the demon. With Jesus' arrival, the demonic distraction of human disagreement (often a useful control tool of evil) must be replaced by another tactic, the distraction of odd and offensive behavior: *"So they brought him. When the spirit saw Jesus, it immediately threw the boy into a convulsion. He fell to the ground and rolled around, foaming at the mouth"* (Mark 9:20). Jesus immediately cuts through the "show" with calm authority. He ignores the demon's antics, focuses on the father, and then expels the demonic.

Second, the victim of demonic oppression here is a child, which calls into question much of evangelical theology and understanding. This boy has been inhabited "since childhood" (*paidiske*), an expression that suggests he was like this from infancy, perhaps even birth. This point is highly significant, for it tells us that demonization, as it is understood by Jesus and the Gospel authors, was not something for which the demonized person was necessarily responsible. As Raymond Brown notes, for Jesus and the Gospel authors, "demonical possession is not so much the result of a league with Satan as an expression of bondage under Satan's dominion."[26] It would be wrong on our part to assume that demonic possession or harassment must always be blamed on the person who is suffering. We are often handicapped by a western understanding that things we don't want, don't believe in, or don't like, can't happen to us. Such is not true. A non-western view (far more prevalent in Scripture) would hold that experiences are communal as much or more than they are individual. What happens to us or in us can be largely influenced by family and culture before they can be explained simply by individual choices.

Jesus' words and actions on that occasion teach us today that pity and compassion must be central to any ministry to those under the influence of the demonic. The pastoral importance is that people are not always responsible for inhabitation. The attitude of the religious leaders in this story presumes guilt and that the person is full of sin. When this view is removed, we shift out of simplistic thinking and see a person's case as a struggle with a holistic and complex reality, which is always connected to the act of deliverance.

This last point is even more emphatic when we realize that this compressed sequence of events—beginning with the disciples' original attempts at deliverance until Jesus expelled the demonic—took significant time, with varying witnesses. The climax in verse 25 tells us, *"When Jesus saw that a crowd was running to the scene,"* He proceeded quickly with the exorcism. His focus was on the individual need, not a display of power for the crowd. Deliverance ministry in an age where everything is entertainment must resist the temptation to make a show out of the work of setting people free. Our attention to the reality of corporate connections mentioned above does not invalidate (and actually highlights) the significance of individual dignity. Jesus didn't make a show out of meeting this child's desperate need; we should never allow this kind of ministry to become a display for the crowd.

Finally, in verse 29, Jesus reveals that some deliverance does not come about without prayer and fasting (in some Marcan texts), and an approach grounded in faith, as is made clear in the parallel account in Matthew 17:14-21. The reason there was no freedom to overcome evil was because power was being limited by the lack of faith in those trying to help.

The narrative is to drive home the need for faith in God if the kingdom of God is going to expand against the kingdom of Satan. We are told that the disciples lacked faith and had not prayed enough in treating the boy (Mk 9:29); all the people involved lacked faith (Mk 9:19); even the boy's father had only a wavering faith (Mk 9:24). Hence the attempted exorcism had been unsuccessful.[27]

Biblically speaking, faith means informed trust. It isn't a "pull myself up by my own bootstraps" kind of internal self-reliance. There must be a specific, and of course, worthy object to that informed trust. When faith is rooted in us rather than rooted back in the God of the Bible, the Maker of Heaven and Earth, we are depending on a very weak and entirely unreliable source of power for action, particularly in the spiritual realm. Our faith must be in Jesus, who has clearly revealed God to us as being utterly trustworthy. When the effectiveness of the effort is said to be dependent on the quality of faith in us, failure will follow. This is why "health and wealth" erroneous teaching is such a plague on the church. The idea that our own level of faith can generate continuous well-being and abundant resources is a not-so-subtle substituting of our dependence on God with self-dependence, or what is more often the case, a self-serving teaching that allows someone to manipulate and confiscate the goods of others. In this particular setting, Jesus could have said the same thing He said during the Last Supper in John 14, *"You believe in God; believe also in Me."* And yet no one had the focused faith that would allow them to participate in what God wanted to do for that young man and his father. The point of reference and the point of decision then, as it is now, is Jesus saying, "Look at Me. I'm right here. You can trust Me to do what is right."

Included in Jesus' closing words after the expulsion of the demon is another significant lesson: *"This kind can come out only by prayer"* (Mark 9:29). The term *kind* or "species" indicates that within the demonic there are different types or kinds of demons. This includes a multiplicity of rank, size, ability—unmistakable diversity in the fallen realm. The implication of Jesus' statement is that our experience in deliverance will include a variety of responses from the demonic depending on the *kind* we encounter. At times, they will readily submit to Jesus' name; at other times there will be a more or less prolonged struggle that includes prayer. Our own experience has confirmed these details of Scripture more often than not. When we encounter something unexpected in deliverance settings, we often find that checking Scripture will remind us of some aspect of Jesus' dealings we have overlooked until we have faced them today.

Discussions like this usually bring out the assumption that because Jesus has all authority (and He does), the use of His name in deliverance settings should cause immediate victorious results. But Jesus' own practice and experience indicates that the struggle is real and the battle isn't easily won. Assured eventual victory doesn't mean the warfare in the trenches isn't still intense and deadly. The demonic argued with, resisted, insulted, and even tried attacking Jesus; why should we be amazed when they dig in their heels with us?

CHAPTER 5
THE GOSPEL ACCORDING TO SAINT MATTHEW AND SAINT LUKE

With our overview of Mark's narration of Jesus' deliverance work, we can now move to the additional details and insights provided by the other two synoptic Gospels.

Though I am focusing solely on the act and environment surrounding the encounters between Jesus and the demonic, I think it's worth noting for theological and practical reasons the battle that was waged before Jesus arrived in the region of the Gerasenes. I didn't deal with this when walking through Mark, but the implications are still the same. Matthew records Jesus rebuking a storm as He heads to His encounter on pagan soil (8:23-27). While on one level, this action on Jesus' part demonstrates His authority over the created order, there are good reasons to include in our overall understanding of this event that this was not simply a naturally occurring storm. There are other forces at work here to influence the weather. Catholic scholar Daniel Harrington gives a great insight to the Old Testament roots of this event, which now brings again the inferred current worldview of the first century into a crystal clear focus. This allows us to go back and see the full scale of combat within the previous generations.

> Whereas in Matt 8:1-17 Jesus showed his power as a healer of various diseases, In Matthew 8:18-9:9 he shows his power over even more formidable obstacles: a storm at sea (8:18-27), demons (8:28-34), and sin (9:1-8). These foes all belong to the kingdom of children of darkness...The background for the stilling of the storm is the ancient Near Eastern idea that the sea (especially a storm at sea) symbolized the powers of chaos and evil over against God. By making the storm subside and controlling the sea, Jesus defeats the forces of chaos and evil. Some see the episode as rooted in Psalm 107:23-30: Some went down to the sea in ships, doing business on the great waters; they saw the deeds of the Lord, his wondrous works in the deep. For he commanded and raised the stormy wind which lifted up the waves of the sea. They mounted up to heaven, they went down to the depths; their courage melted away in their evil plight; they reeled and staggered like

drunken men, and were at their wits' end. Then they cried to the Lord in their trouble, and he delivered them from their distress; he made the storm be still, and the waves of the sea were hushed. Then they were glad because they had quiet, and he brought them to their desired haven. By showing power over the sea, Jesus does what God does according to Ps 74:13-14; 89:10-12. Indeed in apocalyptic texts the sea monsters Leviathan (Ps 74:14) and Rahab (Ps 89:10) become symbols of the evil powers defeated when God's kingdom comes in its fullness (see 2 Baruch 29:4).[1]

Not only does this root the very act of deliverance from the storm within the Old Testament tradition, but the very linguistics connect the act of stilling the sea with acts of power. The word *rebuke* here is the same used in the acts of deliverance between Jesus and demons. The deliverance of the demoniac is, therefore, part of a flow of events in an ongoing battle, not an isolated event apart from the context. Okay, so many of us miss another profound moment. This is the first time God in flesh, the good news Himself is going to non-Jewish communities! This is "go into all the world." Of course the forces of evil used even the natural elements to attempt to thwart the plan by killing Jesus and the disciples. The sudden and fierce storm does scare the half of the disciples who are not sailors and haven't experienced that kind of human helplessness, but even the experienced fishermen among the disciples were terrified. Galilee is a lake on which shore is always in sight (though not at night). The knowledgeable disciples knew that what was happening was bad and could easily lead to their deaths. This makes their shock in seeing Jesus sleeping soundly understandable. Why wasn't He awake and rightfully worried like they were?

These details are not immediately obvious in the text, but give us as the ongoing faith community another key pastoral insight. When you are preparing to be a co-worker with Jesus in this type of ministry, there will be attempts to stop, thwart, harm, and kill as you go to minister. Here is a clear demonstration that there is a battle before the battle, and this should send a strong warning and give us keen understanding about the implications for such an act of ministry. It may seem obvious, but it is rarely thought through by many. In our own experiences with deliverance ministry, we have tracked a consistent pattern of resistance and conflict before a major confrontation with the demonic. Obstacles—which seem on the surface to be purely natural occurrences like malfunctioning cars, plumbing, and electrical systems or sudden people conflicts, sickness, temptations, and social demands—arise to sap energy and infuse discouragement in those who are about to confront evil in Jesus' name. People forget their appointments for prayer or get lost on the way to church to meet with our deliverance team. And more, many times team members will be tempted in ways that are not normal for them and then when the session begins, that is the issue being confronted! The demonic are highly organized and will not be defeated without a struggle. Flat tires and unexpected anger issues are not necessarily demonic in nature, but we don't assume otherwise either.

Next comes Matthew's shortened Gadarenes account. Using Mark as his primary source, Matthew's gospel has many similar details (with his own additions and thoughts), but also has unique encounters to his own writing and some shared with Luke. Within this second series of miracles, the most famed deliverance, the Gadarene Demoniac, is used to point to Jesus' claims and identity. Yet Matthew has it in a different region and now doubles the number of demonized persons from one (in Mark) to two. Again, the point of this book is to look at the history, practice, and theology of the encounter and not to deal with challenges to the Synoptic harmony. Matthew's account of this event is only half the length, but does include the same attempts to overcome Jesus and the same eschatological implications. Matthew's unique understanding also brings some key ideas worth thinking about. Some suggest he doubled the persons because he omits so many other deliverances.

The idea that the healing and the confession of Jesus as the Son of God or the Son of David (in 8:28ff; 9:27ff; 20:30ff) must have a community of witnesses reveals an important Jewish connection. The Law insisted on at least two affirmations and Matthew's writing to the Jewish audience regularly includes the two corroborating witnesses, but still with the main focus on Jesus' authority, not the men's.[2] This caused me to think beyond the Law to the truth that all His encounters and His followers' encounters are done in community, and this infers and sets the precedent that the act of deliverance is a communal act. The power of the community and witness for authority sake and not just testimony, I believe, becomes a key element within the Gospels, Acts, and when developing biblical deliverance models for today's local church.

One other observation that has already been touched on briefly and that I will cover again later is the expressed desire on the part of the demons to be in the pigs. This not only infers geographical wants or even necessities; it would also seem that the demonic, when they are expelled, need a new host or home, which in this case becomes the pigs.[3] Harrington writes, "The assumption behind the demon's request is that they need a dwelling place where they might spend their destructive energy (see Josephus, *Ant.* 8:48)."[4]

At the end of this second grouping of miracles, Jesus again confronts a spirit after healing two blind men. This act will not only bring communal affirmation (the people) and support but also will begin to set up the religious smear campaign (the Pharisees) to sow doubt about the source of the power Jesus uses. "The reaction of the crowds (which is uniquely Matthean) situates Jesus' miracles squarely within Israel...The reaction of the Pharisees does not contest the fact of Jesus healing and exorcism. The point at issue is the source of his power."[5]

The strategy of Jesus' opponents offers interesting pastoral and practical insight for today and can be traced throughout all of church history as the argument used to discredit those trying to help the most lost and desperate. Yet the performance of miracles and deliverance also requires great discernment, for many have gifts or do such acts who are actually exercising power that is not of heaven at all. It is a great tension we experience today, as they did thousands of years ago.

One of the next encounters is found in Matthew 9:32-34. R. T. France writes,

> *Kophos* means both 'deaf' and 'dumb,' the two complaints being naturally linked together. Verse 33 indicates that the latter meaning is primarily in mind as in 12:22, 15:31. In view of the careful distinction normally drawn between illness and demon-possession (see on 18:16), it is surprising that here and in 12:22 a physical complaint is attributed to demonic influence: cf Mark 9:17ff, the only other such instance, again in a case of dumbness. The fact that the language here is entirely that of exorcism (demons cast out; no mention of faith or of touching the patient), whereas elsewhere the deaf and dumb are healed normally (15:30-31; Mk 7:32ff.-but see 12:22, where the blind and dumb demoniac is 'healed') indicates that this case was regarded as primarily one of possession, with the dumbness as a 'byproduct.'[6]

This stands out, both as an example that some physical ailments are directly connected to the presence of the demonic and in giving us needed insight to understand that sometimes what appears to be physical or emotional is not truly the issue; there may well be underlying spiritual factors that should be considered. Today, the growing awareness of the spiritual dimension among Christians has led to a tendency toward extremes, often resulting in everything being classified as demonically based: demons of sickness, mental disorders, feelings, ADHD, etc. A better reflection of biblical emphasis would be to approach people's needs holistically, taking into account a range of physical, medical, and mental factors, but not discounting the possibility of demonic roots in what might otherwise be considered simply natural phenomena. You will see later how we have attempted to include all these possibilities in the way we practice deliverance ministry.

In the task of distinguishing what is going on, we've found it helpful to use an electrical wall socket analogy. Instead of remaining focused or even distracted by the events immediately before us, it's helpful to ask the question: what power source is generating what we're seeing, hearing, and experiencing? Is it physical, social, or mental? Is it God, psychological factors, or demonic? Because all of these can result in observations that are very similar. The Spirit of Christ and the spirit of antichrist can produce what appear to be the same effects. Satan is called the angel of light for a reason. He can lurk behind events that we might easily attribute to God at work. He can imitate Jesus for the purpose of deception. Confronted with a set of behaviors that might at first appear demonic, those with experience in authentic deliverance take time to check their assumptions with power questions.

The challenge of identifying the source behind unusual events drives us to undertake deliverance ministry as a team rather than an individual effort. Certain spiritual gifts like discernment, knowledge, and wisdom are crucial tools in confronting the power of evil as well as recognizing when God is actually at work. When Jesus sent out His disciples to do ministry on their own, including deliverance (see Luke 9-10), He sent them in pairs.

Matthew 12:22-26 not only describes a powerful deliverance but also gives some of the best theological insight into the clash of kingdoms. It starts with a power encounter and ends by revealing Jesus' understanding of His coming, the continuance of His presence on earth, and the effects against the fading kingdom run by the so-called god of this world. Another illness spirit is driven out by Jesus and results in the crowd being moved closer to recognizing Jesus' true identity. As in chapter 9, the religious leaders take aim at both Jesus' ability and the source of that ability, which they believe is from Beelzebub. The reason they came to this conclusion is best summarized in this syllogism:

> Only prophets and magicians can do miracles; Jesus does miracles. Therefore, Jesus is either a prophet or a magician. Prophets enforce God's law; Jesus breaks God's law. Therefore, Jesus is a magician.[7]

The running conflict between Jesus and the Pharisees was based on their repeated assumption that "Jesus breaks God's law," an accusation He repeatedly denied and clearly refuted. His issue was with the way the oral law had been given equal authority with God's written Word. As long as they held that error, they would reach wrong conclusions about the source of Jesus' power.

Before moving into the specifics of this encounter, let's pause to say a word of admiration for the Pharisees of Jesus' day. He was hard on them, yet engaged them in serious dialogue. They were wrong about some things, particularly about Jesus. But they got a lot of things right. They were the foremost defenders of God's Word in their time. Jesus complimented their allegiance to Scripture, but He challenged some of their interpretations and applications. This exchange is an excellent example of how Jesus engaged the Pharisees in authentic conversation about deliverance and challenged some significant theological mistakes on their part.

Beelzebub is a name that comes from the Philistine god of Ekron (Baal-zebub) (2 Kings 1:2), the lord of the flies. Baal means lord, "zebul" means prince, heavenly region, dung, and enmity. Within the Synoptic Gospels (Matt 12, 24; Mark 3:22; Luke 11:16), he is called Satan, the prince of demons.[8]

> *Jesus knew their thoughts and said to them, "Every kingdom divided against itself will be ruined, and every city or household divided against itself will not stand. If Satan drives out Satan, he is divided against himself. How then can his kingdom stand?"* (Matt 12:25-26).

Jesus, with supernatural knowledge (a "word of knowledge" spiritual gift) knows their thoughts, and again enforces the idea of two kingdoms, their battle, and the inability of one to destroy itself. If there are attacks on or destruction of one kingdom, it must come from the other, for this conflict is spiritual in nature. "Jesus' exorcisms are blows against the kingdom of Satan and therefore can't be understood as done by the power of Satan."[9] Within this teaching, there are three other significant ideas that continue to help build understanding and practice for deliverance. First, in the next verse, Jesus compares Himself to other Jewish exorcists of His day. He said, *"And if I drive out demons by Beelzebub, by whom do your people drive them out? So then, they will be your judges"* (Matthew 12:27). This again enforces the idea that similar powers, abilities, and practices may be wielded by opposing sources. No one was challenging the reality of the exorcisms; they were questioning the source of His power. France writes:

> The argument assumes that Jewish exorcism was real and effective, and that it was acceptable to the Pharisees. The next verse will claim a unique significance for Jesus' exorcism; they were differently executed, lacking the magical techniques, generally used and depending on a simply irresistible authority, and the concentration of such activity in Jesus' ministry contrasts with the relative scarcity of reference to exorcism in non-Christian Jewish literature. But if exorcism as such was accepted in Jewish society, why should Jesus' practice of it be suspect?[10]

Again, it is never about formal or special ability but permission, power, and authentic connection to the One who can set people free. This has been and still is a terrible tension and temptation within the church, believing that formula alone is the answer. The formula, though Scriptural, must be done by a person who has permission and is empowered by God Himself. The model is only a vehicle; it is not the place of power. The power is from God, through His chosen servant; in this case, His Son! *"But if I drive out demons by the Spirit of God, then the kingdom of God has come upon you"* (Matthew 12:28).

Given the setting in which the demonic are being confronted, Jesus is responding to the accusation of the Pharisees by stating the issue: Either He or the disciples of the Pharisees might be accomplishing deliverance by the power of Satan. This emphasizes the important, underlying issue that the demonic do have power and this power can accomplish what appears to be healings and other remarkable occurrences. This was confirmed to me early in my ministry with youth when our church group was joined by a young man from a Hindu background. He was very active for quite a while and appeared to have accepted Jesus and made progress as a disciple. Then he vanished. A while later I ran into him and asked what had happened, assuming he had been tempted by the pull of the world that so often draws young people from pursuing God. He assured me that wasn't the case. He said, "I needed healing and I prayed to Jesus and nothing happened. So I went back and prayed to my family's Hindu gods and they healed me." The devil's use of deception to remain in control or destroy people is stunning, including the real possibility that some demonic submit to other demonics for the tactical purposes of gaining greater control in the long run. Jesus illustrated this with the surprising description of the person who has been set free from a demon only to have that demon return later with seven demonic friends to retake the ground they had vacated, with worse results, which we will consider below (Matthew 12:43-45).

Second, the term "Spirit of God" is used again to enforce the idea that the Spirit of God really has been placed upon Him (Matt 12:18, Isa 42:1).[11] Luke uses the phrase "finger of God" and this is "a deliberate allusion to Exodus 8:19. When Aaron on the command of Moses bests the magicians of Pharaoh's court, they are forced to acknowledge, 'this is the finger of God'" (Johnson 1991:181).[12] Those who fail to identify the Spirit of God in action are the ones most in danger of blaspheming against the Spirit, as Jesus points out in this passage. This remains a significant caution to us today to not dismiss the work of the Spirit even as we attempt to evaluate all things by God's Word.

Here in Matthew, as the demonic are removed by Jesus while empowered by the Spirit of the God of Abraham, Isaac, and Jacob, He brings to bear the kingdom of God and the environment of His rule which is experienced and is established. As we will see, that is why this ministry has not stopped, nor can it cease, for it is one guaranteed act that ushers in the kingdom of God within a space or more importantly, a person's life.

Third, Jesus also speaks to a wider issue. *"Or again, how can anyone enter a strong man's house and carry off his possessions unless he first ties up the strong man? Then he can rob his house"* (Matthew 12:29). Now again, this is talking about dealing with Satan and his power. This is "The idea of binding Satan and thus neutralizing his power (see Revelation 20:2-3). The point is that Jesus has already bound up Satan, and his exorcism should be understood as a sign of this victory over Satan."[13]

In this case, Matthew has connected Jesus to Isaiah 49:24-26, where God's people are rescued from evil. The broader picture here includes humanity; under the grasp of Satan are goods that Jesus is removing from the "strong man."[14] This is a statement about the cross and Jesus' ultimate victory.

> The 'binding of Satan' was a feature in Jewish apocalyptic hope (Testament of Levi 18:21, 1 Enoch 54:3-5, 69:27-28) and became also part of Christian eschatology (Rev 20:1-3). First, it may refer back to an earlier binding of Jesus (e.g. the defeat of Satan in 4:11f) but more likely is part of the overall metaphor. Satan is powerless before the victorious incursion of God's kingdom in Jesus ministry of deliverance.[15]

Again, within the same passage, Matthew gives another key aspect to deliverance by dealing with the strategic and persistent nature of the demonic:

> *When an evil spirit comes out of a man, it goes through arid places seeking rest and does not find it. Then it says, 'I will return to the house I left.' When it arrives it finds the house unoccupied, swept clean and put in order. Then it goes and takes with it seven other spirits more wicked than itself, and they go and live there. And the final condition of that man is worse than the first. That is how it will be with this wicked generation* (Matthew 12:43-45).

The thought and goal of this passage is not really the "ontological status of evil, but rather reminding us that we cannot try to at once serve God and mammon."[16] Yet it does really give us needed insight. It enforces the idea seen before, that the demonic are "parasitic"; they need a place to reside and they cannot create such a home.[17] Boyd gives further insight:

> This passage presents the reverse principle of the teaching just before it, namely, that Jesus was stronger than the 'strong man' who guards his house, and that his ministry was about overpowering this tyrant and 'dividing his plunder', in other words, what applies to the kingdom of God also applies to the kingdom of Satan. The teaching states that when a demon has been cast out of a 'house', one can expect it to return with stronger reinforcements to attempt to reclaim what it regards to be its territory. It needs 'rest', and it will do whatever it needs to do to find it. In the context in which these words are spoken, it is clear that this principle applies not only to individuals but to whole generations...implying that it is possible for an entire generation to be demonized by multitudes of demons. An apocalyptic conception of demonic national gods is perhaps implied here. As much as such a notion may lash with our modern Western individualistic assumption, in the light of our modern experience of Nazi Germany, we should perhaps not reject it too quickly.[18]

We also see that the demonic have needs, exhibit personality, and have rank by wickedness. The words "live" or "dwell" (Matthew 12:44; Luke 11:26) mean to "settle down," "live permanently." "No one can live for long in a moral vacuum. The kingdom of God does not bring about such a vacuum but a victory over evil is replaced with good and with God."[19]

THE GOSPEL ACCORDING TO SAINT LUKE

Leon Morris argues that the "Triumph of God" is a key theme within Luke's writings. Luke shows that Jesus does expel demons (4:33-37, 41; 6:18; 8:2, 26-39; 9:37-43; 11:14; 13:11-16; 13:32).[20] Yet, it is the flow of the narrative within Luke that reveals this theme. Luke, unlike the other Synoptic authors, spends little time around Jesus' baptism (Luke 3:21-22) but places the emphasis on the giving of the Spirit for ministry and the affirmation of identity (His Sonship) at Nazareth. Joel Green summarizes the idea by saying,

> His mission and status are spelled out in relation to God's Servant and Son who fulfills his mission of redemption and establishes his peace with justice in ways that flow out of his uncompromising obedience to God. It is this notion of the boundaries determined by obedience to God's purpose that the devil will test in 4:1-13.[21]

Luke's understanding is that the kingdom of God is now going to be established within the established kingdom of darkness, during which the god of this world (2 Corinthians 4:4) meets God in flesh in direct confrontation. He outlines the encounter in Luke 4:1-13. Jesus resists the temptations which Israel failed to do during their 40 years in the desert and His stern obedience is connected to His "commitment to one aim, God's eschatological agenda" and also proves His "competence to engage in ministry as God's Son."[22] Satan's withdrawal from the situation is "concession of defeat and concomitant shameful withdrawal."[23] It is only then that Jesus outlines His mission at Nazareth.

> *The Spirit of the Lord is on me, because he has anointed me to preach good news to the poor. He has sent me to proclaim freedom for the prisoners and recovery of sight for the blind, to release the oppressed, to proclaim the year of the Lord's favor* (Luke 4:18).

"Release" is a central theme found in this Isaiah passage. This theme comes from the phrase "release from debts" (see Luke 11:4).

> This draws our attention to Jubilee legislation (Lev. 25) the freeing of slaves, the cancellation of debts, the fallowing of the land, and the returning of all land to its original distribution under Moses...now the

time of God's gracious visitation, with Jesus himself presented as its anointed herald.[24]

Humanity is portrayed as poor, captive, blind, and oppressed, yet salvation will deal with all of the above both on a physical and spiritual level as this new kingdom manifests itself in the now and the future. Further, "release," according to scholars, in this context means both forgiveness of sin and freedom from the demonic.[25]

One of the first communal encounters is also seen within this chapter (and Mark 1:23ff). The outline is from Mark. In Luke we find the first of five healings that will take place on the Sabbath, which will not only cause conflict but also point the reader to His real power and identity.[26] Luke 4, like Mark, presents the incident as a conflict and attack against Jesus. The word here again that gives insight to the rebellion is "Ha!" *"Ha! What do you want with us, Jesus of Nazareth? Have you come to destroy us? I know who you are—the Holy One of God"* (Luke 4:34).

The meaning roughly translated is "let us be!"[27] Again, how amazing that the demonic, who were made by Jesus, their Creator, would have the rebellious gall and ability to stand in such defiance. It should be assured that as they behaved toward Jesus, so they will act toward us. It is not just because we are weak and wrong.

The story of Mary Magdalene and her former demonization is unique to Luke. Her case is further confirmation that one human can be inhabited by more than one spirit at a time. But unlike church history, the Scripture does not say she was demonized because she was a sinful woman coming from an immoral life, leaving open the other possibility, that her demonization led to immoral behavior. Once released from the demonic, she and her companions were the women who would accompany Jesus in His ministry (8:1-3), His death (23:49), His burial (23:55), and this Mary would be the first to be told about His resurrection (24:10).

Next, in Luke 8:1-3 and also in 11:26, there is a repeated number of seven spirits being confronted by Jesus. Timothy Johnson, when commenting later on chapter 11, says there is no "special significance" to the number 7,[28] but as I pondered this apparent coincidence, I wondered if this could be an inferred mockery and intimation of truth. Does not God's number 7 represent perfection? I just wonder sometimes if even down to the smallest detail the demonic are involved in imitation, mockery, and deception?

The other key deliverance unique to Luke is found in 13:10-13, where again Jesus heals on the Sabbath and deals with the all-so-important question, who can be saved (13:23)? Here we see a woman with a terrible affliction, which is only there because of a fallen angel. The summary by Luke reads that a *"woman was there who had been crippled by a spirit for eighteen years. She was bent over and could not straighten up at all"* (13:11) As Morris points out, "It was *'spondylitis deformans;'* the bones of her spine were fused into a rigid mass."[29]

Jesus removes this "spirit of weakness" by declaration and by physical touch. The placing of hands, though not usually done in deliverance, was a frequent gesture of healing used by Jesus (4:40; 5:13; 8:54). After 18 years of darkness, she is set free and begins to worship. But not all are worshipping along with her. The one who represented God had the opposite view:

> Indignant because Jesus had healed on the Sabbath, the synagogue ruler said to the people, "There are six days for work. So come and be healed on those days, not on the Sabbath." The Lord answered him, "You hypocrites! Doesn't each of you on the Sabbath untie his ox or donkey from the stall and lead it out to give it water? Then should not this woman, a daughter of Abraham, whom Satan has kept bound for eighteen long years, be set free on the Sabbath day from what bound her" (Luke 13:14-16).[30]

The result of the miracle makes the religious leader very angry and reveals the true battle Jesus wants to address. Dealing with the demonic always gives God the opportunity to confront the human heart and the religious community.

> This leads Jesus to a more direct charge of hypocrisy: the allowance made for the 'loosing' of animals on the Sabbath to give them relief is a light thing, compared to the heavy matter of 'loosing' a human person (and a 'daughter of Abraham') from the bondage of Satan. Indeed, faced with such a human need, it is necessary to heal on the Sabbath.[31]

This again shows the terrible and wrong view of many evangelicals who argue over the nature of this act. They are not seeing the many who are either rejoicing with Jesus or who remain in darkness—still in bondage, yet desiring freedom. How sad that today, even as in Jesus' day, most are more concerned about theological categories and views than kingdom, freedom, and salvation. Yet for this study, Jesus' use of the title "daughter of Abraham" is most important. Zacchaeus was called a "son of Abraham" by Jesus at the point of his conversion, when salvation comes to his house (Luke 19:9). Later in Acts 13:26, Paul calls the community in Antioch of Pisidia "sons of the family of Abraham." Yes, since she is a neighbor (in the spiritual/ethnic sense) there should be compassion shown.[32] But that does not go far enough. Jesus is not just saying she is a neighbor. It is a phrase of religious standing. It implies that she is a "godly woman" and is the only place in all of Scripture where the title is given. It is about being a child, but more than Jewish heritage, it is a declaration of genuine faith. She is in a relationship with God.

> She is bent over in a shameful position, demonized, this is a daughter of Abraham? Hers was no position of honor, but through Jesus' gracious ministry she is fully restored as a member of the community.

She and other children of Abraham in the Luke's narrative, evidence how God's promise to Abraham is fulfilled through Jesus' ministry are thus confirmed as Abraham's children.[33]

The other implication from this incident is that even one who knows God in a relational way can be affected and demonized to such a degree that the body is deformed and the person is inhabited. This insight, which is missed by most, has informed our practice and theological reflection in the greatest of ways. Really, it is the most important implication of the Luke 13 account, which underlies every other account. The question is, can someone who knows God be demonized? Often, the word used to pose the question is *possession*, which has become a misleading English phrase. The term *possession* immediately sets up tension with terminology Paul uses in places like 1 Corinthians 6:20, *"You were bought at a price. Therefore honor God with your bodies."* In almost all conversations I have ever had, I hear the statement that a Christian cannot be *possessed*. What they mean is *owned*, but that is not what the Greek implies in Luke 13 or any other passage on the subject.

The word possession never even appears in the Bible in the passage where Jesus or the apostle cast evil spirits out of an individual. The expression demon possessed or demon possession does occur in some English translations of the Greek text, but there is never a Greek word for 'possession' that stand behind it. 'Demon possession' is always the translation of a single Greek word, *daimonizomai*. Words for ownership or possession (e.g. *huparcho, echo, katecho, ktaomai,* or *peripoeio*) are absent in the original text. The idea of possession is the interpretation of the Greek term by Bible translators. This translation of the word became the standard because the most popular English Bible translation for over three centuries-the King James Version-used 'demon possession' or 'possessed with the devil' to render the Greek...In other occurrences of *daimonizomai* these other verses employed expression such as 'tormented', 'vexed', or 'troubled' to translate the term...the obstacle for us is that in popular contemporary usage we have a difficult time disentangling possession from the concept of ownership. To avoid this confusion, some Christian leaders have suggested that we begin transliterating the term *daimonizomai* by the expression *demonized*. This has the advantage of providing us with a new term to use without the baggage that comes with 'demon possession.' It might also be advisable to use other common translations of *daimonizomai* that we noted earlier. I am convinced that there would be far greater agreement among Christians on this issue if we framed the question differently, leaving out the word possession. We might ask, 'Can Christians come under a high degree of influence by a demonic spirit?' or 'Is it possible for Christians to yield control of their bodies to a demonic spirit in the same way that they yield to the power of sin'?[34]

This theological understanding has been the most clarifying and groundbreaking for us, for the many who question, and for those who go through our process. I summarize it this way: You can be in right relationship with God positionally (elected, called, adopted, sealed, seated with Jesus, and sealed unto the day of redemption Ephesians 1), as well as in right community with other believers, under the very Word of God, yet still be inhabited by a demonic being, even though it does not own you.

If that didn't just give you serious pause, you should read it again. That statement challenges certain deeply held evangelical assumptions that have taken on an inerrant and unquestioned tone among believers. Again, the confusion comes from our inaccurate translation of the Greek term for ownership, which is far more nuanced than in the English language. Ancient Greeks had at least five ownership concepts, but none of those terms are used in Scripture to describe the relationship between the demonic and victims. We tend to use *possession* as a synonym for *ownership* when a moment's thought reminds us this is often not really the case. We possess or have things in our possession or under our control all the time which we do not own. Another way to put it is that it's not ownership, but impact.

Declaring believers to be immune or protected from demonic attack, influence, and control actually flies in the face of biblical witness and Christian experience. When Paul made his well-known charge about spiritual weapons for spiritual warfare in Ephesians 6, he began by setting the stage with, *"For our struggle is not against flesh and blood, but against the rulers, against the authorities, against the powers of this dark world and against the spiritual forces of evil in the heavenly realms"* (v. 10). There is no hint throughout this passage that believers are automatically immune or protected from real danger. The intervention, help, and deliverance God offers us is in the valley and in the trenches, not a life above this world, but deeply in it, needing God's ever-present help (more on this when we look more closely at the book of Acts and Paul).

It is this idea that truly is the lynch pin to this view of ministry. Without this understanding in place, confusion, suspicion, and wrong categorization will break down unity and disrupt environments designed to minister to those who are bound. As we have worked over the years to evaluate and improve our hybrid deliverance matrix—whose roots are fully biblical and faithfully historical—the question we have repeatedly asked is, "What are the basic and repeatable lessons about the environment, the acts, and the results of deliverance seen in the writings of Mark, Matthew, and Luke?" Seeing the sometimes surprising parallels in our situation today has consistently shown us a way forward.

Jon Thompson

SUMMARY OF THE SYNOPTIC GOSPELS

From the preceding biblical data, a simple summary can be established. The demonic can inhabit a person and there can be one or many. They can manifest themselves in various ways and have different strengths. They can cause great harm and they can move into other people, animals, or environments. There are varied reasons why the demonic can have rights, grounds, accesses, and privileges to people. They may have territorial rights or powers. *Possession* is not an accurate term to describe the relationship between believers and the demonic, but there can be no denying that the demonic can impact, infect, and affect believers in devastating ways. The full range of positional truth about what believers have in Christ, with a full range of applicable terms like election and predestination, doesn't nullify the very real experiences of continued life in the fallen world where demons do all they can to challenge the kingdom of God.

There must be a greater power to overcome and remove demons, which shows us that this act is truly and always in some form a power encounter. They will always resist leaving their hosts. They can reside in people for short and long periods of time and can even be in people who are sitting under the written Word of God and in environments dedicated to the true living God (synagogue). Jesus, when dealing with them, always spoke directly to them and sometimes asked for their names. Jesus did this in large and small groups, but never used it as a show. We should expect the same experience and responses. Clinton Arnold, writing for *Christianity Today*, gives a good but not complete outline. He writes,

> We can pray and ask God to deliver someone from evil, but it may be necessary to address a spirit directly in the way that Jesus did. If the spirits resisted even Jesus before they departed, it should come as no surprise if demons resist our commands. Jesus issues a command to the demons based on his own authority. In contrast to exorcists of his day, who used elaborate rituals and incantations…. Based on our union with Jesus Christ, our being filled with the same Spirit by which he cast out evil spirits (Matt 12:28; Luke 11:20), and our right to exercise authority in his name over this realm, we can issue a firm and direct command to an intruding spirit with the expectation that it will leave.[35]

At this point in the book, we face the same situation that those disciples did when Jesus ascended and was taken from them physically. Two millennia have passed, but the same core issues of life remain. They, like us, had to take Jesus' commands, practices, teaching, and example, and put them into practice in a world where Jesus' promise to be with them had to be lived out in action. We will see that by the second century, as Christianity spread through lands and cultures long under the influence of the demonic, that the

Church Fathers had to take into account the real possibility that almost any new convert was demonized. The baptismal confessions coming from the early church include the consciousness of the need to renounce the world, the flesh, and the devil in turning to Christ for salvation. But more on this later.

Now we move to Luke's second volume, Acts, to root ourselves in the opening phase of church history, the experiences and practices of those who first received power when the Spirit came upon them and were witnesses in Jerusalem, Judea, Samaria, and to the ends of the earth.

At a personal level, the challenging news of this chapter is not meant to instill fear. In fact, believers who have sometimes struggled for years under the influence of the demonic find the truth liberating. They don't have to be plagued with constant insecurity about their relationship with Christ based on the assumption that their experiences are contradicting God's acceptance of them in Christ. Post-conversion demonization is a matter of sanctification, not justification. It should not surprise us that the struggle goes on. We will be able to confront the demonic with greater confidence in Christ if we are not constantly second-guessing our position in Christ based on the conflicts we're facing.

I close with the picture of a house.[36] It represents every human life. If this house has been surrendered to Christ, Jesus is present in the house. He owns it. But for one reason or another, a window has been left open in the back and now there are squatters living in the house. They are not in the whole house and they have no ownership claim on the house, but the un-locked window has given them access to it. The process of clearing the house, filling it with wholesome things, and locking the windows is an illustration of what the Bible calls the process of sanctification—a struggle that goes on until the point of transferal to the eternal kingdom. What is the condition of your house and those of your closest neighbors?

Jon Thompson

CHAPTER 6
ACTS OF THE APOSTLES AND DELIVERANCE

The necessity for a study in the book of Acts when we are focused on under-standing spiritual conflict is sixfold. First, Luke's outworking of the spiritual conflict theme continues in Acts 1:8, promising indwelling power to believers. Second, there are new insights on deliverance as the gospel moves into many new cultural arenas, particularly since every time a new area is opened with the gospel there is a demonic reaction—every time. How often in church leader-ship today do we acknowledge in our plans to minister in a new area, culture, or neighborhood that we expect there to be demonic conflict as a reaction to the gospel? Third, there are new insights on personal demonization and its connection to family, religion, or geography. Fourth, there are new case stud-ies to reflect on because those who never walked with Jesus are now joining those who did, now participating in this act of freeing. Fifth, we see this prac-tice now done within the established, post-Pentecost church community, a setting which was not yet a reality in the Gospels. This leads to the last and most important point: did these acts of power cease? Did the gifts of the Spir-it that are used during such encounters end with the Apostles alone? The fact that within the book of Acts itself there are recorded at least two post-apostolic generations exercising the gifts seems to make a powerful case against cessationism (the teaching that the spiritual gifts were only for the New Testament age to confirm the apostolic witness and ended with the close of the Canon of Scripture).

At the end of the Gospel of Luke, the cross is the culmination of the battle. Satan entered into Judas (22:3), he tries to sift Peter like wheat (22:31), and as Moffatt translates Jesus' arrest, "this is your hour, and the dark Power has its way" (22:53).[1] Yet at the resurrection, Jesus overcomes the kingdom of darkness and ensures the inevitable victory of the kingdom of God. This is where the book of Acts begins. Acts 1:8 fleshes out Jesus' command in Mat-thew 28:18-20 that those that follow Him now must go and tell this great news in Jerusalem, Judea, Samaria, and then to the ends of the earth. The im-plication here is that the ministry of Jesus and His acts will continue through His Spirit in His new community (Acts 2:42-47). As the late John Wimber frequently argued, the miraculous acts, including the removal of evil, are seen in the Apostles, the second generation of non-Apostles (Stephen, Philip, Ananias; Acts 7, 8:26-40, 9:10-18) and even the third generation of Barnabas, Silas, and Timothy.[2]

This sets the stage for Luke's intentional writing about the cosmic war as expressed through direct encounters between God's community and those working within the kingdom of darkness. As the messengers of this new kingdom follow the directive of Jesus, Luke creates a sub-theme of conflict, which could be labeled "turf wars."[2a] Every time there is a move into a new geographic area, Luke notes a confrontation with the demonic—two kingdoms clashing against each other as their masters did from the wilderness to the cross. The difference in Acts, compared with the Gospel accounts, is that the power of evil is fully broken (John 8:36; 1 John 3:8; Col 1:13).

JERUSALEM/JUDEA

The first battle is fought in Jerusalem, more specifically, within the church itself. Satan, being the Father of Lies (John 8:44) and knowing the heart is the source of all decisions, recruits from within. Like Judas and Peter earlier, Ananias and Sapphira are the next in a larger attempt to shut down the church. At this time, people like Barnabas were willingly selling property for the sake of the church and its mission (Acts 2:42-47), yet this couple brought only part of the money while still claiming to the apostles that it was the full amount. They were attempting to claim wholehearted generosity despite a half-hearted effort. Like Achan's sin (Joshua 7:1), they lie to God's people and to God Himself. Peter knows it was not just their actions, but that *"Satan had filled their hearts"* and they had *"lied to the Holy Spirit"* (Acts 5:1-11). It is reasonable to infer from Peter's words that the willingness of Ananias and Sapphira to lie opened the door for demonic filling.

God gives divine insight to Peter, which protects the community. We see spiritual gifts being exercised here to unveil spiritual corruption in a setting where everything seemed—on the surface—to be praiseworthy and God-centered. Peter had a word of knowledge (information) that this couple had lied about the money and discernment (knowing the source) that Satan had walked into that door.

The death of both of those at fault provokes a new holy fear in the community of God. This is not to say that the couple were not true believers, for even they can lie (1 Corinthians 11:30, 5:5).[3] Elsewhere, Ajith Fernando points out that Satan targets those of faith and this is an excellent example of the demonization of the believers, thus being a significant turf war to win.[4] It is after this act that the apostles do many miracles, including the casting out of demons. Luke shows that crowds come to them from Jerusalem and the surrounding area (Judea; Acts 5:12-16). Gregory Boyd points out that

> This passage mentions, as a matter of course, that freeing people from evil spirits was a standard aspect of the ministry of the apostles.

We are not surprised, then, when we read that Philip exorcised many shrieking evil spirits out of people while evangelizing Samaria (Acts 8:7).[5]

For our purposes here, it's worth noting from this early example that every time there is a genuine revival and outpouring of the Holy Spirit, the first spiritual resistance and effort to undermine the Holy Spirit's work will occur within the church. The first pushback is always an inside job, often masked by superficial righteousness as in the case of Ananias and Sapphira. Today, when a church is experiencing an outpouring of God's Spirit in any way, those in leadership ought to include in their oversight a prayerful watchfulness for the counterfeits that will undoubtedly arise.

Another important principle is that hiddenness cloaks demonic activity. They work in lies, half-truths, and hidden motives. Also, when believers hide sin, pain, shame, and vulnerabilities, they are leaving a door open for demonic activity or revealing the effects of demonic suggestion or influence. The number of believers in a typical church who have never come clean about their history, weakness, and sin through lack of desire or opportunity creates an obvious weakened spiritual condition that lacks the vitality of the Holy Spirit. A significant obstacle to revival in the church is our reluctance (even as we pray for revival) to have things revealed that are hidden, because we know when Jesus shows up, everything and everyone is exposed. In the meantime, the war rages—a real war—and if the primary tactic of the church at large is to deny the war's existence, there will be painful loss of ground. People too often leave the church or reject Christ, not because the gospel isn't compelling, but because of all the chaos created by the failure to take evil seriously. The unrepentant disunity and hypocrisy in the church remain strong indicators that the devil has invaded the house of God either by invitation or by our providing entry points of sin. He is up to no good.

SAMARIA

The second direct reference to conflict is found in Samaria. New territory has again been entered. Philip predictably confronts evil, and during these clashes of power, we witness the next attempt to stop and distort the kingdom. Simon was a powerful warlock and many followed him because of the demonic power he displayed (Acts 8:9-11). Yet he was overwhelmed by the power in Philip, became a follower of Jesus, and was baptized. All seems well, until Peter and John arrive. Simon offers them money for the power they have. With power and anger, Peter responds that Simon was not right before God, that he must deal with God, and then maybe he will be forgiven. If not, he would perish (Acts 2:19-23). F. F. Bruce, while reflecting on this incident writes, "The poisonous root of superstitious self-seeking had not been eradicated from his heart, his soul still held fast in the 'fetters of unrighteousness.'"[6]

Bruce's observation raises the question of the actual state of Simon's spiritual condition. Was the description of his conversion in Acts simply the record of appearances with no genuine repentance, or was there real conversion followed by ongoing influence by the demonic that had been so dominant in his life? There does seem to be plenty of evidence, possibly even in our own lives, of the way pre-conversion attitudes and values survive to skew the way we see kingdom values. In places in the world where the demonic powers have been openly displayed, the kind of response Simon gives to the display of God's power, offering money for the same abilities, is not that unusual. Unlike the situation with Ananias and Sapphira, who we concluded were probably believers making a serious error, Simon doesn't die as a result of Peter's rebuke, leaving us with the possibilities that either as a recent convert he was still unaware of the hold of the demonic on his life or he was not yet converted.

But there are more participants and larger issues at play in this episode than just Simon. The kingdom of darkness, realizing power over many people would be lost, does not attempt direct confrontation but a more subtle approach through Simon—syncretism, the idea that power and belief can be used and blended, thus making truth and lie indistinguishable. Syncretism describes the mixing of belief systems under the assumption that a deeper unity can be found or that the results will not damage the individual components. But if one of the components is truth, syncretism undermines and ignores it.

Satan overplaying his hand, and the Spirit giving Peter the needed insight, prevent a possible deathblow. In the flow of the account of the Church expanding in the book of Acts, this is yet another example of the turf wars being fought in the spiritual realm and involving human participants. At the height of an explosive revival in a new area, someone appears who is used to create a potentially destructive influence among all the good that God is bringing. Those involved in a work of the Spirit cannot let down their guard by ignoring the almost inevitable counterattack by the demonic. Any revival situation will involve a somewhat chaotic setting in which Godly power, demonic power, and predictable human erratic behaviors will all be present, and what is odd or uncomfortable to observers should not be discounted as false. Genuine revival among deeply sinful people can generate some shockingly odd responses. In as staid and dry a setting as John Wesley's sermons during the Wesleyan revival in Britain, it was not uncommon for the congregation to be bursting with such a cacophony of sounds—weeping, crying out to God, indistinguishable utterances, and confession—that it made hearing the preacher difficult. Some of it was genuine, some of it was silly, and some of it was demonic. In the radical shift from a setting in which the devil is in control, to a place where Jesus is now Lord, there may well be increased chaos before order is restored—because the war is real. Understanding the power source of anything we witness will require a full exercise of spiritual gifts to sort out the participants in the conflict.

Further light on Simon indicates the significance of Peter's rebuke. Church history tells us that Simon does great damage in the future. He is widely thought to be the father of the Gnostic heresies and the founder of the Simonians. His followers were found in Rome and Samaria until the time of Claudius (Justin Martyr confronted them) and represented in such writings as the non-canonical books, *Acts of Peter and Pseud-Clementien (Recognition and Homilies)*. These contain uncorroborated accounts of Simon opposing Peter and Paul in different situations and is only defeated by a direct power encounter.[7] No matter the biblical/traditional record, the demonic attempt again is to stop the gospel from spreading into a new area, Samaria.

We can leap forward for a moment to modern settings as we see these same principles still at play. Syncretism may well be the most effective weapon being used by the demonic to oppose God. One of the current places of explosive gospel expansion is the African continent, where there are genuine and ongoing moves of God in various cultural situations. The growth of the church is evident. But those on the ground report the same pattern of syncretistic undermining that we see in the actions of Simon. Large numbers of people participate in obviously orthodox settings—with enthusiastic worship, earnest repetition of the classic creeds of the church, and fervent prayer meetings—and yet can also be seen engaging in pagan rituals of animal sacrifice and appeasing offerings to spirits. The temptation to keep a foot on each side of the battle line is sometimes evidence that conversion has not yet happened and at other times evidence that we remain in the world and are subject to ongoing demonic influence. For us in Toronto, the world is here. So those practices happen everyday. Even Christians are regularly involved in spiritual activities such as New Age spirituality, eastern inspired self-help, etc. For many others, the evidence of ties to the old life are not as obvious as ancestor worship, but the ongoing hold of money, un-biblical sexual activity, and power are real aspects of syncretism among believers. Wise leaders keep all the possible sources of power in mind while fluid spiritual situations are unfolding.

The new life of a disciple of Jesus must work out the reality of how allegiance, truth, and power affect every part of life. Commitment to Jesus must be lived out, day by day, as a learning experience of sanctification; truth from Jesus and His Word must confront the lies that have infected my life and which may remain as residue in my mind for a long time; and the power of the demonic in my past must be confronted and rooted out by the power of Jesus. Speaking truth to power (to use a modern expression) will only be partly effective—the devil already knows the truth and must be dealt with through and with God's power. All three aspects of a healthy relationship with

God must be increasingly present: commitment, truth, and power. Growing disciples experience encounters in all three of these areas.

ENDS OF THE EARTH

The third direct power confrontation with the demonic is found in the next outworking of Jesus' instructions in Acts 1:8, following the remarkable conversion of Saul of Tarsus who will be known best to us as Paul. This would be the first time into the Gentile world as Paul and Barnabas are confirmed, directed, and released by the church in Antioch, thus starting the first missionary journey (13:1-14:28). It is also the first in a consistent pattern in which the spread of the gospel among largely Gentile areas is met by demonic resistance every step of the way.

Traveling to Seleucia, then Cyprus, the pair arrived at Paphos, which at the time was the senatorial official capital. After preaching in local synagogues (13:5), they went to speak to Sergius Paulus, an intelligent man interested in the Gospel. The kingdom of darkness has a key player in this place of power by the name Bar-Jesus, which in Aramaic means "Son of Salvation." He is identified as a sorcerer, which is one with great demonic power, not just trickery. He is part of the proconsul court because it was believed he had the ability to break the bounds of fate and give power to his employer.[8] I. Howard Marshall is quick to point out that it was by

> ...the direction of the Spirit that the missionaries were sent out and brought into a situation of conflict with the forces of evil (vs. 9); are we intended to see a parallel with the equipping of Jesus with the Spirit at the outset of his ministry followed by his conflict with Satan (Lk 3:22, 4:1f.,14)?[9]

The answer to Marshall's question is "yes." Knowing his influence and power could be lost, Bar-Jesus opposed Paul (Lk 21:15; Acts 8:22) and more importantly, his message of light. Paul, empowered by the Holy Spirit, understood the root of the confrontation and called him a "child of the devil" (1 John 3:9,10), meaning "one that twists the path that leads to salvation" (Hos 14:9; Ps 119:1; Isa 40:3,5; Luke 1:79; Acts 8:21). Unlike the previous encounter, this is direct opposition. This is a real turf war. Don't miss the cunning of this—two leaders, both Jewish, both have real power, both have names connected to Jesus. This is a classic move of the enemy. And it is no mistake that this happens again when the gospel is given in the formal Roman setting for the first time. Again, everytime the gospel goes into a new family, neighbourhood, people group, etc., expect the demonic to be present to stop it in any way.

Paul, in the power of God, blinds Elymus, and the proconsul believes (13:11-12). It is significant for our purposes to recognize that the combination of the clarity of the verbal presentation of the gospel along with the demonstration of God's power over evil moves the Roman pro-council to faith. Everett Harrison, in his commentary on Acts, rightly points out this power encounter is central in how God distinguishes Himself from false forms of the divine:

> It was the first presentation of the word of God to the Roman's world: and naturally it was not easy for Sergius Paulus to detect the vital distinction between the true prophets and the false ones. Once and for all that distinction and the separation of Christianity from all trafficking in spiritualism must be demonstrated.[10]

Although Evangelicalism has tended to emphasize the importance of rational understanding of the gospel as central to conversion, it's probably safe to say that a vast majority of conversions originate from experience while a smaller amount flow simply from cognition or intellect. In the West we have downplayed experience and elevated intellectual capacity in response to the gospel, but the vast majority of the world knows through experience, not just intellect. Today, we need the ongoing brilliance of apologists making the rational case for faith, but we also need to expose the world to genuine experiences of God's power at work. The point, illustrated in Paul's dealing with Sergius Paulus, is that both intellect and experience have a place in an effective presentation of the gospel.

When I was a youth pastor, the churches in our area decided to work together to promote an Alpha-styled experience for teenagers called Quest. This was an unusual effort because it cut across a lot of denominational lines—Baptists, Pentecostals, and Anglicans working together. For seven nights during a break in school, the kids gathered for these Bible encounters. I'm not aware of anything in our area quite like it before or since. The teens in our youth groups were challenged to invite their unbelieving friends, and among those who showed up was a girl involved in witchcraft. When the word got to me about her, I went over, sat down, and engaged her in conversation. She informed me quickly that she wasn't a black witch, but a white one. I responded by saying, "So, I know you're not a Satanist and you are welcome here." After she thanked me, I continued, "As a white witch, you're involved in trying to bless and help people, right?" She agreed. Next I said, "Do you want to have this conversation we're about to have or not?" Puzzled, she said, "What?" I repeated the question and she said, "Sure." My next question caught her even more by surprise: "So, how strong are you spiritually?" I could see the wheels turning in her head. I was treating her not as crazy or weird, but as someone to be taken seriously. I was acknowledging that what she was wielding and experiencing was great and real power. But then I challenged her with, "You've got nothing on me." Her incredulous response meant I had to repeat my words and then add, "I'm much more powerful than you—well not me, but the One in me, who is actually the Creator of everything including what's in you. So where do you want to go with this? Because we can do this right now."

Those listening in were a little shocked. She was stunned. Now this response on my part wasn't about a prideful attitude or putting on a show. I was exercising confidence in the power of Jesus over the demonic, even when it was masquerading as benevolent, white witch power. My responses were based on both experience and reliance on God's Spirit to guide. I was confronting her with the truth that as enticing and even intoxicating the power seemed to be in her, there was a limit. I was inviting her to turn to a greater power. Very much like the rich young ruler who met Jesus, who blinked when the power that anchored life was challenged, she turned away.

This story is a continual reminder that the church must be able to pivot depending on the situation. Sometimes an argument is needed; sometimes power must be met with the overwhelming power of Jesus. If our only weapon is intellectual arguments, the demonic will run rings around us (and unfortunately often does). Having truth, commitment, and power in our spiritual arsenal doesn't ensure victory every time, but it means we're bringing the right weapons to bear depending on the battlefield.

Luke now takes the reader to the second missionary journey. God calls Paul and his companions to Macedonia and there a most unique encounter takes place. In Acts 16:16-24, the mission to the Jews and to the Gentiles continues, but a slave girl who is both economically bound (trafficked, used for money; 16:16) and possessed by a demonic spirit, attempts to stop this new thrust.[11] The spirit has been translated "python" or a "spirit of divination" (NIV). Python would make sense, for the prophetess of Delphi was called "Ipythia," inspired by the god Apollo who defeated the dragon python. It also could be translated a spirit of "ventriloquism" for they were also called pythons.[12] For days the girl calls out (crying out repeatedly) that these men are *"servants of the most High God, who are telling you the way to be saved"* (16:17). Paul is deeply troubled (strongly irked or provoked at something or someone)[13] and though he does wait a few days, finally turns around, and casts out the demon in Jesus' name. It leaves her. Still, we are left wondering why the kingdom of darkness was affirming the apostolic missionaries as a way to discredit their mission. To the Jewish mind, the cry of the demonized woman (Acts 16:17) rings of truth (Holy God/*el-elyon*) but to non-Jews (most of the audience), these shouts actually undermine the message that would bring the light of the gospel into this area. The divine name being used is generic, allowing each listener to fill in the identity of that god according to their views. She's telling the truth in a way that undercuts the truth—and this irritates the apostle. Larkin summarizes,

> But to polytheistic pagans, who were henotheists as opposed to monotheists, there were many 'highest gods'; the title had been at-

tached to Zeus, Isis, the mother-goddess of the kingdom of Lydia in Asia, and Baal. A pagan hearer would understand the term to refer to whatever deity he or she considered supreme ... And a way of salvation? For the pagan it was release for the powers governing the fate of humanity and the material world.[14]

This expression of opposition to a new move of Jesus is done in an attempt to confuse Paul's hearers by using their natural presuppositions and worldviews, thus promoting a false or distorted gospel. Though Paul and Silas are beaten (Acts 16:22) and thrown into jail (16:24), God reverses the situation. The jail is shaken open (16:27-32), and the jailer and his family hear the clear message and are brought from the kingdom of darkness to light (16:32-35). Luke here, unlike the other encounters, continues to show that during this second missionary journey, the battle for the control of lives does not end.

Traveling 100 miles, they arrive at Thessalonica (Acts 17:1-10a). After preaching in the local synagogue to both the Jew and the Gentile, a mob tries to arrest Paul and Silas. Unable to find them, they take others (Jason), allowing the missionaries to leave towards Berea that night. This incident would seem to be a turf war lost. Paul later reports he has repeatedly wanted to visit again but *"Satan blocked our way"* (1 Thessalonians 2:18). Paul argued that the "rulers of the world" (1Corinthians 2:8) were behind the provoking of the crowds and authorities at Jesus' trial and crucifixion, and he saw the crowds in this situation influenced by Satan as well. "The contrast of Paul's earnest desire with Satan's obstruction also says something about Paul's view of just how powerful and successful Satan could be in his opposition to the ministry."[15]

The last great clash takes place on Paul's final missionary journey within a great centre of the occult, Ephesus. This was to become the second main focus of Christian outreach to the Gentiles.[16] Here the great goddess of Artemis was worshipped, for she supposedly had power over fate itself. Four key occultic elements were prevalent in Ephesus: Spiritual powers were rampant (Acts 19:11-20), artisans made objects or charms of power in silver shrines (19:24), people revered a sacred stone that supposedly fell from heaven (19:35), and finally, the city proudly proclaimed itself home to a place of false worship, the temple of Artemis (19:27).[17] Fernando also notes, "Its reputation in this respect is indicated by the fact that the phrase, 'Ephesian writings' (ephesia grammata) was commonly used in antiquity for documents containing spells and formulae."[18]

Paul preached in the Ephesus synagogue and after establishing good relationships there, spent two years arguing for the faith in the Lecture Hall of Tyrannus. During this time, God did such miracles that even Paul's handkerchiefs and aprons were used to heal and cast out demons (19:11). We should not read into these descriptions a list of practices we ought to also undertake, such as certain evangelists hijacking the handkerchief idea as a fundraising gimmick with promises that the cloth sent out upon receipt of a donation will have been blessed by the ministry with special healing or other beneficial powers. In this case, these were already existent practices that God co-opted for His purposes, using these objects to demonstrate real power where there had previously been merely disappointing amulets. These were power encounters appropriate to those settings, not necessarily transferable to today.

In this atmosphere, much attention was given to Paul and other Jews, for they had the ability to speak their God's name with powerful results. It wasn't long before attempts were made by others to use this name.[19] The Jewish high priest's sons came against a demonic man and tried to invoke the name of Paul's Jesus as a magical word. The demon knew both Paul and Jesus, but not them, and beat them almost to death. Ed Murphy suggests that these are evil spirits fighting each other.

> The evil spirits in the possessed person battled the demonized exorcists... Demons can expel and attack other demons to enhance the control of demons over people. Such demon-to-demon attacks only increases Satan's hold over people.[20]

Satan overplays his hand again and Jesus' name and message are embraced. Many in the occult believe, confess evil deeds, and renounce the occult by burning their scrolls. The summary is that *"the word of the Lord spread widely and grew in power"* (19:20). As Larkin writes,

> Luke highlights the power of the message through adverb phrases and verses (keta kratos, NIV grew in power, possibly 'prevailed'; compare Lk 1:51, Eph 1:19, 6:10). Luke's theology places proclamation of the gospel message at the centre of any 'power advance' in the church's mission.[21]

Luke ends his account of the spiritual conflict in Ephesus with a riot (Acts 19:11-41). Demetrius and many others throw the city into chaos over their lost income, status, and commerce, because of the message of Jesus. This conclusion is almost predictable, because every time major inroads are made into the kingdom of darkness, not only do many come to faith but the fabric of society is changed forever (19:18-20). Religious, cultural, and economic realities change, for when the human heart is transformed, so are lives, families, communities, and society with it.

> At the very centre of each culture is a religion, whether sacred or secular, expressed in a set of myths of origin, power and destiny. These in turn spawn the culture's worldview, which generates social structures and behavioral patterns. Paul's message here shakes the Ephesians, indeed the Greco-Roman culture to its very core by showing one of its religious power centers, the Artemis cult for what it is:

nothing. In that sense it does mean the death of the culture, as it does for any culture today with its gods, whether they be a traditional pantheon of tribal deities or the media and educational icons of secular humanism.[22]

The process we are describing includes the reality that aspects of the culture will, at least for a time, influence how new believers go about worship. But neither the unique disruptions the gospel and revival bring nor the cultural trappings that survive change should be seen as permanent features or policies as the church develops and disciples grow. We look to Scripture for ongoing and reliable truth and direction, while recognizing that the ways we apply Scripture may change with the times and environment. The old Youth for Christ motto was, "Geared to the times, anchored to the Rock." The danger comes when we take temporal and seasonal expressions of spiritual realities and try to spiritualize them and make them permanent. We've already mentioned the danger of taking the handkerchief mention from Ephesus and making it a permanent feature of current spiritual practices. Another major example of this would be recognizing that if we want to know what Hillsong and Bethel, cutting edge, vibrant worship was in the fifth century of the Church, all we have to do is visit an Orthodox church, where that millennium-and-a-half-old pattern is still preserved today, though some of it has outworn its earlier meaningfulness. Visit a Roman Catholic church anywhere in the world and you will experience the same ritual, and until recently, even the same language though not even understood by the majority of those present. The Latin Mass institutionalized their entire spiritual practice to the point where there is little or no cultural flexibility. When worshippers can't explain why they are doing what they are regularly doing, it's likely a past practice has ossified into permanence without effective results in those worshippers.

One of the values that has been more or less preserved in Protestantism is the church as seed/husk, where the seed should remain unchangeable while the husk is in continual adaptation. To admit that my current role as a pastor in a mega-church in the suburbs of Toronto, Canada has the same feel as the local Walmart and Starbucks is simply to say that externally our church reflects our surrounding culture, which is constantly in flux. If I expected churches elsewhere in the world to look like my church in architecture and internal décor, I would be dangerously spiritualizing what is worldly. I anticipate ongoing changes in our church in many ways and would not be surprised if it takes on a significantly different shape by the end of my ministry, or if the environment changes radically, so that it ceases to even exist in its current form. The more we look at the material side of the life of a follower of Jesus, the more we should expect change and adaptation, even while we remember that Jesus Himself is the same yesterday, today, and forever. What flows out of Jesus, His Spirit, and His teachings are permanent, eternal things. And the closer we get to the world side of spiritual expression, the more we are looking at vapor and constant change.

Now, a major secondary theme that has been hinted at in this overview of Acts is the ongoing ministry of Jesus through His people. Yet many today would argue, starting with Acts, that these encounters and gifts began to cease as the Apostles died and as the New Testament canon was formed. The arguments below transcend Acts, but this is a good place to deal with this issue since the seeds of the battle are found in Acts. The so-called cessationist position is that the power gifts phased out during Acts or just after, since they were no longer needed to confirm the authority of the apostles. Yet the Biblical evidence already seen and outlined below contradicts this idea. Also, the whole next chapter is a narrative journey over generations disproving such a theology.

CESSATION OF THE GIFTS?

Coming from a church and association that was heavily influenced by the idea that all supernatural acts of God had ceased, I have had to deal with the four largest arguments from our history in order to give proper weight to Scripture as well as to experience and tradition. The four challenges are: (1) Are not all acts such as exorcism tied and limited to the Apostles? (2) Doesn't Paul in 1 Corinthians 13 say gifts will cease? (3) Does not Jude 9 imply Christians should not cast out demons? And (4), is it not a historical fact that the miraculous gifts ceased within the early history of the church? Wayne Grudem gives an honest, humble, yet all-encompassing response to cessationism, both in his *Systematic Theology*[23] and his article in *The Kingdom and the Power*.[24] The most common argument we grew up with was 1 Corinthians 13 as the reason we should not expect the New Testament experience to be our own. It was Grudem's work here that brought clarity and needed freedom:

> Many have used 1 Corinthians 13:8-13 to argue cessation of the miraculous. They argue 'the perfection to the gift of Holy Scripture'. Yet this does not follow the logic of Paul here and in his other writings. When dealing with the 1 Corinthian text, he points out that this group of verses is about gifts ceasing when Jesus returns back to earth. 'When perfection comes' is about the second coming of Christ. In summary, here are the three main reasons for this conclusion. "This means that the time when 'the perfect comes' must be the time of Christ's return. Therefore we can paraphrase verse 10, 'but when Christ returns, the imperfect will pass away.' Or to use our conclusion above that 'the imperfect included prophecy and tongues, we can paraphrase, 'but when Christ returns, prophecy and tongues (and other imperfect gifts) will pass away.' Thus we have in 1 Cor 13:10 a

definite statement about the time of the cessation of imperfect gifts like prophecy: they will 'be made useless' or 'pass away' when Christ returns. And this would imply that they will continue throughout the church age, including today, right up to the day that Christ returns".[25]

Paul's purpose in 1 Corinthians 13 is to show the supreme prominence of love. Love is what will last forever, unlike gifts, which will no longer be needed when God Himself, who is love, returns. In 1 Corinthians 1:7, Paul also wrote, *"You are not lacking in any spiritual gift, as you wait for the revealing of our Lord Jesus Christ."* Paul teaches that the church is gifted and empowered for His kingdom and will be until the Lord Jesus Himself returns (to see all the arguments and responses read Grudem's outline).[26]

The most used argument within my tradition is about the unique gifting of the Apostles. Yet this does not agree with the biblical text. First, in the book of Acts, many beyond the original Apostles were empowered to do exorcism, healings, etc. Second, in 1 Corinthians 12 there is mention of "workers of miracles" (12:10) and other gifts (12:4-11 and Galatians 3:5), which seem to indicate the normative experience of the church. The Holy Spirit is at the heart of the new covenant age. The implication of resurrection power for all generations is not only word, but also power experiences within one's life and without (2 Corinthians 3:1-4:18; Philippians 3:10; Ephesians 5:17; 2 Corinthians 10:3-4; 2 Timothy 1:7; Ephesians 6:10-12).

Grudem again summarizes that the ongoing Christian community would:

> ...also have the ability to minister the gospel not only in truth and love but also with accompanying miraculous demonstrations of God's power. It is difficult to see, from the pages of the New Testament, any reason why only the preaching of the apostles should come *"not in plausible words of wisdom, but in demonstration of the Spirit and of power, that your faith might not rest in the wisdom of men but in the power of God"* (1 Cor. 2:4-5). Though there does seem to have been an unusual concentration of miraculous power in the ministry of the apostles, this is not a reason for thinking that there would be few or no miracles following their deaths. Rather, the apostles were the leaders in a new covenant church whose life and message were characterized by the power of the Holy Spirit at work in miraculous ways.[27]

Others use Jude 9 to argue that neither the angel Michael nor we are called to be involved in deliverance ministry. Therefore, the practice of direct confrontation of demonic powers must have ended. Yet within its context, this argument misses the pastoral heart of Jude. *"But even the archangel Michael, when he was disputing with the devil about the body of Moses, did not dare to bring a slanderous accusation against him, but said, 'The Lord rebuke you!'"*

Therefore, the lesson of the verse is simple. Don't try to go beyond the authority God has given you! When Jude 9 is viewed in this way, the only question that arises for a Christian from this verse is, What authority has God given us over demonic forces? And the rest of the New Testament speaks clearly to this in several places. Not only Jesus, and not only His 12 disciples, but also the 70 disciples, Paul and Philip (who was not an apostle) are *given* authority over demons by the Lord Jesus. Jude 9, therefore, simply cannot mean it is wrong for human beings to rebuke or command demons, or that it is wrong for any but the apostles to do so. Both Peter and James encourage *us* Christians to "resist" the devil, and Paul encourages believers in general to put on spiritual armour and prepare for spiritual warfare.[28]

Again this is included because in both my personal history and in our church we either taught that all power gifts and experiences had ceased or we were functionally cessationist out of fear of the unknown or of the disruptive. We taught about the gifts or preached from the texts but did not expect, train, and apply these parts of Scripture to our daily lives as individuals or as a congregation. Our journey has been from one extreme to a more balanced biblical worldview. This whole ministry would be dismissed and removed from our context if we had not made this significant shift in worldview.

CHAPTER SUMMARY

I realize that many good biblical scholars caution against using Acts for building theology and ministry philosophy. The idea is that narratives don't yield principles as readily as written instruction. Yet there must be balance between historic content alone and continuing history. I affirm the hermeneutical notion that Acts is not just recorded holy history, but is also the outworking of the Gospel in many cultures. This provides a diversity of models for leadership and missional engagement for all generations of Christians. Grant Osborne has rightly challenged the idea that by using a narrative text one cannot determine the author's intent since he has not produced a didactic text. He writes,

> Moreover, I also oppose the current tendency to deny the theological dimension on the grounds that narrative is indirect rather than direct. This ignores the results of redaction criticism, which has demonstrated that biblical narrative is indeed theological at the core and seeks to guide the reader to relive the truth encapsulated in the story.[29]

This diversity of experience and practice is undergirded by the command in Acts 1:8 and the implications of shared mission, power, and kingdom presence. Ben Witherington has also pointed out that we can know what Luke intends to be normative by affirmed patterns in his account:

> (1) look for positive repeated patterns in the text, (2) look for when there is only one pattern, or (3) look for when there is clear divine approval or disapproval in the text for some belief or behavior or experience or religious practice.[30]

The practical implications for deliverance derived from the Acts account are five-fold. First, Satan will attack the church from within once it has been established. Ananias and Sapphira stand out as a sad but real example of personal sin and the demonic attempt to divide, discredit, and even counterfeit the work of God through His people. Second is the theme of "turf wars." That is, every time the gospel comes into a new area, there will be a new clash between the two kingdoms. Satan opposes evangelism. Acts 5, 8, 13, 18, and 19 are all progressive examples of this reality. Third, Satan utilizes occultic religious practices, which can hold whole communities in bondage. Yet when the gospel comes and is accepted, it can break the evil ones' power in great ways as seen in personal confessions and the burning of magical scrolls in chapter 19. This enforces the need to acknowledge the true Lord, to confess all sin, and to remove all objects connected with that old life. Again it goes back to functional harmony between allegiance, truth, and power.

The story of the seven sons of Sceva in Acts 19 graphically points out that there must be a personal relationship with Jesus to do this type of ministry. Our epistemology is relational, and all of our ministry flows from that relationship. Formula and ritual are not the place of power and they are not real weapons. Truly, they are merely tools if, of course, they have theological integrity. This is a conflict between the One residing in us and the enemy residing in others.

Lastly, the very idea of cessationism is invalidated within the book of Acts. The power gift experience is at least three generations deep in the account itself. And in later chapters, we will see how the practice of deliverance has been persistently performed since that time.

Jon Thompson

CHAPTER 7

HOW THE EPISTLES FOCUS ON DELIVERANCE

When we move from Acts into the Pauline epistles and further, a lot more of the information useful in deliverance ministry is from "upstairs"— didactically—than it is from "downstairs"—narratively. It's always helpful to read Acts along with the Epistles, particularly in connecting Luke's account of the founding of churches and visits to specific locations with the correspondence later sent to those same believers. Acts provides us with case studies that give practical pointers to the principles included in the Epistles. Paul himself spends a great deal of time on the demonic, giving us terminology and theological pictures to summarize the experiences of the early church.

Paul tells us it is the demonic that blinds the eyes of unbelievers (2 Corinthians 4:4), calling it *"the god of this age."* He identifies Satan as an angel of light who can appear right and true but is actually evil and wrong (2 Corinthians 11:14). When we turn to the letters of Ephesians (1:21; 3:10; 6:11-12) and Colossians (1:16; 2:10; 2:15), we discover a Pauline understanding of structure or hierarchy when it comes to the demonic. The terms principalities, powers, rulers, authorities, and dominion are used to describe ranks of demonic opposition that Paul warns about (see Romans 8:37-38). Ephesians and Colossians, both prison epistles, originated close to the same time and share similarities. They also help clarify one another. Although Paul is fighting different heresies in these two communities, his tactics in responding to what are demonic distortions or attacks on the gospel reveal a pattern that can instruct us in our own time.

In Colossians 1, Paul includes a great statement of Creation. Even as John's Gospel begins with an unveiling of the Word's participation in Creation, Paul here further reveals the intimate and exacting role of Jesus in the details of Creation. He celebrates the deliverance of believers, including those in Colossae in verses 13-14, *"For he [Jesus] has rescued us from the dominion of darkness and brought us into the kingdom of the Son he loves, in whom we have redemption, the forgiveness of sins."* He can't help but continue with one of the greatest doxological profiles of Jesus in Scripture:

> *The Son is the image of the invisible God, the firstborn over all creation. For in*
> *him all things were created: things in heaven and on earth, visible and invisible,*

whether thrones or powers or rulers or authorities; all things have been created through him and for him. He is before all things, and in him all things hold together. And he is the head of the body, the church; he is the beginning and the firstborn from among the dead, so that in everything he might have the supremacy. For God was pleased to have all his fullness dwell in him, and through him to reconcile to himself all things, whether things on earth or things in heaven, by making peace through his blood, shed on the cross (Colossians 1:15-20).

Among significant exegetical notes on the passage above is the idea that the phrase *"the image of the invisible God"* means that Jesus shares the DNA of the Creator, being one with God and therefore God Himself. This is a clear statement of divinity. And the phrase, *"firstborn over all creation,"* does not mean "first to be created," but "supreme over the order of creation." God, who would eventually become the child born to a virgin in Bethlehem, was "hands on" in every aspect of Creation. Jesus' supremacy over everything is seen in His role in Creation and confirmed by His work on the cross.

This passage is a go-to passage in the work of deliverance. We have found it a helpful passage to force demons to admit the identity of their Creator. Scripture declares that Jesus holds all things together. Specifically, it spells out that before the Fall, Jesus created everything, including *"thrones or powers or rulers or authorities"* (v.16). The entire seen and unseen realm owes its existence to Jesus. Every angel and demon that exists at this moment was created by Jesus and He knows them by name as surely as He knows you and me—as only the One who fearfully and wonderfully made us could know us. Positionally, Jesus is before all things and above them all.

After reviewing their spiritual history and describing his view of his ministry, Paul again returns to the central matter of Jesus. The shift is from what has happened in the past to what they should do in the future, as we see in Colossians 2:6, *"So then, just as you received Christ Jesus as Lord, continue to live your lives in him."* After a brief explanation of what "living your lives in him" means, Paul again elevates his language to doxological expression about Jesus, leading up to a resounding declaration of past and ongoing victory over the demonic in Colossians 2:9-15,

For in Christ all the fullness of the Deity lives in bodily form, and in Christ you have been brought to fullness. He is the head over every power and authority. In him you were also circumcised with a circumcision not performed by human hands. Your whole self ruled by the flesh was put off when you were circumcised by Christ, having been buried with him in baptism, in which you were also raised with him through your faith in the working of God, who raised him from the dead. When you were dead in your sins and in the uncircumcision of your flesh, God made you alive with Christ. He forgave us all our sins, having canceled the charge of our legal indebtedness, which stood against us and condemned us; he has taken it away, nailing it to the cross. And having disarmed the powers and authorities, he made a public spectacle of them, triumphing over them by the cross.

The closing verse announces that through the cross, Jesus stripped these enemies of their power and made mockery of them by His victory. Paul is using a powerful image derived from current Roman culture. The term *triumph* wasn't just a word for victory; it referred to the elaborate practice of marching the defeated enemies in a grand procession through the streets of Rome as the crowds jeered them and cheered the victorious general and his armies. The apostle used this familiar experience to say that by the cross (an assumed symbol of defeat), Jesus actually accomplished a stunning victory that left the *"powers and authorities"* weaponless and humiliated. Even their greatest and apparently unbeatable weapon (death) was taken on by Jesus and shown to be beatable in His resurrection.[1]

Elsewhere, Paul himself can jeer at the impotence of mortality:

When the perishable has been clothed with the imperishable, and the mortal with immortality, then the saying that is written will come true: "Death has been swallowed up in victory." "Where, O death, is your victory? Where, O death, is your sting?" The sting of death is sin, and the power of sin is the law. But thanks be to God! He gives us the victory through our Lord Jesus Christ (1 Corinthians 15:54-57).

Back to Colossians, we saw in chapter 1 that Jesus is the Creator of all things; He has exercised and confirmed His power through the cross. Then Colossians 2:15 tells us that on the cross Jesus was doing more than simply reconciling humanity back to God and inaugurating the eventual arrival of the new heavens and the new earth; He was also, in that ultimate place, routing the principalities, powers, rulers, and authorities who were disarmed, paraded in shame, and mocked in Jesus' presence. Time and time again I will read Colossians 2:15 to the demonic and command them to confess if this happened and if it is true. Every single time they, after trying to resist, say yes it is all true and Jesus is stronger and Jesus has won!

In Ephesians, Paul establishes in chapter 1:20-23 that all authorities—whether human or demonic—are underneath Jesus' feet. Ephesians 2 presents the amazing picture that we are seated in Christ (v.6). And by extension, if we are seated with Christ, then everything that is under His feet, including Satan and his forces, is under our feet! This is just one of the benefits of being positionally in Christ. Orthodox theologians have described God's action as inviting broken human beings into the dance of the Trinity. Through Christ we have access to the Father and the Spirit. We are not, nor do we become God, but we are graciously included in Him. By the time we reach Ephesians 3:10, God's shocking intent becomes plain:

> *His intent was that now, through the church, the manifold wisdom of God should be made known to the rulers and authorities in the heavenly realms, according to his eternal purpose that he accomplished in Christ Jesus our Lord. In him and through faith in him we may approach God with freedom and confidence* (Ephesians 3:10-12).

It was God's plan all along to use you and me to display His grace and power to the evil one. We, the Church, are God's billboard announcing every demon's defeat. It was God's will to use small, weak, ineffective things in this world to display His greatness. The most apparently insignificant storefront church, Bible study, gathering of believers is actually a bright and glaring spiritual announcement to every passing demon that their days are numbered and their defeat is inevitable. Our existence is evidence of God's manifold wisdom. To summarize, in Ephesians 1, Christ wins; Ephesians 2 says you're in Him; and in Ephesians 3, we're the biggest advertisement for the reality of the largest win in history.

Now we return to our immediate setting in Ephesians 6. If all the above is true, then we are called now to take a stand:

> *Finally, be strong in the Lord and in his mighty power. Put on the full armour of God, so that you can take your stand against the devil's schemes. For our struggle is not against flesh and blood, but against the rulers, against the authorities, against the powers of this dark world and against the spiritual forces of evil in the heavenly realms. Therefore put on the full armour of God, so that when the day of evil comes, you may be able to stand your ground, and after you have done everything, to stand. Stand firm then, with the belt of truth buckled around your waist, with the breastplate of righteousness in place, and with your feet fitted with the readiness that comes from the gospel of peace. In addition to all this, take up the shield of faith, with which you can extinguish all the flaming arrows of the evil one. Take the helmet of salvation and the sword of the Spirit, which is the word of God. And pray in the Spirit on all occasions with all kinds of prayers and requests. With this in mind, be alert and always keep on praying for all the Lord's people* (Ephesians 6:10-18).

The emphasis on *stand* (4 times) is not only a reference to Roman military strategy (to take a stand and hold ground against all counterattacks), but also serves as a warning that we will be called to stand under attack. Ephesians 6:13 doesn't say *if* the day of evil comes, but *"when* the day of evil comes." The items of armour are not a stylish spiritual wardrobe, but issued with the assumption that they will be necessary to protect against blows, arrows, and other violence. Each of the pieces in our armour refers to an aspect of the work of Christ (salvation, His righteousness, His truth, etc.). The armour is positionally ours in Christ and yet we are instructed to actually put it on. This action is summarized by the ongoing discipline of "putting on Christ" and all that He is for us, rather than picturing the armour as our effort or ability in the face of evil. The spiritual/mental/devotional practice of dressing in the armour of Christ each day is a healthy practice in recognition that it's a battle out there.

I do this in my own daily practice established over a number of years as part of my early morning shower. I acknowledge again that Jesus is my Savior and Lord, confirming and affirming my faith. Next, I pray for the fruit of the Holy Spirit to be evident in my life, asking Him to show me what fruit I will particularly need that day so I can depend on Him for it. I rededicate my marriage vows each day and reaffirm my commitment to my ministry vows. Then I pray through the rest of the armour, even when I can't see how it will be specifically useful to me that day. I don't want to ride out to the field of battle half-dressed.

The Scripture doesn't lie about reality. Following Jesus is not a life-style of escapism. Buddhism promises if we will divorce ourselves from ourselves, we will attain nirvana. Secularism directs us to drown ourselves in sex, money, and power while avoiding reality at all costs. But Christianity says we are to walk through suffering with Christ. The way of Jesus is fundamentally antithetical to anything the world or the devil offers us. Ephesians 6 drives home the point that Paul knew spiritual warfare would be the reality of every-day Christian life.

A lot could be said practically, devotionally, and theologically about the usefulness of each part of the armour of God. For example, the breast-plate refers to Christ's righteousness (not ours) and protects the vital organs. Nothing is said about back protection—the enemy must be faced at all times. The sword is not a long but a short weapon, used in close quarter battle. All of this equipment is immediate and functions in conjunction with others who are wearing armour because we go to battle in community, not alone.

PRINCIPALITIES, RULERS, AUTHORITIES, POWERS

In Ephesians 6:12, Paul mentions four categories of opposing spiritual forces: rulers, authorities, powers of this dark world, and spiritual forces of evil in the heavenly realms (NIV). The NKJV lists them as: principalities, powers, rulers of the darkness of this age, spiritual hosts of wickedness in the heavenly places. The transliterated list in Greek is *archas* (rulers), *exousias* (authorities), *cosmocratopas* (world powers), and *pneumatica tes ponerias* (spiritual forces). Though they have become evil, they are part of the original Creation, remain under Christ's ultimate authority, and therefore are subject to the authority of those who are in Christ.

What are the interpretive options when dealing with this list? Some have put forth the idea that these categories don't refer to demons at all, but rather are terms referring to broken parts of this world, or are examples of brokenness like fake idols, secular errors, institutional racism, sex trafficking—

Jon Thompson

natural phenomena that display unusual rebellion or distance from God's ways. These are the wicked ills of society personalized by Paul, but not in fact actual sentient beings. This rationalistic naturalism replaces the supernatural tones of this passage with explainable human and societal depravity.[2]

Others appear to give Paul credit for presenting these as spiritual beings in his letter, though they also claim we now know his view was limited by ancient superstition and spiritualizing of the natural world. So, while the interpretation is kept spiritual in Paul's day and age, the usefulness and application to our day is strictly naturalistic, settling on similar conclusions as the previous position.[3]

A third group points out that the language Paul used had parallels in political terminology of his day. In this view, Paul is calling out movements, structures, or systems that may even be global in nature, but are inspired or directed by demonic beings. Large movements like human trafficking, communism, radical Islam, or uncaring capitalism, while populated by humans, have, at their heart, demonic inspiration or leadership.[4]

A fourth interpretation holds that when Paul was writing this passage he actually meant specific demons in positions of power acting on their own. The phrase *in high places* is seen as indicating actual beings capable of exercising authority in a way that allowed them to control or shape movements, but also allowed them to function directly—impacting persons and events.[5]

In practice, we have to decide how we are going to apply Paul's description in this passage, choosing whether to explain these terms as impersonal evil movements and influences in the world or conclude that Paul was naming personal beings who work in various ways to carry out the schemes of the devil in the world. Taken in whole, Paul consistently demonstrates his view that evil is personal, with real beings in the kingdom of darkness ranked to carry out mayhem in the world. These beings exist "in the heavenlies," can function in and through movements, and can directly attack an individual. To be clear, Paul was not using this demonic language to personalize bad stuff happening in the world. His view was organic rather than materialistic. He pictured himself and other believers locked in a struggle with personal beings (not people) in a clash between kingdoms.

Paul's practice gives us language and terminology to understand some of what Jesus had in mind when He spoke of "kinds" of demonic. The battle space includes events happening in the spiritual realm (up there) as well as clashes occurring in the worldly realm (down here). Though these demonic beings are neither omnipresent nor unlimited, they may have significant global influence, familial capacities, and personal influence. Entire movements or chains of events may be traced back to specific demons. Political spheres may be under the control of demons. From a biblical point of view, it doesn't take much direct exposure to the demonic before we discover a divergence in what demons can do.

Paul's overall language and tone remind us that the mistake we make as Christians is confusing who the real enemy is and insisting on making enemies out of other humans. Human beings are not our true enemies; what inspires, drives, and twists them is. We are facing off against structured ranks of opposition arrayed against us yet over which Jesus is still ultimately in control. And as John put it so well in 1 John 4:4, *"You, dear children, are from God and have overcome them, because the one who is in you is greater than the one who is in the world."*

When I am involved in deliverance, the vast majority of verses I use are not from the Gospels, but from the Epistles. The passages we have been discussing form a sharp two-edged sword against the demonic. I remind them of their origins and the authority under which they must function. Ephesians 1 is my favorite passage in confronting the demonic. I read the passage on God's sovereignty and ask the demons if they have more authority than God the Father's predestination before the beginning of time. Do they have more power than Jesus' adoption of the person and the seal of the Holy Spirit on their lives in place until the day of redemption? Do they have more authority than Jesus of Nazareth who is above all authority? Confronted with these questions, various levels of the demonic have consistently had to admit they were not. I find the greatest applied strength, when dealing with the demonic, is the declaration of the sovereignty of God the Father, expressed in Jesus His Son and the residing power of the Holy Spirit. I find it crucial to confront the demonic as a Trinitarian.

Now, beyond the categories given to us by Paul, we are immediately on shaky ground if we attempt to further unravel the power structure of the demonic. C. S. Lewis pointed out that we make two equally dangerous mistakes with the devil and his forces: the first is to ignore or pretend they don't exist, and the second is to become fascinated with evil to the point of becoming drawn in by the reality of the power.[6] The naturalistic bent of our age makes us susceptible to the first error, but also creates a vacuum by officially denying the spiritual and setting people up to be attracted to any unusual experience and captured by the second error. Either mistake is welcomed by the enemy. Once we step beyond what God's Word tells us, we are simply going by limited experience and must tread cautiously. Experience is real enough, but it isn't authority. And since we are dealing in a realm whose currency is in lies and deceit, we dare not make our own experience the final test of what is true and right. Our aim is to remain firmly under the guidance of God's Word in its totality and the Spirit of God within us. And if these two ever seem to be in conflict, we submit our experience to the Word of God.

It remains a strategic position, based on the testimony of Scripture and backed up by experience, that the world is saturated with the demonic. We may not always understand how they are involved, but it makes perfect biblical sense to assume that they are. In Ephesians 6:12, Paul identifies the two primary areas of the battlespace: *"against the powers of this dark world and against the spiritual forces of evil in the heavenly realms."* Paul is pointing out that we will experience the effects of spiritual warfare occurring in *"this dark world,"* which is the physical universe, also called at Creation "heavens and earth" (Genesis 1:1). But it also includes the *"heavenly realms,"* "heavenlies," or "high places" (epouranios), which refers to the spiritual dimension that is very much a part of our reality. Note he is not speaking about "heaven" or God's dwelling place, where evil cannot invade. Paul is referring to what some call "the excluded middle,"[7] or the almost universal realization that there is something in existence beyond our immediate senses. Our enemies are powers and forces at war throughout the expanses of our experience, whether seen or unseen.

The term *"wrestle"* that Paul uses in the passage conveys the intimacy and intensity of the battle. It also reminds us there is a significant time factor in our struggle with evil. It is ongoing and includes bouts of concentrated effort. An expectation that we will employ the name of Jesus and instantly overcome our opposition is not, as we saw even in Jesus' own dealing with the demonic, a realistic way to picture what and who we're up against. They have power to resist, to wrestle against us! If God didn't provide instant and easy victories to His own Son and to the early apostles, why should we expect quick resolutions in our day? If God's purpose is to actually develop us and produce maturity and grown up faith, then James' opening words to believers strike a clear chord of reality in spiritual warfare:

> *Consider it pure joy, my brothers and sisters, whenever you face trials of many kinds, because you know that the testing of your faith produces perseverance. Let perseverance finish its work so that you may be mature and complete, not lacking anything* (James 1:2-4).

All of this is significant because our tendency is to lose heart or think we've done something wrong when the battle isn't over in a hurry. Instead, resistance will be a reality check, a reminder to acknowledge your dependence on an infinitely greater power, refusing to be cowed by the struggle because you know your faith and perseverance are being developed in the struggle. Ministering with others who need deliverance, you may find the struggle lasts years or a short time, depending on factors you may never figure out. But expect to learn in any number of ways the true meaning of the word *wrestle* if you are led into setting people free. And realize that you will be deluged with disheartening suggestions from the demonic: "See, you're not strong enough;" "You don't love Jesus enough;" "What's wrong with you?;" "You don't have enough faith;" "Jesus doesn't really love you;" "Maybe His Word doesn't really work;" "Maybe this is all psychological and you've got a problem!" If your attention swerves from Jesus and onto your role, qualifications, or abilities, then the person you are trying to help will remain un-free. But if you know what Jesus has done, if you know what He has given us, then when you face down evil, everything falls into the right perspective.

Jon Thompson

CHAPTER 8
HISTORY OF DELIVERANCE MINISTRY (PART 1)

Since the idea of theological cessation of spiritual gifts is not found or truly implied within the Word of God, the logical question is: where are the records of pastoral care involving the act of freeing people from the demonic within church history? And what do they teach about the "what and how" of this needed ministry? Of course, all orthodox Christians believe in God, the devil, his defeat, and the ongoing battle, but many do not publish or issue authoritative statements on pastoral encounters on this subject. Yet, as one reads holy history carefully, a pattern does emerge. The same work done by Jesus and the earlier church has been done in every time period of church history in varying degrees. The personal journals of many of the most recognizable names in church history include remarkable accounts of dealings with the demonic. Names such as Athanasius, Calvin, Luther, and Wesley confronted the devil's work in their own lives and were called to intervene in the lives of others.

After the death of St. John, the next generation of church leaders continued the work of Jesus as empowered in Acts 1:8. As part of that ongoing work in and through the church, the act of exorcism was normal, expected, and practiced again and again within the first three centuries of the post-apostolic faith community. The following examples not only show a non-cessationistic worldview, but also record a living history of a variety of church leaders dealing with the demonic in the area of theology as well as pastorally as people came needing freedom.

The following is a short survey of experiences spanning from 100 AD to 1950 that includes not only documented cases but also gives us a glimpse into the models used by different leaders in different time periods. We start with stories from twelve key leaders from the 1st to the 5th centuries summarized by David Bercot in *A Dictionary of Early Christian Beliefs*.[1]

CHURCH FATHERS
Justin Martyr (100/110-165 AD) was a Palestinian philosopher who became a Christian apologist and was killed for his faith. As Bercot points out, Martyr wrote about the demonic again and again:

For numberless demoniacs throughout the whole world, and in your city, many of our Christian men exorcising them in the name of Jesus Christ, who was crucified under Pontius Pilate, have healed and do heal, rendering helpless and driving the possessing devils out of the men, though they could not be cured by all the other exorcists, and those who used incantations and drugs. . . . We call Him Helper and Redeemer. Even the demons fear the power of His name at this day, when they are exorcised in the name of Jesus Christ…they are defeated.[2]

Also, He said, 'I give unto you power to tread on serpents and scorpions'…And now we have all the demons and evil spirits subjected to us, when we exorcise them.[3]

Second is Theophilus (180 AD), who was the Bishop of Antioch and had direct influence on Irenaeus and Tertullian.[4] Bercot quotes Theophilus as saying: "Even to this day, the demon-possessed are sometimes exorcised in the name of the living and true God."[5]

Next is Irenaeus (135-202 AD), who speaks extensively about dealing with the demonic. As a bishop (Lyons) and the key leader who stopped Gnostic thought, Irenaeus understood the need to deal with the demonic.

Those who are truly His disciples, receiving grace from Him…perform (works) in His name, in order to promote the welfare of others….Some truly and certainly cast out devils. The result is that those who have been cleansed from evil spirits frequently both believe and join themselves to the church. Others have foreknowledge of things to come. They see visions, and they utter prophetic expressions. Still others heal the sick by laying their hands upon them, and the sick are made whole. What is more, as I have said, even the dead have been raised up and remained among us for many years. What more can I say? It is not possible to name the number of gifts which the church throughout the whole world has received from God, in the name of Jesus Christ….For just as she has received without charge from God, so does she minister without charge. Nor does she perform anything by means of angelic invocations, incantations, or any other wicked curious art….Calling upon the name of our Lord Jesus Christ, she has worked miracles for the benefit of mankind, and not to lead them into error. The name of our Lord Jesus Christ even now confers benefits. It cures thoroughly and effectively all who anywhere believe on Him.[6]

Tertullian of Carthage (160-225 or 250 AD), who built much of the foundational Christological and Trinitarian views of the West, dealt extensively with this issue. He wrote,

> Let a person be brought before your tribunals who is plainly under demon possession. The wicked spirit, ordered to speak by a follower of Christ, will as readily make the truthful confession that he is a demon. . . .We daily hold them up to contempt. We exorcise them from their victims, as multitudes can testify…What is nobler than to tread underfoot the gods of the nations, to exorcise evil spirits, to perform cures, to seek divine revelations, and to live to God? These are the pleasures–these are the spectacles–that befit Christian men…. See how many men of rank have been delivered from devils and healed of diseases.[7]

A native of Africa, Mark Minucius Felix, lived in the 2nd or 3rd century and was a spokesperson for Jesus in Rome.[8] He wrote,

> The demons themselves confess concerning themselves as often as they are driven by us from bodies by the torments of our words and by the fires of our prayers….when renounced by the only and true God, the wretched beings unwillingly shudder in their bodies and either at once leap forth–or else vanish by degrees.[9]

Later, Novatian of Rome (235-258 AD), a Roman theologian, who though orthodox, started another church after losing the job of being Pontiff[10] and wrote,

> This is He who places prophets in the churches, instructs teachers, directs tongues, gives powers and healing, does wonderful works, offers discrimination of spirits, affords powers of government, suggests counsels, and orders and arranges whatever other gifts there are of the charismata.[11]

One of the greatest minds and leaders of this time was Origen of Alexandria (200-254 AD). One of the first systematic theologians and exegetes, he wrote multiple times on the subject of exorcism and the demonic. He wrote, "Traces of those signs and wonders are still preserved among those who regulate their lives by the teachings of the Gospel."[12] There are many other key references to this ministry. "The name of Jesus can still remove distractions from the minds of men, expel demons, and also take away diseases."[13]

There are still preserved among Christians traces of that Holy Spirit that appeared in the form of a dove. They expel evil spirits, perform many cures, and foresee certain events.[14]

Even at the present time, the demons and other unseen powers show that they either fear the name of Jesus as that of a Being of superior power, or else they reverentially accept Him as their lawful ruler. For if the commendation had not been given Him by God, the demons would not have withdrawn from those whom they had attacked. For they withdrew in obedience at the mere mention of His name.[15]

Cyprian of Carthage (248-258 AD) was the bishop of Carthage and was killed for being a leader in the community of Jesus. He wrote:

This is also done in the present day. For the devil is scourged, burned, and tortured by exorcists – by the human voice and by divine power. . . . Oh, if only you could hear and see them when they are adjured by us. For they are tortured with spiritual scourges and are cast out from the possessed bodies with tortures of words. Howling and growling at the voice of man and the power of God, they feel the stripes and blows and confess the judgment to come. Come and acknowledge that what we say is true.[16]

Later in the next century, one of the earliest leaders to speak about the continuing need and ministry of deliverance was Lactantius (260-330 AD). A teacher of rhetoric at Nicomedia, he lost his job when he became a Christian. He ended up tutoring the son of Constantine and was the author of a book called *The Divine Institutes*. He wrote, "The same demons, when adjured by the name of the true God, immediately flee."[17]

As long as there is peace among the people of God, these spirits flee from the righteous and fear them. And when they seize the bodies of men and harass their souls, they are adjured by (Christians) and are put to flight at the name of the true God.[18]

Athanasius (295-373), as one of the most famous leaders of this time period, gives us insight into the Desert Fathers, ascetics like Antony who spent time alone in the wilderness working out spiritual disciplines that continue to affect our understanding of what it means to live in the world but not of the world. He very clearly spells out that the solitary life of these believers subjected them to intense demonic attention. He even defines the life of a desert father as, to a great extent, a continual daily battle with the demonic. Athanasius, who included the reality of the demonic when dealing with the arguments for the resurrection, also connects the act of exorcism as proof of the living Christ. He wrote,

And how does it happen, if he is not risen, but is dead, that he expels the false gods who by the unbelievers are said to live, and the demons whom they worship, and persecute and destroy them? For where Christ is mentioned, and faith in him, all idolatry is eradicated, all demonic deceit is revealed, and no demon even tolerates that the name is mentioned, but hurries to flee, as it hears it mentioned. This is not the work of a dead man, but a living and first and foremost God.[19]

It is clear that if Christ were dead, then he would not expel the demons..., for the demons would not obey one who is dead. But when they obviously are chased away at the use of his name, then it should be clear that he is not dead, especially because the demons who see the things that are not visible for humans - should know it if Christ is dead. Then they would simply deny him obedience. But now the demons see exactly what the ungodly do not believe; that he is God, and therefore they flee and fall down for him and say that which they also said when he was in the body. 'We know who you are, you the Holy One of God.'[20]

All of this is crucial because the names we have just surveyed represent some of the most influential thinkers in the first centuries following the closing of the canon of Scripture. We rely on their writings for the best direction in understanding how early Christians developed the core theology and practices of the Church that continue to shape us today. It is curious, then, that we have failed to listen very carefully to all they had to say about the reality of dealing with the devil as an integral part of the rest of their lives in following Jesus. When Athanasius wasn't writing his classic treatise on the Incarnation or assisting to craft the Nicene Creed to confront Arianism, he was fully engaged in pastoral ministry. His day job involved laying hands on the sick, casting out demons, and pushing back the kingdom of darkness. How have we lost this picture?

Also during these first three centuries in church history, three different streams and understandings of exorcism came to be, which set the agenda for all further conversations. As the Church spread, it became clear that the need to consider exorcism regularly arose at three different stages of spiritual life. Today, in developing our own ministry of deliverance, we have made it our practice to keep these three emphases in mind. These stages are baptismal exorcism, major exorcism, and the post-baptism/conversion exorcism. Major exorcism or exorcism in general was already seen above when Christians who are practicing the act of evangelism show the power and existence of the risen Jesus to those in bondage and to those who are seeking.

The exorcism functions so to speak as a 'miracle of confrontation', where the demons loudly are forced to proclaim who Jesus really is,

and that he is their superior. This is the reason for the great significance ascribed to exorcism in the missionary literature of the ancient
church.[21]

The apostles and other frontier evangelists and church planters were invading
territory and lives held under the kingdom of darkness. The necessity for exorcism in these settings was clear. Power over the demonic was often a confirming witness to those hearing the gospel that Jesus did have authority over
any being who currently controlled them.

By the second century, the act of baptism and exorcism were joined
together because most, if not all, new Christians were converting from pagan
religions and thus needed an act to deal with other spiritual influences which
were often overtly or covertly demonic. Failure to address these deep-seated
influences created situations we can already see occurring in the New Testament in the sexual confusion evidenced in the church at Corinth. Unless the
trappings and assumptions of their previous spiritual understanding were dealt
with, new believers were bringing into the Church all sorts of demonically
inspired behaviors that involved immorality, finances, habits, latent idolatry,
etc. Baptismal exorcism was seemingly both a preventative measure and a way
to assimilate people into the church. In other words, the very act of immer-
sion baptism included a verbalized renunciation of the devil and works as well
as a declaration of faith in Jesus Christ. Preparation for baptism included time
spent on the matter of demonic influence. Oscar Skarsaune, writing for the
Lausanne Committee, summarizes the rise of this "act" still done by many
traditions today.

> Already in the church order of Hippolytus (ca. 210 A.D.), there exists
> a broadly developed pre-baptismal exorcism; several repeated exor-
> cisms during the time immediately prior to baptism. In Hippolytus'
> conditions for admission for those who want to follow the baptismal
> instruction we read the following, "If anybody has a demon, then let
> him not hear the Word from the teacher before he has been cleansed
> (Apostolic Tradition 16, 8). And further: "From the day that they
> (who are to be baptized) are elected, let there be laying on of hands
> with exorcism every day. When the day of baptism approaches, let the
> bishop perform exorcism on each one of them, so that he may be
> certain that the baptized is clean. But if there is anybody who is not
> clean, he should be set aside because he did not hear the instruction
> with faith. For the alien spirit remained with him." (Apostolic Tradi-
> tion, 20, 3). In Hippolytus it seems as if the pre-baptismal exorcism is
> meant diagnostically so to speak: It will reveal and heal possible pos-
> session in the baptizands. The possession is here presupposed to be
> something that may occur in baptizands, but not necessarily often.

Secondly, there is reason to believe that a preventive effect is ascribed to the exorcism; it is supposed to prevent possession. Exorcist prayers often include a phrase where one prays that the spirit in the future may stay away from the person for whom the prayer is made, or the spirit is ordered to do so in direct speech.

When it is so important that the exorcism take place before baptism, it is undoubtedly connected with the understanding of baptism as a seal, as a protective wall against possession. It is imperative that the enemy be outside the city at the moment the wall is being built. If the enemy is inside the city, the wall will work against its purpose. It is important that the demon not - so to speak - slip under the seal of baptism. Then it would be more difficult to drive it out afterwards (so clearly in the Gnostic material in Clement of Alexandria, Excerpta ex Theodoto). We also, however, encounter a slightly different conception. This idea would in the future become the most important interpretative key for the pre-baptismal exorcism, which became a part of the baptismal ritual of the church - and still is in the old churches. Here all unbaptized people are thought of as being "dwellings" for unclean spirits before baptism. So for instance in the Epistle of Barnabas (ca. 130 A.D.): "Before we believed in God the habitation of our heart was corrupt and weak, like a temple really built with hands, because it was full of idolatry, and was the house of demons through doing things which were contrary to God. But...we became new, being created again from the beginning; wherefore God truly dwells in us" (Barnabas 16,7f)".[22]

As a result, by the end of the third century not only were all Christians baptized, they had also formally renounced the devil in that act of baptism. The average new believer was assumed to have been infected with the demonic in one way or another. Living in modern-day Toronto, Canada, with its mind-boggling assortment of mixed cultures from around the world, we have found it helpful to assume that we also are dealing with people very much like the early Christians—confronting and evangelizing in pagan contexts. In fact, I have often encouraged my students that we need to give more attention to the writings of the early church fathers than we do the giants of the Reformation. We no longer live in a world like the one Calvin and Luther faced. The bulk of their audience was already Christianized peoples who held to various distortions of biblical faith. Today we deal with post-Christian people who neither accept nor understand the biblical worldview the Reformers could assume in their audiences. Most everywhere in the world today has much more in common with first century Corinth, Ephesus, and Rome than with sixteenth century Geneva or Wittenburg.

Also within this church period, they wrestled with the key question: Can those who have been baptized (this being viewed as conversion at the time) be demonized even though the Holy Spirit has now taken residence in and sealed a follower of Jesus? It would again seem the answer is yes, but only in one case. That is if a follower of Jesus goes back and connects with the kingdom of darkness through forbidden practices. Tertullian gives an account of this involving a woman he prayed for. "She went to the 'theatre.'" Unlike today, the theatre at that time involved killing and mutilation of animals and people. This church father wrote, "In the out casting, accordingly, when the unclean creature was upbraided with having dared to attack a believer, he firmly replied, "And in truth I did it most righteously, for I found her in my domain."[23]

Within Clementine's writings (Clement of Rome 92-101 AD), he also affirms the possibility of the demonic inhabiting a Christian.

> Therefore the demons themselves, knowing the amount of faith of those of whom they take possession, measure their stay proportionately. Wherefore they stay permanently with the unbelieving, tarry for a while with the weak in faith; but with those who thoroughly believe, and who do good, they cannot remain even for a moment...The labor, therefore, of everyone is to be solicitous about the putting to flight of his own demon (*Clementine Homilies 9:11; see also Recognitions 4:17*).[24]

This gave rise to acceptance of post-conversion possession or oppression that Church leaders knew they had to confront.

Lastly, it must be noted that within this time period there was established an office called exorcist. The Older Traditions have replaced this office by allowing priests to act with understanding, but they do need permission from an ecclesial authority.

> Already from the third century the church has instituted the office of the exorcist, which in ecclesiastical language is a cleric who has received the third of the four minor orders. The order of exorcist invests the one who receives it with power and authority over evil spirits, deputing him to perform the exorcisms that are part of liturgical function. It is noteworthy that this office is not part of the priestly office instituted as a sacrament, but is an ecclesiastical institution. The exorcist originally performed the exorcisms in the context of baptism. The Catholic Church is, however, well aware that originally in the early church exorcisms of energumens (people possessed by evil spirits) were performed both by lay people and clerics. This was true even after the institution of the order of the exorcist.[25]

Today this structure remains in place, with every Roman Catholic diocese around the world having a priest assigned as an exorcist. From a developmental point of view, we see exorcism become an institutionalized practice as the emphasis shifts from Spirit-gifting to role or assignment, more organizational than organic as fewer ordinary Christians were aware of this aspect of the faith.

MIDDLE AGES

It would seem that exorcism began to decline during the Middle Ages, possibly because the number of those becoming Christians within the West was drastically reduced after Constantine. Yet there are still experiences and references during this period. As Christianity spread north there were power encounters. The Norwegian King Olav (known today as St. Olav) had an encounter with pagan cult leader Dale-Gudbrand. This power encounter leads to the conversion of this king and his tribes.[26] Here is the summary:

> Skarsaune comments that King Olav's answer is similar to that of an ancient apologist: "You frighten us with your god, who is blind and deaf and neither can save himself nor others, and who cannot move an inch without somebody carrying him. But now I believe that it is not long before something bad happens to him. Look up, and see toward the East, where our god comes with a great light!" One of Olav's men then struck the idol so that it fell down, and "mice as big as cats, and lizards and snakes" ran out of it. The peasants who had opposed Olav were so frightened that they ran away, but later Dale-Gudbrand returned and drew the only possible conclusion: "We have suffered great damage to our god. But since he was unable to help us, we will now believe in the god that you believe in and then all of them received the Christian faith.[27]

In the British Isles, accounts coming through the Venerable Bede and the non-mythological aspects of St. Patrick's life include episodes in which the demonic play a significant adversarial role.[27a]

The next major event in Church history is the East-West rupture in 1050 AD. The two major branches of Christianity kept alive but handled somewhat differently the matter of the demonic. But the fact remains that recognition of the need for exorcism survived the split in both the Orthodox and Roman Catholic churches down to today.

ORTHODOX (EASTERN CHURCH)

The Eastern Church, being so grounded within the Church Fathers, has never removed nor blushed at the need for exorcism of both types. In the *Longer Catechism of the Orthodox, Catholic and Eastern Church* we can see the baptismal rite of exorcism started within the 2nd century and is still used today. Following the classic question and answer pattern, we quickly see the Patristic worldview still in effect.

> 296. Why before baptizing do we use exorcism?
>
>> To drive away the devil, who since Adam's fall has had access *to* men and power over them, as his captives and slaves. The Apostle Paul says, that all men, without grace, *walk according to the tonne of this world, according to the prince of the power* of *the air, the spirit that now worketh in the children of disobedience.* Eph. ii. *2*.
>
> 297. Wherein lies the force of exorcism?
>
>> *In the name of Jesus Christ,* invoked with prayer and faith. Jesus Christ gave to believers this promise: *In my name shall they cast out devils.* Mark xvi.17.
>
> 298. What force has *the* sign *of the* cross used on this and other occasions?
>
>> What the name of Jesus Christ crucified is when pronounced with faith by motion of the lips, the very same is also the sign of the cross when made with faith by motion of the hand, or represented in any other way.

Cyril of Jerusalem writes: "Let us not be ashamed to confess the Crucified; let us boldly make the sign of the Cross on the forehead, and on everything; on the bread which we eat; on the cups from which we drink; let us make it at our going out, and coming in; when we lie down to sleep, and when we rise; when we journey, and when we rest: it is a great safeguard, given to the poor without price, to the weak without labor. For this is the grace of God; a token for the faithful, and a terror for evil spirits (Cat. Lect. xiii. 36)."[28]

The heart of the Orthodox rite of exorcism, beyond baptismal vows, is built on Scripture and on a grouping of prayers from some key leaders later in the Patristic period. The first is Basil the Great (330-379 AD), a Cappadocian father, bishop of Caesarea, and the great defender of the Trinity at Nicaea.[29] The other one is John Chrysostom (344-407), the Bishop of Constantinople, one of the greatest preachers of his time. Rev. George C. Papademetriou's writing on the website of the Greek Orthodox Archdiocese of America summarizes the modern view.

> All the Orthodox prayer books include prayers of exorcism used by priests to fight the power of evil. The Orthodox Book of Prayers (Euchologion To Mega) includes 3 prayers of exorcism by Saint Basil and 4 by Saint John Chrysostom. They are read 'for those who suffer from demonic possessions and every other malady.' Through these

prayers, the devil is exorcised (renounced) 'in the name of God Almighty and the Lord Jesus Christ, and commanded to come out of the victim, who is liberated and redeemed by the eternal God from the energies (powers) of the impure spirits. The great ills that humanity suffers are attributed to the devil and demonic power.' In summary, the 4 prayers of exorcism by Saint John Chrysostom and the 3 of Saint Basil ask in the name of God to deliver the possessed from the captivity of the devil. Some can be healed by faith, accompanied by fasting and purification. The use of exorcism must be made with discretion and great care.[30]

The Priest's Service Books outlines the rite under the title "Exorcism." This "major act" is done by a priest with the prayers.

ROMAN CATHOLIC

The Roman church, like the Eastern Church, has never removed the rites dealing with evil. There have been additions and minor changes, but overall their worldview is firmly influenced by the Church Fathers and a medieval philosophical and theological outlook.

As far as the understanding of possession is concerned, the Catholic Church distinguishes between diabolical oppression, which is a "hostile action of the devil or an evil spirit besetting anyone from without" (cp. 2 Cor. 12:7-8), and "diabolical possession" which is "the state of a person whose body has fallen under the control of the devil or a demon." The great theologians of the Middle Ages (Thomas Aquinas and Bonaventure) maintain that what occurs in possession is the "entrance of the demon into the human body, the faculties (physical) of which he proceeds to control." The soul, however, cannot be entered or overcome and thus remains free, though its functions in respect to the body it informs are as it were, suspended. The signs of possession were developed in the 17th century by P. Thyräus. He emphasized that the physical indications like spastic movements and hysterical convulsions were not to be considered decisive by themselves, but that the true criteria were knowledge of secret things and the knowledge of languages not learned by the possessed. All writers also mention lack of memory as a criterion. This means that it precluded normal human consciousness. It is also mentioned that maybe in the final analysis the effect of the exorcism settles the question.[31]

The actual rite stems from the Council of Carthage (393 A.D.) and in the 7th canon there is the instruction to affirm an exorcist. The Bishop would say:

...receive and commit to memory, and possess the power of imposing hands and energumens, whether baptized or catechumens." Importantly also, in the Apostolic Constitutions (V 3; P.G. I 1122) says "the exorcist is not ordained', i.e. for the special office of exorcist, but that if anyone possess the charismatic power, he is to be recognized, and if need be, ordained deacon or sub deacon.[32]

Yet even today the Catholic Church has been open about the need for and their continuing practice of the act of exorcism. The new *Catechism of the Catholic Church* deals with both styles of exorcism while making sure to show the difference between the spiritual and emotional. It reads,

> When the Church asks publicly and authoritatively in the name of Jesus Christ that a person or object be protected against the power of the Evil One and withdrawn from his dominion, it is called *exorcism*. Jesus performed exorcisms and from him the Church has received the power and office of exorcizing. In a simple form, exorcism is performed at the celebration of Baptism. The solemn exorcism, called "a major exorcism," can be performed only by a priest and with the permission of the bishop. The priest must proceed with prudence, strictly observing the rules established by the Church. Exorcism is directed at the expulsion of demons or to the liberation from demonic possession through the spiritual authority, which Jesus entrusted to his Church. Illness, especially psychological illness, is a very different matter; treating this is the concern of medical science. Therefore, before an exorcism is performed, it is important to ascertain that one is dealing with the presence of the Evil One, and not an illness.[33]

The rite called "Roman Ritual for Exorcism" (Rituale Romanum) was issued in 1614 and was reaffirmed in 1989 under Cardinal Medina.[34]

CHAPTER 9
HISTORY OF DELIVERANCE MINISTRY (PART 2)

THE PROTESTANT REFORMATION

As one comes to the birth of the Protestant movement, there are signs that exorcism, or as they preferred to call it "dispossessing," was not considered among the aberrant theological developments in the church that needed re-forming. Because of this, general instruction on exorcism wasn't emphasized. But there was great debate around the now ancient act of baptismal exorcism.

> The Calvinists claimed that it implied the exclusion of children from God's covenant of grace, while the Lutherans contended that its omission amounted to a denial of original sin. In England, Archbishop Thomas Cranmer retained baptismal exorcism in *The Book of Common Prayer* of 1549, but the second Edwardian book of 1552 omitted it.[1]

Yet there are key documents and historical occurrences that show this practice remained in effect. In the larger Lutheran circle, Melanchthon wrote that a demon could be removed by prayer and fasting. That is, by "the prayers of pious men" and by commands from them to depart but not by the "worshipping of bread."[2] Johannes Marbach allowed for the act and pastors from Frankfurt and der Oder (1536), under Luther's permission, helped set free a sixteen-year-old, using prayers during a divine service. In northern Europe, Johannes Bugenhagen, the one who brought the reformation to both Denmark and Norway and became the Lutheran Bishop, writes a letter to Luther and other theologians in Wittenberg about this issue. He describes a young woman who is possessed, and we know Luther refers to this letter from Bagenhagen and does not dispute the request or the fact of the demonic.[3] There are other cases in Augsburg (1560) and in the English church. The act of exorcism was never disallowed, but in 1604 (even after the removal of the practice of baptismal exorcism) one had to receive "Episcopal permission" to pray over an afflicted person.[4]

In 1547, Bishop Peder Palladius gave a lecture on how to deal with the demonic. He called on his audience to read Scripture and use the baptismal act.[5] The Church's *Ritual of 1685* outlines the guidelines, which again give insight into the model used at this time.

If the pastor is called to someone who is held to be possessed, or in any other way is tormented by the Devil, one must not at all decline it; but he ought to, according to the duty of the office, in the name of the Lord, after serious prayer and calling upon God, go to the sick (sick) and investigate his condition." The pastor is not to assume that possession occurs often "for ... such examples are at the present time rare in Christendom," but he should also not think "that we now are totally free from these attacks by Satan." Together, with doctors and other pastors whom the bishop appoints, the pastor of the area should evaluate the case, whether it is a natural disease or whether the person is "bodily possessed by the devil, so that he either rules and governs in the whole body and all its members, as well as mind, reason and the attributes of the soul, or if he only has conquered for himself one or other limb on the body, in which he lives and lets his power be seen, as he did with the dumb in the Gospel. (Luke 11:14).

The Ritual further makes it plain that it might be difficult to discern the spirits, but that a servant of God does not easily err if he seeks the guidance of God and tests the case on the Word of God. Possession can either be caused by the possessed himself if he has made a pact with Satan or in any other way voluntarily has given himself to his service by sin or ungodliness, or it can be undeserved. The bishop should write a special prayer for the possessed to be prayed by the pastor and the relatives of the possessed.[6]

Luther himself was involved in more than one act of "dispossessing." When I first reviewed the literature of the Reformation, looking for examples of dealing with the demonic, I was perplexed to find so few references. It took a while to discover that the term used for discussing deliverance from demonization in that age was "dispossessing," a literal description of the process, which is awkward today given the misunderstanding of what "possession" actually means. Below is a needed and insightful rendition of one encounter:

Once, during the life of Dr. Martin Luther, a young woman was brought to Wittenberg who was born in the land of Meissen, who was often vexed and tormented by the devil. And a letter was written to blessed Dr. Martin that he should save and rescue this young woman, who was 18 years old, from the evil spirit. When this virgin was brought to Dr. Martin, he asked her at that time whether she could say her faith (the creed). She answered, 'Yes.' Then the blessed Dr. Martin commanded her to say it. As she now began and came to the article (of the creed) and these words, 'And I believe in Jesus Christ, His only-begotten Son, our Lord,' she could no longer speak, but the evil spirit began to convulse and torment her. Then Dr. Luther spoke, 'I know you well, you devil. You would really like it if someone would set up a big ceremony with you and celebrate you greatly. You will find none of that with me.' Then he commanded that she be brought to his sermon in the church on the next day, and afterwards be brought into the sacristy, and he told the other servants of the church to come into the sacristy in addition. The virgin was obedient and came to the sermon of the doctor, but afterwards, when they wanted to bring her into the sacristy, she fell down and struck and convulsed around, so that several students had to carry her into the sacristy and lay her at the feet of blessed Dr. Martin, and they locked the door to the sacristy, and all the servants of the church with several students stayed therein.

Then Dr. Martin began, and made this short admonition to the servants of the Church, which should be well observed by all preachers of the divine Word who find themselves in the same situation, and they should do nothing different.

1. He began and spoke: 'Now and at our time, people should not drive out devils as it was done at the time of the Apostles and shortly thereafter, when it was necessary to do miracles and signs for the sake of the Gospel, to confirm it as a new doctrine, which now and at our time is not necessary, since the Gospel is not a new doctrine, but has been sufficiently confirmed. And if anyone wants to drive them out as was done at that time, he tempts God,' he said.

2. 'One should also not drive out the devils with conjurations, by commanding, like some in the papacy and even some of our own people do, but one should drive them out with prayers and contempt. For the devil is a proud spirit, who cannot stand prayer and despising, but desires a ceremony. Therefore no one should make a ceremony with him, but should despise him as much as possible.'

3. Dr. Luther spoke further, 'One should drive out the devil with and through prayer in such a way that one prescribes for the Lord Christ no rule, no means and manner, no time or place when and how he should drive out the devils, for that would be tempting God. But we persist in prayer so long, knock and rap (at the door) so long, until God hears our prayer, as He Himself says, Matt. 7, "Ask and you will receive, seek and you will find, knock and it will be opened to you." But Uzziah, he tempts God by setting and prescribing the time for Him, in which He should help him, Judith 7. Therefore he is rightly rebuked by Judith, Judith 8.'

4. Dr. Luther laid his right hand on the head of the virgin, just like one lays hands on those who are being ordained and consecrated to the preaching office. And he commanded the servants of the Gospel to do the same, and commanded further that they speak after him: First, the Apostles' Creed. Next, the Our Father. Third, Dr.

Luther spoke these words, John 14. 'Truly, truly, I say to you, whatever you ask the Father in My name, that will He give to you. Until now you have asked nothing in My name. Ask, and you will receive, that your joy may be full.' After these words, the blessed doctor called upon God mightily and prayed that He would rescue and save the poor young woman from the evil spirit, which was in her for the sake of Christ and of His holy name, that thereby He would be praised, honored, and glorified. After this prayer and admonition, he stepped away from the girl and shoved her with his foot, and mocked Satan, saying, 'You proud devil, you would gladly see me set up a ceremony with you, but you will not experience that. I won't do it. Do what you want, I will not give up.'

After this procedure, they took the young woman the next day back to Meissen from Wittenberg. And afterwards they wrote and reported several times to Dr. Luther and others that the evil spirit after this no longer tormented and convulsed the girl as previously.[7]

Even Calvin, who was much more conservative and seemed to not believe the miraculous gifts were available for his day, did see and speak about the reality of demon possession. In the following letter we see not only his experience, but also his pastoral heart to see freedom.

The man lived on the Ager Tugurium and Calvin described him as 'a wicked worthless creature, known all his life long as a drunken, dissipated blasphemer', who came to a tragic end. But the reformer was distressed by the fact that many members of the Council of Geneva 'were making a just of the whole affair.' In the face of continuing skepticism, Calvin cried, 'If you believe that there is a devil, you have here a manifest instance of his power. Those who believe not in God deserve to be blind in the midst of light.' Immediately after the strange and fearful end of this man, Calvin preached on the matter to the Council. 'I went indeed so far as to say that, during these two days, I should have preferred death twenty times over, having seen those unfeeling countenances, could I have them witness the judgment of God. The ungodliness of our people was more than ever discovered by this affair. Few only agreed with us. I know not if even one really believed us from the heart.[8]

John Foxe (1516-1587), a moderate English Puritan, is most renowned as a martyrologist and preacher of his day.[9] What many don't know is that he was also known for dealing with the demonic. One of the most famous cases is of a 30-year-old father Brigges, who was in his last year of studies for law. Known as a good husband and father, when he chose to become a Protestant he began to experience physical, emotional, mental, and spiritual attacks, which were later discerned as demonic. I won't recount the whole story (which Sands does in great detail in the article quoted below), but only outline a short part of the encounter which points to the model used by this puritan leader and pastor. The encounter ended with the prayers and commands seen below,

> Emphasizing this significance of Words by making a first and separate prayer for the restoration of Brigges's speech alone, Foxe adjured Satan to depart Brigges's body in the name of Christ Jesus. This adjuration demonstrated the power of the five-letter `weapon' (J-E-S-U-S), for at the moment Foxe pronounced Jesus' name, Brigges recovered his speech and cried out, `Christ Jesus, magnified and blessed be thy name, at whose name the devil ceaseth to molest thy creature. Blessed and glorified be thy name, who by the humble prayer of thy penitent servants and by the pronouncing of thy most glorious name, Jesus, the devil departeth.' The word is the way of God: `he hath promised me by his word I shall have a way out' -- a way out of sin and into grace, a way out of death and into life. Foxe then made a second prayer for the restoration of Brigges's other senses. Following this prayer, Brigges's feeling, hearing, and sight were immediately restored, with bystanders testifying that `sudden sparks of light flashed' from his eyes, which had formerly been `as dark and dim to behold as horn'. The assembled company believed a miracle had occurred, and Brigges's words of thanks were `Glory, praise, and power be unto thee, oh Christ, by whose power the dumb receive their speech, the deaf their hearing, and the blind their sight.'" Unfortunately, Foxe's routing of Satan proved merely temporary. Satan returned the next day and continued to torment Brigges for another week, again depriving him of sight, hearing, and touch; engaging him in theological argument; undermining his faith in God and in his community. But May 1st marked the last battle between the two: Satan inexplicably never returned after this date. Brigges was able to resume his studies, accept his call to the bar, swear the oath of supremacy, and maintain a practice as a London barrister for nearly three decades.[10]

Other Puritans would follow after Foxe. John Darrel and George Moore would do the act of dispossessing through prayer and fasting. They highly publicized these acts in order to refute the idea that the Catholic Church was proved as God's true church by the ability to cast out the demonic.[11]

Now before I move to the rise of the Evangelical movement (1700-2000) and outline a few other needed examples, I want to note that the above and below have nothing to do with the witchcraft trials within the Catholic and Protestant traditions. For the distinction, reading Tormod Engelsviken's paper[12] and John Warwick Montgomery's paper (Chapter 6) in the book *Demon Possession*[13] will give you the needed clarity and separation. Also, given the notable names mentioned in the last few pages, it is important that we recognize the error it would be to continue quoting the great figures of the Reformation while ignoring the unmistakable dealings they had with the demonic. Because they took "sola Scriptura" seriously, they took the demonic seriously.

EVANGELICAL MOVEMENT
In the aftermath of the Reformation, some of its children formed the Evangelical Movement. And it is here within the West that we see a greater resurgence of understanding and involvement in setting people free. Among the greatest examples are John Wesley and his colleagues. This Anglican renewal movement, which would birth not only Methodism but a full range of holiness groups (Salvation Army, Church of the Nazarene, Missionary Alliance, and even, in many ways, the Pentecostals), has reported multiple examples dealing with the demonic. Again, the sources for these accounts are journals written by the figures involved, not necessarily their formal published writings. Wesley kept meticulous daily accounts of his activities, including encounters with evil. Below is one account from John Wesley dealing with the demonic in a young woman.

> Tuesday, 23. In riding to Bradford I read over Mr. Law's book on the new birth. Philosophical, speculative, precarious; Behemish, void, and vain! Oh, what a fall is there! At eleven I preached at Bearfield to about three thousand, on the spirit of nature, of bondage, and of adoption. Returning in the evening, I was exceedingly pressed to go back to a young woman in Kingswood (The fact I nakedly relate and leave every man to his own judgment of it). I went. She was nineteen or twenty years old, but, it seems, could not write or read. I found her on the bed, two or three persons holding her. It was a terrible sight. Anguish, horror, and despair above all description appeared in her pale face. The thousand distortions of her whole body showed how the dogs of hell were gnawing her heart. The shrieks intermixed were scarcely to be endured. But her stony eyes could not weep. She screamed out, as soon as words could find their way, "I am damned, damned; lost forever! Six days ago you might have helped me. But it is past. I am the devil's now. I have given myself to him. His I am. Him I must serve. With him I must go to hell. I will be his. I will serve him. I will go with him to hell. I cannot be saved. I will not be saved. I must, I will, I will be damned!" She then began praying to the devil. We began: Arm of the Lord, awake, awake! She immediately sank down as sleep; but, as soon as we left off, broke out again, with inexpressible vehemence: "Stony hearts, break! I am a warning to you.

Break, break, poor stony hearts! Will you not break? What can be done more for stony hearts? I am damned that you may be saved. Now break, now break, poor stony hearts! You need not be damned, though I must." She then fixed her eyes on the corner of the ceiling and said: "There he is: ay, there he is! Come, good devil, come! Take me away. You said you would dash my brains out: come, do it quickly. I am yours. I will be yours. Come just now. Take me away." We interrupted her by calling again upon God, on which she sank down as before; and another young woman began to roar out as loud as she had done. My brother now came in, it being about nine o'clock. We continued in prayer till past eleven, when God in a moment spoke peace into the soul, first of the first tormented, and then of the other. And they both joined in singing praise to Him who had "stilled the enemy and the avenger."

Saturday, 27.—I was sent forth to Kingswood again, to one of those who had been so ill before. A violent rain began just as I set out, so that I was thoroughly wet in a few minutes. Just as that time the woman (then three miles off) cried out, "Yonder comes Wesley, galloping as fast as he can." When I was come, I was quite cold and dead and fitter for sleep than prayer. She burst out into a horrid laughter and said, "No power, no power; no faith, no faith. She is mine; her soul is mine. I have her and will not let her go." We begged of God to increase our faith. Meanwhile her pangs increased more and more so that one would have imagined, by the violence of the throes, her body must have been shattered to pieces. One who was clearly convinced this was no natural disorder said, "I think Satan is let loose. I fear he will not stop here." He added, "I command thee, in the name of the Lord Jesus, to tell if thou hast commission to torment any other soul." It was immediately answered, "I have. L---y C---r and S---h J---s." (Two who lived at some distance, and were then in perfect health). We betook ourselves to prayer again and ceased not till she began, about six o'clock, with a clear voice and composed, cheerful look: Praise God, from whom all blessings flow.

Sunday, 28.—Returning in the evening, I called at Mrs. J---'s, in Kingswood. S---h J---s and L---y C---r were there. It was scarcely a quarter of an hour before L---y C---r fell into a strange agony; and presently after, S---h J---s. The violent convulsions all over their bodies were such as words cannot describe. Their cries and groans were too horrid to be borne, till one of them, in a tone not to be expressed, said: "Where is your faith now? Come, go to prayer. I will pray with you. 'Our Father, which art in heaven.'" We took the advice, from whomsoever it came, and poured out our souls before God, till L---y C---r's agonies so increased that it seemed she was in the pangs of death. But in a moment God spoke; she knew His voice, and both her body and soul were healed. We continued in prayer till nearly one, when S---h J---'s voice was also changed, and she began strongly to call upon God. This she did for the greatest part of the night. In the morning we renewed our prayers, while she was crying continually, "I burn! I burn! Oh, what shall I do? I have a fire within me. I cannot bear it. Lord Jesus! Help!"—Amen, Lord Jesus! When Thy time is come.[14]

John Cennick, one of John Wesley's close preacher associates writes about exorcisms also:

One night more than twenty roared and shrieked together while I was preaching... (some of whom) confessed they were demoniacs. Sally Jones could not read and yet would not answer if a person talked to her in Latin or Greek. They could tell who was coming into the house, who would be seized next, what was doing in other places etc... I have seen people so foam and violently agitated that six men could not hold one, but he would spring out of their arms or off the ground, and tear himself as in hellish agonies. Others I have seen sweat uncommonly, and their necks and tongues swell and twist out of all shape. Some prophesied and uttered the worst blasphemies against our Savior.[15]

One other that deserves mention in this summary is another leader and friend of both John Wesley and also George Whitefield. Ralph Humphries is recorded in Whitefield's journal as saying,

I think the case was often this, the word of God would come with convincing light and power into the hearts and consciences of sinners, whereby they were so far awakened (that) the peace of the strong man armed would be disturbed; hell within would begin to roar; the devil, that before; being unmolested lay quiet in their hearts, would now be stirred up.[16]

From the late 18th through the 19th century, a series of revivals broke out in the English-speaking world, during which there were reports of dealing with the demonic. Alongside the Awakening accounts above, there are many encounters in the Cambuslang Work in Scotland recorded by Arthur Fawcett. Later, the Ulster Revivals (1859) and the Welsh revivals (1903-1904) both include accounts of physical and spiritual conditions that the leaders of the day concluded were not from God, nor a human invention, but demonic in origin.[17]

Martin Lloyd-Jones is a good bridge between the old and coming Evangelical moment in the West. He was reformed, independent, and a prolific preacher and writer. Yet he also understood the need for the Holy Spirit and His unique workings. To my surprise, he wrote and spoke about deliverance and had the unique insight of being both a medical doctor and pastor to evaluate certain cases he came across. Geoff Thomas reports the following from Lloyd-Jones:

> Dr. Lloyd-Jones writes of one example he came across of a person he believed to be demon-possessed: "Here was a poor girl who was supposed to be paralyzed, and many doctors had fallen in the trap of thinking that since she could not walk she had an organic disease. But they could not say which one it was, for none of the doctors could fit the paralysis into any known disease. Then it fell to my lot to see her - partly as a doctor, and partly as a minister - and what struck me immediately was that this was not an organic disease at all, but clearly a case of devil possession. How did I know that? Well, one of the reasons was that when I approached her bed with her doctor and her own minister, the expression on her face changed to something I shall never forget, and though she had not been able to walk for eight years, she began to make the most violent movements with her arms and legs and head, and this continued for ten minutes. Later, as the result of the conversion of two of her sisters, one after another, with a good interval between, that poor girl began to attend a place of worship - she was carried there at first - and finally she herself was converted. Nothing was ever said about her paralysis, but it just completely disappeared.
>
> Another memorable case of the conversion of the medium or spiritist in the 1930s in the Forward Movement Hall in Sandfields, Aberavon, where Dr Lloyd-Jones was then the pastor. It is often quoted, and it is a salutary incident. Dr. Lloyd-Jones tells the story like this: "Here was a woman who made her living as a spiritist medium, earning her three guineas almost every Sunday night. One Sunday she was unable, because of a slight illness, to go and do what she normally did. As she was sitting in her house she saw people walking to a place of worship. Quite suddenly she thought to herself, 'What if I went with them? I wonder what they do there? I wonder what that place is like in comparison with what we do?' So she went to that place of worship, and that led to her conversion. She never again did what she had been doing before.
>
> "But I want to quote to you her reply to my question, 'What did you feel like when you came to this service?' 'Well,' she said, 'this was what really convinced me and finally convicted me. When I came into this place I felt immediately that there was a spiritual power here, exactly as we have in our meetings. I was always conscious of power

in our meetings, and I was conscious of power in your meeting, but there was one great difference. The power in this building here, in some indefinable way, seemed to me to be clean. I didn't think of it. I wasn't reasoning. I was just conscious of power and cleanliness and of purity such as I had never known before.' That is it. Spiritism is unclean...the mediums are not in touch with the spirits of the departed dead, but with evil spirits impersonating the dead."[18]

Within the last hundred years, more accounts have emerged which give a great living narrative of deliverance ministry.

Much has been talked about and recorded within classical evangelicalism, the Pentecostal experience, and subsequently in the Charismatic renewal. Deliverance has been experienced in all three streams. There are significant examples not just of theological affirmation, but actual experiences. Pastors, Christian counselors, theologians, missionaries, and lay people all affirm this part of Christian ministry.[19]

Many of the greatest sources on deliverance come out of historic missional activity, which is recorded in articles, mission reports, and journals. Now many have gone into cultures without this understanding and in doing so have never been able to support the church in one of their greatest needs. Charles Kraft's story (confession) is a key example of this struggle in modern missions. He humbly talks about his "powerless Christianity" and Western rationalistic worldview, which did stop needed ministry. He calls for a change.

> Many of us former missionaries who presented a deficient (powerless) Christianity but have now experienced the missing dimension can do seminars leading people into that missing dimension in non-Western areas, including the places we once served. We can repent and return to a fully biblical view of ministry in God's power. We can teach, demonstrate, and lead our people out of the need for dual allegiances into a powerful, biblical Christianity.[20]

Once a quest is undertaken, we discover God has led others to help in this area. One of the oldest authors is John R. Nevius, a Presbyterian missionary in China, who included accounts of his experiences with the demonic in two books. He spoke of the neglect of this subject and also "found that the proximity of strong Christians and the reading of Scripture was enough to drive off many of the possessing spirits he encountered."[21] In the book *Demon Possession*, W. Stanley Mooneyham (chapter 11) gives 10 direct accounts from three continents between 1890-1974 of exorcism and the demonic reality. Other such missional reports can be found in books such as *Demon Experiences in Many Lands*[22] and *Wrestling with Dark Angels*.[23] Lastly, the Lausanne gathering in 2000 was about the issue of spiritual warfare. There were case studies from

Latin America, India, Europe, Brazil, West Africa, and one on Folk Religion. Each report gives a first-hand account of Evangelicals dealing with the demonic within their own cultural setting.[24]

PENTECOSTAL EMERGENCE

Beyond classic Evangelical theology and denominations, a new movement within Protestantism called Pentecostalism has not only guaranteed new life for our faith on a global scale, but has also reintroduced the biblical mandate of preaching with signs and wonders. Christian scholars estimate that by the year 2050, Pentecostals will number one billion. That means there will be twice as many Pentecostals than Buddhists and equal amounts of Pentecostals and Hindus.[25] This rapid growth has taken place for varied reasons, but one key reason is deliverance. From their outset, Pentecostals have taken the spiritual gifts enumerated in Scripture and the reality of the demonic at face value. They broke from the increasing naturalism in the rest of the church, understanding that most of the world remains instinctively supernaturalistic. Paul Pomerville, a Pentecostal Missiologist, rightly argues that the act of deliverance has been and is an intentional growth strategy among this group.[26] Other mission thinkers agree. McGraven cited exorcism as a part of the answer to his question,

> What Makes Pentecostal Churches Grow? Pentecostals he said, 'accept the fact that men and women today believe that demons and evil spirits (varying forms of Satan and dark thoughts) do invade them, bind them, and rule over them. Pentecostals believe that the mighty name of Jesus drives out evil spirits and heals them.'[27]

Now it needs to be said that Pentecostalism, like every move of God in a broken world, has its share of challenges and problems: lack of full biblical teaching, imbalance of emphasis on the experiential, some incorrect interpretations—all consistent with other movements of the Spirit across the ages. As long as the human factor is involved, we can expect things to be less than perfect. Yet despite shortcomings, God has worked in mighty ways among Pentecostals as they have pushed the Gospel into places where it came with power against the dark forces of power in this world.

This massive growth is part of a wider move of God, where the church in all its forms is truly Global and its key centers of thought, practice, and numbers are now in Asia, Latin America, and Africa. Viewed globally, the Church has now moved south, and with that numerical shift has come the needed shedding of Western rationalism and skepticism. Again, at the heart of ministry are many stories of deliverance done from Pentecostals, to Anglicans, to Baptists, to self-grown churches.[28] One of the most fascinating and significant reintroductions is found in the Congolese community, which contains many models of this type of ministry.

> In some Congolese dioceses, the transition from catechumen to baptized Christian has taken on many of the features of traditional initiations ties. Candidates may spend time away from their communities, learning both religious knowledge and new world skills, and the Easter baptism ceremonies may involve the exchanging of masks, signifying the shedding of old pagan identities. The baptism is accompanied by an exorcism, which is given far more weight than the symbolic vestige that this rite occupies in the West. In the twenty-first century Africa, as in second-century Rome, baptism is an awe-inspiring symbol of the believer's separation from a failing pagan world, an act of divine rescue. The point about the catechumenate reminds us that, in many ways, Southern Christianity today stands in much the same relationship to the wider society that the church did in the Roman Empire, before and during the great age of conversions.[29]

As I read this I can relate to their situation in so many ways. Again, they are actually living in conditions similar to those that faced Christians in Rome in the first century just as we are in Toronto. Our experience and culture may be different, but the encounter, pressure, and conversion call are becoming more and more similar.

SUMMARY OF DELIVERANCE THROUGH CHURCH HISTORY

Within this section on the history of the act of exorcism, we see some key emerging themes. First and most obvious, this function of ministry has been consistently performed by every generation of Christians, especially those within areas where the gospel has first been introduced or in areas where the gospel is being reintroduced. The pattern found within the book of Acts (turf wars between light and darkness) has been seen again and again throughout holy history. Second, it would seem that both lay leaders and ordained leaders are involved in this ministry, but the majority of this type of work is done by clergy. Third, no matter one's theological background or the ritual used, there are common themes used by all that recur in every generation. Fourth, there is the universally shared understanding that it is the given power of Jesus through the use of His name and the presence of the Spirit, which allows the community to remove the demonic. Fifth, the act of prayer is used in every session. Sixth, deliverance is always a communal act, not an individual work. There is power within the gathered body of Christ, which is seen in especially vivid ways in this form of ministry. Seventh, many if not most of the encounters took extended time, which underscores the notion from Ephesians 6 that spiritual warfare is a wrestling match. Many, including myself in the past, assumed that the demonic would be removed by one prayer and by using the name of Jesus. But Scripture, history, and experience give us a fuller and more mature understanding. Eighth, the conditions that set off or cause an encounter vary. We see that the presence of Christians engaged in the reading of Scripture, preaching, baptism, singing, prayer with fasting, and reciting creeds and liturgical prayers all are used to reveal and to deal with the demonic. It should also be noted that as in the summary of the Scriptural evidence, the demonic causes people to convulse, speak in unknown languages, and give supernatural ability or strength. Another key observation from Scripture and then throughout Church history has been that both the Christian and the non-Christian could be demonized.

Holy history is full of Christians who not only believed in, but personally encountered demons. Time and time again famed leaders have not only felt compelled to minister as Jesus and the Apostles did, but they have also understood that effectiveness was not attributable to personality, rite, gift, or position, but that it was the living Jesus, present through the Spirit of Christ, who overcame evil in all its forms. The pattern of new ground and conflict emerges just like in Acts, and the ebb and flow of need seems to grow and dissipate depending on evangelism and revival-like experiences. Yet this history provides much needed insight.

The analogy in Charles Hummel's book *Fire in the Fireplace,* when taken in a different direction, was helpful for the next part of my work. The fire is, of course, the Holy Spirit, the Spirit of Christ, and the will of the kingdom expressed, but the mantel or fireplace is, for me, the different expressions or rites of deliverance.[30] It would seem the various rites or activity of deliverance, though within the bounds of orthodox practice, are widely diverse. Yet all have the Spirit—the One who empowers, guides, leads, and the fire is the same. We can have unity in our diversity because the work is primarily about presence over cultural practice and allows the Church to continue the work of Jesus through these miracles of confrontation. The next chapter will work through the commonality of architecture between fireplaces to establish a hybrid model.

As I arrive at the end of this chapter, I am again affirmed in my need for such a study, the conclusions we have reached, and the continual growing edges of our ministry. I am working in one of the most multicultural cities in the world. My culture has become more pagan, more violent and cruel. Our society is going back not to holy history but to pagan roots found not only in Europe but wherever one comes from. The world's best have come to Canada, but all of us have brought the spiritual baggage of our history as well. I feel that, like my African brethren now and those who lived back during Roman rule, our churches are and will end up dealing with many of the same issues. Our church (like the rest of Christianity) is increasingly at the fringe of culture. As people come to Sanctus Church and become Christians, we are having to deal with demonic baggage. Yet I am comforted because I know that Jesus is leading me and others to show that the kingdom is still among us. The gates of hell are still not able to prevail against the Church that Jesus is building generation after generation.

CHAPTER 10
FOUNDATIONS OF OUR MATRIX

If you are one of those imagining how a deliverance ministry would look in their church, let me begin by saying I don't expect it would look like ours. Ours is continually under construction because we are responding to a cultural and historical situation undergoing rapid change. We have had to incorporate increased sensitivity to medical and mental health concerns alongside the spiritual focus of deliverance. In today's environment, people coming from a mental health or medical point of view are having to engage in some thinking about events that can't be explained within their worldview or disciplines. And we don't want to ignore symptoms or behaviors that may at times not be evidence of mere spiritual activity but are, in fact chemical imbalances, mental disorders, or disease. Our approach sees biblical value in a holistic approach because it is truthful.

The fact that we begin with God the Father and rely on Jesus Christ and the Holy Spirit in really caring for people gives us much greater flexibility than if we tried to help within the limits of a naturalistic view. We've had to deal with some contemporary medical or mental health workers who give passive assent to the reality of spiritual warfare "because you need to believe in it, but once you're whole and healthy you won't need those primitive beliefs any more." We find that approach unhelpful and suspect it would be the kind of devious tactic the demonic would be happy to use. Satan doesn't mind being described with horns and a tail as long as we're not actually treating evil with deadly seriousness.

We also realize that in one sense it is tempting to make everything demonic rather than something like mental illness. The demonic can be expelled; mental illness might be a life-long burden to bear. Faced with those possibilities, many hope they are dealing with the demonic when their actual case may be significantly more complicated. And we're not saying that a purely medical or mental health problem can't be healed by Jesus, but we do recognize that healing in this life is not guaranteed. The only guarantee of complete healing we have is at the resurrection—everything before then is partial and temporary. We don't ever lose sight that we live in a fallen world with messy reality. Neither deliverance nor healing are magic bullets that solve issues or secret pills that remove all consequences and relieve us of any responsibilities for the conditions in which we find ourselves. We have certainly noted that each person who is freed from the demonic in our ministry has invariably had to face other issues and problems that were masked by the presence of personal evil. Other sin issues or disorders suddenly seem clearer. In fact, many of those set free, after the initial time of euphoria in freedom, experience a let down or depression when the rest of life comes crashing back in with reality.

The most important thing to remember is that you are still left with you after the demonic leave. There's always more work to do—sanctification doesn't come to an end this side of eternity. At the end of the day, our lives are in His hands, and no matter what we perceive our needs to be when we come in faith to Jesus for help, our deepest attitude must always be, "Lord, I believe; help my unbelief." The best thing Jesus could ever do for you or me He has already done with His work on the cross, confirmed by His resurrection! Anything and everything else He does beyond that is simply an unmerited blessing for which we seek to live gratefully.

The great example of Lazarus comes to mind. He was brought back to this life by Jesus and had to eventually die again. Not only that, his resurrection still left him wrapped in the burial trappings. Don't miss the significance of Jesus' command to those who witnessed the miracle: *"Take off the grave clothes and let him go"* (John 11:44). Miraculous work in one area doesn't mean everything is repaired or made right. The focus in all this must be the resurrection power of Jesus and our eternal hope in Him, not any temporal circumstances, good or bad. He is risen, indeed! That ultimately makes all the difference.

Developing an authentic deliverance ministry will not be easy or quick work. We are not offering a plug-and-play approach to helping people who have been demonized. The stakes are too high for dabbling. So, to minimize superficial copying, I want to include here an outline and summary of each model we have reviewed, accessed, and used, at least in part, before I take the time to outline our current matrix. We have tried to learn from others while at the same time seeking the Holy Spirit's guidance for our time and place, as well as studying the dynamics of our congregation, which are probably unlike yours in significant ways. The almost two decades-long process of continual reflection and experience has become a key pillar to our current practice today. We are increasingly documenting everything we do and the results we are seeing God bring about among us.

In the pages to come I will summarize each model, but I'll also point out what we have liked and questioned and even disliked from each perspective. We realize where we have landed at this point is not perfect. And we tell anyone who will listen that we've made at least as many mistakes and wrong moves as right moves along the way. It grieves me to realize that errors we have made have caused injury to our team members and those we have been trying to help. We have had to face the reality that whether or not we engaged seriously in spiritual warfare, people were going to get hurt. Only God can account for all the variables in every life situation, and He has demonstrated in His Word and throughout experience that He is willing to do great work through imperfect servants and in those who will continue to need help. One of our biblical heroes is Moses who despite all he accomplished, was a flawed human being with multiple shortcomings. God called him to service, gifted him with a staff of power, referred to him as "friend," yet didn't let him enter the Promised Land because his character failed him and he sinned. Like Moses, we can sin and make mistakes even while wielding spiritual gifts from God. The human factor makes us all aware of the need to get better at the process of helping others.

In fact, the process, we've discovered, matters as much as the content. The result or destination is important, but so is how you get there. And since some of us tend to be mostly about process and some of us mostly about results, the wise way forward is to account for both. Because I am results oriented, I desperately need process people to help me.

But before I walk through the five contemporary deliverance models, I need to go back to the Fathers one last time. All the models in use today and all the current disagreement between faithful Christians over approaches to deliverance can, I think, already be seen functioning in part in the Church between 95-300 AD.

HISTORICAL BACKGROUND

Graham Twelftree's book, *In the Name of Jesus: Exorcism Among Early Christians*, was very helpful and transitional in my thinking. His summary of the New Testament and the Early Church Fathers offered some other needed insights that help define and shape the models still called on today. Also, the observed themes he uncovered in our forefathers' practices truly shape the theological and practical implications of dealing with the demonic almost two thousand years later. Like all theological debates ongoing today, the roots of honest disagreement between Jesus followers of every generation seem to be found within the dialogues and disagreements in the early years after the death of St. John. As I already mentioned, there is one strand and one theme that binds the whole New Testament and post-Apostolic period together related to this vein of ministry. Twelftree correctly argues that it is the living Jesus who matters within any encounter. He writes,

> We have seen that the New Testament writers held the conviction that exorcism was a confrontation between the divine and the demonic in which the demonic was defeated. In the exorcism among early Christians, the incantation, the words or prayers of the exorcist were important, not because of any inherited 'power' to evict the de-

mon but because they brought about a confrontation between Jesus and the demonic.[1]

This insight is what will keep us on the right path—humble and not self-reliant, but following the pattern of Jesus Himself. Yet Twelftree's work went farther than I did. My goal in the last chapter was just to point to the ongoing tradition of this ministry using living examples from varied sources and times in holy history. He gives more insight to frequency and functionality, which becomes helpful when speaking into today's challenges as churches try to build and evaluate a matrix and appraise many of the models offered. He writes,

> It is not possible to say that exorcism was the primary engine of evangelism 'a very powerful method of mission and propaganda.' Only in some churches was exorcism used and in fewer churches did it seem to be of such significance....We can see more clearly that there were other ways in which the demonic was confronted. Thus, through the lens of literature of the second century, the great anomaly of the fourth gospel avoidance of exorcism is less startling and more readily explicable. For many Christians, demonic encounters were not confined to individual maladies but alternatively encounters involved theological error, as for example also in Ignatius. In turn, the demonic was not confronted by an exorcist but by an encounter with God in Jesus through conversion or more generally expressed with the Truth. It is not that there was a reluctance to become involved in exorcism perhaps because of an increasing intellectual sophistication but an understanding that the demonic could be doctrinally dealt with and defeated other than through exorcism. In this approach to exorcism, we can see more clearly that, while Jesus may have been considered of profound and central importance to Christianity, the modeling of his ministry was not seen to be important by large sections of the church.[2]

His insights here point out that though this act of mercy was used, it was not the only point of evangelism or ministry. Second, there is a shift or the building of multiple traditions within the proto-orthodox church to deal with the demonic.

As pointed out above, we can easily see glimpses of contemporary models such as the Truth Encounter Model, the Power Encounter Model, and the Gospel Model, which still holds that when Jesus is truly embraced, His work and His Spirit will remove any and all demonic footholds at conversion. What we see in the proto-orthodox church has now translated into current traditions when dealing with the demonic—from MacArthur to Kraft, Anderson, and the Catholic Church. Nothing is truly new under the sun. Now this is encouraging and gives balance, but when looked at more in-depth, it also reveals the loss of a New Testament worldview as the movement matures. This was best summarized by Gerald L. Bray's work on the Nicene Creed in the book *Ancient Christian Doctrine, We Believe in One God*. He wrote,

> This doctrine can be summed up in a single word-monotheism. Scholars debate whether the early Israelites were monotheists in the strict sense, since there is at least a possibility that they worshiped Yahweh, the God of Israel, as one deity among many. But whatever truth there may be in that idea, it is clear that by the time of Jesus, Jews were monotheistic in the modern sense of the term. The only argument was whether pagan gods were demons or illusions-that is, did they exist in some form, or were they nonexistent? For most Jews this must have been an academic question, of little practical significance for their lives, which were lived in separation from the non-Jewish (Gentile) world around them. Christians found it more difficult to ignore the issue, because they were engaged in active evangelism among pagans and therefore had to deal with the claims made for their gods. It is probably fair to say that the more intellectual the Christian, the more he would be inclined to argue that pagan gods were nonexistent. But the reality of the early church was that many believers came from the lower classes of society, where belief in demon possession was extremely prevalent. Christians in that milieu could not afford to be too intellectual in their approach, and what we find is an insistence that pagan temples were the haunts of demonic forces, against which Christians were protected by their faith in God and by the intervention of guardian angels, who watched over them on a daily and individual basis. But even on this interpretation, it is obvious that no Christian ever imagined that the pagan gods were real in the sense that the claims made for them were true. There was only one God, and he was the God of the Bible, the God of Abraham, Isaac and Jacob (Israel), who had now revealed himself in the world as the Lord Jesus Christ.[3]

This shows that some of those in the faith community who were more educated took the seeds of theology from above (essentially prioritizing John's gospel over the synoptic gospels) and ended up seeing deliverance (actual or allegorically) by conversion, not by encounter. Salvation, then, is seen as the reduction of or removal of demonic presence in many or all cases. Further, while there is agreement with the biblical view that idols are not actual gods, for some to say there is no spiritual power or beings behind them is a very different conclusion. These views, which essentially ignore or minimize demonic activity, are not reflected in Paul (see 1 Corinthians 10:1-22), Peter, or Jesus, and set us up for the battles we have today over responding to the presence of the demonic. That is, there are some genuine followers of Jesus who confess their love for Holy Scripture but use a lens that is not fully grounded within the Canonical framework and therefore fail to account for real demonic activity.

Yet the fairly widespread teaching I've just mentioned does not change the day-to-day reality of what many of us face within our ministry context. So, using Scripture, church tradition, and almost two decades of experience and practice, the goal below is to summarize the models we have been influenced by, see the similarity and differences in those deliverance approaches, and then outline our current practice in light of the models and our own hard-learned lessons.

To start with myself and the team, we would say the reason we even began this journey was because we kept bumping up against the "middle reality" which we knew about in theory, but not in reality. Demonization manifested itself within Christians, baptized followers of Jesus. I was struck dumbfounded and unsure why there was such a pattern. Now, more than fifteen years later, I know for certain that what we face within our churches is no different than what the Global church has always faced, right from the start. "Split-level Christianity" is the most serious issue present in every church expression. It took thinkers like Hiebert to give me the global view and language to translate my everyday pastoral experiences into a practical and workable framework. When I read the statements below, it was like the light bulb turned on and the fog began to clear.

> Around the world Christian churches face the challenge of folk religions. Missionaries brought formal Christianity encoded in systematic theologies, churches and institutions such as schools and hospitals. They assumed that traditional religions would die out as the gospel displaced animistic beliefs and practices. Today it is clear that old ways do not die out but remain largely hidden from public view. Christianity is an overlay and the two co-exist in uneasy tension. People affirm orthodox theologies but go to witch doctors, shamans, diviners and healers during the week, often in secret for the fear of the condemnation of the church leaders. They are baptized in the church and initiated in traditional rites in the forest. There is also a resurgence of folk religion in the West, which contradicts the assumption that religion dies as science and secularism gain ground. The questions folk religions raise have less to-do with heresy than with syncretism-the mixing of different beliefs and practices in ways that distort the truth and power of the gospel.[4]

This untaught but everyday experience was seen in all facets of ministry but became most clear when we started to deal with the demonic. Here we began to see why this was a Lordship issue, a holiness issue that needed to be addressed with grace and truth, teaching and deed, with prophetic power and mercy. This gave us hope that we were not inviting or inventing issues, nor was our church somehow missing the mark, but was truly a normal reflection of the war that rages and the discipleship needs we as the Church have faced since Pentecost.

OUTLINE AND EVALUATION OF THE FIVE MOST INFLUENTIAL MODELS FOR SANCTUS CHURCH

Five deliverance models have been key to our journey. Some we originally brought to the table and others were explored as we have continued to deal with the demonic over more than a decade. The rest of this chapter and the next several include a summary of each model, highlighting what we applied as well as what we rejected because of theology or experience. The logical place to start is with the worldview that was strongly held by myself and most of the team just before and early on in this ministry experience.

THE GOSPEL MODEL

This first view is one that must be mentioned even though we quickly found it inadequate and therefore rejected parts of it. As mentioned above, it was actually the default model most of us as evangelicals from non-Pentecostal backgrounds had grown up with. In most cases, it was mixed with a strong dose of cessationism which denied most overt evidence of the Holy Spirit's presence. The seldom-stated but unhelpful assumption was that with the end of the New Testament age the Holy Spirit no longer needed to do signs, wonders, or anything weird and the demonic were prevented from doing anything unusual either.

This first approach to deliverance was not one we rejected as false teaching, but as incomplete and too narrow. It is what some have called the "*Gospel Encounter.*" It is summarized below by Gerry Breshears from Western Seminary in Portland and is held by leaders such as John MacArthur, Hank Hanegraaff, and David Powlison. He writes,

> Either a person has a demon and isn't a Christian or he/she is a Christian but only *thinks* he/she has a demon. And so the procedure or model is salvation, which removes any form of internal demonization and sanctification because the way to continue to resist the external attacks the average Christian will experience within the fallen world. Thus the Procedure goes something like this. "Proclaim the gospel with prayer, a godly life, and clear truth. Remember that when the person becomes a Christian, the Spirit indwells and no demon can also be inside the person. Teach and urge application of the truth to deal with demonic deception, accusation and temptation. Do not fall prey to the lie that you must cancel curses, cast out a demon from a

believer or do binding prayers or the like (Key Passages: 2 Corinthians 6:14-15;1 John 5:18)… Argument: The Holy Spirit and a demonic spirit cannot occupy the same space/person. Nowhere in the epistles do you see any commands or instructions to cast a demon out of a believer. Just preach and apply the gospel and look to the Spirit for growth in righteousness. Resist all satanic temptations by standing on the Word.[5]

David Powlison, a Christian leader of great depth and who was a great gift to the church wrote simply that spiritual warfare is a "pastoral and theological term to describe the moral conflicts of the Christian life."[5a]

Now I realize this is a widely held and cherished position that should not be casually dismissed. And I would readily find agreement with its champions in many other areas of theology. But I have been led to a different conclusion when it comes to confronting the reality of evil in the world. Let me simply outline a few of our responses to explain why we have rejected part of this teaching even though all of us on the team did hold to this view for most of our ministry lives. First, the fundamental mistake or misunderstanding is that Gospel Model defenders confine the problem to the theological category of soteriology (salvation), where it should be placed in many cases under the category of sanctification (holiness). The best and simplest way to describe this is when one looks at the theological definitions of holiness. Millard Erickson, a Baptist theologian, defines sanctification as "a process by which one's moral condition is brought into conformity with one's legal status before God."[6]

Recognizing the two sides of this one coin brings the debate from fog to clarity. A believer begins with legal or formal holiness, which is given to all Christians. You might call it positional holiness. Thus,

> Sanctification in this sense is something that occurs at the very beginning of the Christian life, at the point of conversion, along with regeneration and justification. It is in this sense that the New Testament so frequently refers to Christians as 'saints' even though they are far from perfect.[7]

Yet there is, at the same time, a call to grow in this faith by personal, everyday holiness, saying "no" to sin and "yes" to God and His will through the Spirit of God. It is a process of developed holiness experienced over a lifetime—becoming more like Jesus. It was St. Paul who outlined it best to a very holy/unholy church: *"To the church of God in Corinth, to those sanctified in Christ Jesus and called to be holy, together with all those everywhere who call on the name of our Lord Jesus Christ—their Lord and ours"* (1 Corinthians 1:2). The kind of high positional theology we find in the great evangelical theologians and consistent throughout Church history is profoundly affirming and is worth giving more attention to from the pulpit. Who we are and what we have in Christ can always stand more careful teaching. It is foundational to everything else in the Christian life. They get so much of the "upstairs" right but they are wrong in how they apply it "downstairs."

For to say that at conversion all demonic, internal influence must be gone is not a pattern that fits the full biblical record. Each believer, though positionally right before God, must also be changed in the now through His community, His Spirit, and His Word. Likewise, we would say that dealing with internal spiritual conflict also occurs during this phase of our life in Christ. The believer is now truly free, the war is won, the power is broken, and the allegiance is now replaced with a new Lord, but the battles must be worked about in the everyday, over time. Second, to say that the demonic cannot be in the same space as God is unbiblical. In Job 1, Satan stands in the counsel of the gods and God is still there. Jesus and Lucifer shared space more than once over a period of time—look at the temptation in the wilderness (Matthew 4). Proponents of the view that the demonic are excluded from God's presence would not make the same jump in "biblical logic" about sin—putting a middle finger in the face of a holy God—the same act Lucifer did within heaven (Job 1). The fact that God is omnipresent leads us to realize that creatures infected with sin (demons and us) do exist in God's presence by His gracious patience.

Every time we sin, God does not leave. The Spirit is grieved, but not removed. The issue isn't loss of salvation, but the ongoing need for repentance even after we have been sealed by the Holy Spirit. Ephesians 1:13-14 affirms our position in Christ *"guaranteeing our inheritance until the redemption"* but that word *"until"* leaves a lot of room for in-between experiences. And so it is the same here. This is not about ownership but influence and presence, and by the way, how very rational, western, and engineer-like it is to speak so spatially about the soul, the spirit, and that whole dimension. The view described above has no grounding in Scripture, but is really a physical/spatial worldview that is more western and naturalistic than biblical. The most striking Scripture that contradicts this is found in Ephesians 4:27 where Paul uses *"topos"* in the context of the believer:

> It is crucially important to recognize that *topos* is spatial language that occurs in a letter loaded with spatial language: "be filled with the Spirit" (5:18); "be filled with all the fullness of God" (3:19); Jesus ascended higher than all the heavens "in order to fill the whole universe" (4:10); Paul prays that Christ may "dwell in your hearts" (3:17); and Paul describes the church as a holy temple that is "a dwelling in which God lives by his Spirit" (2:22). It would be consistent with this widespread use of spatial imagery throughout Ephesians to interpret *topos* spatially in 4:27….In summary, Ephesians 4:27 holds out the po-

tential for succumbing to demonic inhabitation on the basis of excessive anger over time. Because the context of this passage points to a variety of vices that should be replaced with Christian virtue, it would be inappropriate to limit the susceptibility to demonic inhabitation to only the one vice of anger. It is significant, however, that Paul warns against anger more than anything else in this context with a variety of terms (see v. 31: "bitterness, rage, anger, and brawling"). Ephesians 4:30 gives perspective to this demonic inhabitation and influence. Paul affirms that the sinning believer is still the property of God through the use of the "seal" image. But, he teaches that the Spirit of God is grieved over the sinful behavior and the *topos* yielded to a demonic spirit.[8]

While it has become widely customary when preaching on Ephesians 4:27 to refer to *topos* as *opportunity*, 98% of usage in the New Testament is to use *topos* spatially, referring to foothold, room or place, space etc. Too often we let a theological discomfort cloud our application of Scripture rather than allowing God's Word to speak with an ominous warning that renders this verse, "If you as an elect, predestined, sealed believer, seated with Jesus in the heavenlies are consumed with anger, you have made room for the devil to invade your life." This is not an anomaly in Ephesians, which turns out to be a distinctly spatially oriented letter (just think of the spatial aspects of Paul's description in Ephesians 3:18 of the love of God as *"wide... long... high... and deep"* along with verses such as 1:20-22; 2:6, 13, 17, 20-22, etc.). Again, this warning is given to believers and pictures them as being in danger of allowing the demonic space to operate in their lives. And anger becomes simply one example that nullifies the claim that Paul doesn't contain post-conversion conflict with the demonic. The principle he is exemplifying is that the danger in habitual, unrepentant sin in a Christian's life (like anger) is the making of space for demonic presence and harassment. And, given the immediate context of Paul's passion about unity among believers, he is including among his concerns that not only the presence of ongoing sin, but also the allowed impact of the demonic will seriously undermine effective unity among believers. How often, when facing breakdown in fellowship and rampant disunity in the church, are we guilty of leaving the demonic completely off the list of suspects?

Those wrestling with the implications of this teaching might wonder where—in the believer who is indwelt and literally possessed (owned) by the Spirit—might the demonic find space to operate. Some imprecision in our language can challenge us at this point. While we may say that at conversion the Holy Spirit takes up residence in our heart, it would be more biblically correct to say that He takes up residence in our spirit—*"The Spirit himself testifies with our spirit that we are God's children"* (Romans 8:16). If our understanding of the human being is limited to a spirit and body, it's difficult to answer the question. But if we see humans as spirit-soul-body (spirit—dead before Christ, alive in Him; soul—made up of mind, will, and emotions; and body—physical aspects of humanity), there's a lot of territory in believers who are undergoing sanctification that can be affected and infected with the demonic. All three enemies—sin, the world, and the demonic—are capable of affecting our body, mind, will, and emotions as Christians! One cannot be called less dangerous in the now just because we have the guaranteed not yet.

From a pastoral perspective, all of the above is crucial. I am challenged to preach my heart out every week as I face my congregation. But if I restrict my view of the setting to be my words, their ears and attention span, and the Holy Spirit's presence without accounting for the demonic, I've ignored a significant level of malevolent resistance in the room that is determined to prevent the kind of changes biblical truth can bring to lives. If I have theologically discounted the presence of the demonic as impossible, I'm left preaching in an environment where I'm being drowned out and where I'm not using the rest of the spiritual armour designed to help me do battle. As important as the *"foolishness of preaching"* (1 Corinthians 1:21) is (and it's my job!), I know there is much more to what God is doing and wants to do in an average congregational gathering than I could ever hope to accomplish through preaching alone. But when the preacher is accounting for the presence of the demonic every week and when people in the congregation are being delivered from long-standing harassment by the demonic, the atmosphere for preaching is radically changed. People can actually listen when they are not hearing competing voices in their heads. The tone of prayer changes and anticipation of wholehearted worship becomes palpable. We have found that ongoing revival rests in part on the reality of spiritual warfare.

I also think those who believe Christians have a spiritual inoculation against demonic attacks have become, in a strange way, like the health and wealth teachers, confusing what is given in the now versus the not yet. More times than I can count I have heard teachers say that by the atonement all is given now—healing, happiness, and wealth. Shalom peace, in their mind, is given on a very limited, individualistic scale. They sadly miss that much of what they promise is not present, but will only happen post-resurrection in a new heavens and new earth. The above teachers say the same thing in this case and do not see that reality says otherwise. Their assumption is that if you convert to Jesus, every problem in this area will be dealt with now, at conversion. The future is given and sealed or you are not saved. They would never say this about premature death or sickness, but since the ongoing possibility of demonic influence is, in their minds, uncomfortable and undefinable, they are driven to an all-or-nothing response. Their attempts to bind Satan and his forces by definition rather than by active deliverance are not only ineffective, they leave believers vulnerable to debilitating attacks from the demonic. How sad that they teach the right things against those that promise too much in other categories, but on this narrow issue change positions without even knowing they are committing the same practice of promising more than God has promised about relief from Satan this side of eternity.

Connected to this is a question we have posed frequently as our deliverance ministry has developed: why does most of our ministry involve believers when it would seem many or most cases within the Biblical narrative of direct encounter involve non-believers? After I shared this in a seminary class, my professor, Charles Kraft, roared, "Not true, not true!" and then sent me this email with a section from a forthcoming revision of his book *Defeating Dark Angels*. This idea challenged my most cherished assumptions. Where do I stand with this? My answer is for now, "I am unsure, but the below is thought-provoking."

> To test our theory that Christians can carry demons, we need go no farther than the New Testament. We define "Christian" as one who has faith in Jesus as Savior and Lord. If we look at those whom Jesus healed and delivered from demons and ask the question of whether or not they had saving faith, I think we have to conclude that most, if not all of them came to Jesus in faith—faith that probably needs to be seen as saving faith. Why else would Jesus say to some, *"Your faith has made you whole"* (e.g. Lk 8:48)? When Jesus said that, he was certainly not saying that there is some magic in faith. He would not have said the same thing about Buddhist faith. He was saying that their faith in him, their Savior, was the vehicle through which Jesus could heal them. However, those who assume Christians cannot be demonized are partly right. A demon cannot live in the Christian's spirit—that is, the person's central core, the part that died when Adam sinned, because Jesus now lives there. Demons can, however, live in the other parts where sin also can dwell—body, mind, emotions and will. For some, the process of battling the Enemy as they grow in Christ involves battling indwelling demons as well as overcoming sinfulness within.[9]

Finally, not only is the conversation misplaced into the wrong theological categories but as already discussed, the very linguistics have not helped us as more conservatively inclined evangelicals. The word *possession* is the most problematic and as already pointed out, once the Greek is understood, the term rightly removes all confusion and misunderstandings. When we move from the bias of *ownership* to *presence* then the arguments above hold little water. Only then does the sanctifying work of Jesus and ongoing necessity of freedom become more obvious. Again, we fully agree with this view from a positional perspective and stand together with our brothers and sisters calling for genuine conversions to Jesus as Lord and Savior.

The Gospel Model, then, gave us some foundational truths that have kept us grounded over the years. Besides the commitment and confidence in Scripture, the evangelical proponents of this view have definitely gotten it right with the core principle of our position in Christ as sure and settled in heaven. Where the model fails, we have found, is in not accounting for the realities of continuing to live in this fallen place, exposed to the world, the flesh, and the devil as God does His sanctifying work in us. As we now take time to look at the four other models that have contributed to our own model of deliverance, let me define the terms again. When we're speaking of categories, we are using the word *possession* as positional, and believers by definition are now possessed by God, the Holy Spirit. *Demonization* is internal in a major or minor way and may be a factor we bring into salvation from the past or something we allow into our lives in the present. *Oppression* is external, and is the experience of every Christian. We have an enemy who is diligent in carrying out attacks against us. Jesus promised His church would prevail against the gates of hell; He didn't promise the Church would never be under siege.

Jon Thompson

CHAPTER 11
THE TRUTH MODEL AND POWER MODEL

For us at Sanctus Church, after almost two decades of trial and error in doing ministry in an area we never wanted or dreamed of doing, one of the most influential systems of dealing with supernatural evil within the evangelical community is called affectionately a "Truth Encounter," pioneered by Neil T. Anderson. In my opinion, he brought spiritual warfare into the spotlight for the conservative side of the evangelical church. In my early days of exploring how to resolve the shortcomings of the Gospel Model, Anderson's non-Charismatic, biblical approach seemed like a safe starting point. His model is best expressed in the title of one of his chapters in the book *Bondage Breaker,* "Helping Others Find Freedom in Christ." This is the heartbeat of his minis-try, which has helped millions. He outlines four presumptions to his base model, and in his later writings adds a fifth.[1]

First, he starts out by declaring that "we have mistakenly formulated our methods for dealing with demonic powers from the Gospels instead of the Epistles."[2] He argues that all acts of exorcism in the Gospels were the his-torical events that occurred before the death, resurrection, and accession of Jesus. Thus all authority had not been given to Jesus on *"heaven and earth"* (Matthew 28:18). He was working under the self-imposed emptying described in Philippians 2:5-11 that ensured he operated under human limitations. Also, Anderson points out that as St. Paul said, it was not until the cross that the kingdom of darkness had *"been made mockery of,"* that is, they had not yet been disarmed and exposed. And so, "during this period a special agent with heav-en-sent authority was needed to demonstrate the presence of God!"[3] He goes further by saying that since the fulfillment of the Law and the coming of grace has changed how we deal with evangelism post-Pentecost, our dealing with the demonic should change also.[4]

Finally, in this vein, he argues that Acts "is the historical account of the period of transition between the cross and the completion of the canon of Scripture…Therefore I stress caution in translating examples of demonic ex-pulsion from Acts as the sole basis for methodology."[5]

Second, Anderson also deals with the opposite viewpoints: "Some have mistakenly argued that no continuing ministry of setting captives free exists in the church because the epistles contain no specific instructions for it."[6] He outright rejects this and insists the model has changed from Jesus' time to now. From his viewpoint, this is dealt with when one realizes that personal freedom and overcoming evil, whether internal or external, is a personal responsibility. The believer, not an "outside agent," is key to his model. It is the person embracing Jesus and His truth that brings freedom. The person or community that encourages the person is there only to support them in their personal responsibility and claim of God's truth over their life. He writes,

> As helpers, our success is dependent upon the cooperation of the persons we help. We say with Jesus to those we help *'be it done to you according to your faith'* (Matthew 9:29). Helping people understand the truth and assume personal responsibility for truth in their life is the essence of ministry.[7]

His third idea, which is the foundation to his whole ministry and worldview, is that freedom is not the result of a "power encounter" but a "truth encounter." It is the truth that sets a person free (John 8:32). In his mind, James 4:7 and James 5:16 provide the source of his model. Consistent with this, he insists we should never talk to demons; they are liars, so we must ignore anything they say. We must submit to truth first, resist with truth second, and then Satan will and must flee. He writes in his book the *Bondage Breaker,*

> There is not a verse in the Bible, which instructs us to pursue power because believers already have all the power we need in Christ (Eph 1:18-19). The power for Christian living is found in the truth, the power of Satan is in the lie! Satan does not want you to know your power authority as a believer in Christ because his power is only effective in the dark.[8]

Fourth, Anderson argues that it is not a calling or unique spiritual gift that must mark the "helpers" but is in character and in the ability to teach. In other words, he downplayed the role of spiritual gifts in the process of deliverance. He believes that anyone who is in Christ has the authority to deal decisively with the demonic by dependence on the truth and standing in Christ.

> Focusing on character and teaching will keep the counselor from polarizing into a psychotherapeutic procedure which ignores the reality of the spiritual world or into a deliverance ministry which ignores the whole person.[9]

Lastly, he rightly rejects cessationism, liberal anti-supernaturalism, and strongly argues for the idea that the average Christian can not only be tested and tempted, but can also be vexed and demonized.[10] All Christians will be tempted and if one gives in, then they become influenced, which is deception (1 Peter 5:8). If this deception and accusation is believed, then it can give the kingdom of darkness control and entrance into their life (Acts 5:3), but a Christian can never be owned or possessed in the modern English sense of the word (1 Peter 1:18-19).[11]

The Anderson applied model is outlined in four steps. First, he believes that a person's background and environment are key to understanding where rights, grounds, accesses, and privileges have been gained by evil, if any. There are two guides he created to gather the confidential and needed information so patterns and life can be revealed and truth received, understood, and applied. The *"Non-Christian Spiritual Experience Inventory* and a *Confidential Personal Inventory"* have now been compiled into one form as *"Steps to Freedom in Christ."*[12] Using these questionnaires, a person walks through their life and their family's physical, emotional, mental, and spiritual experiences in detail. Also, here is when you make sure the person has crossed the line of faith and has accepted Jesus Christ as Savior and Lord.

In this step, Anderson is rightly urging the person to replace lies with truth. He is ensuring that the person has accepted the core truth of the Gospel and the salvation offered in Christ. But he is also acknowledging that demonic bondage relies on the person continuing to believe lies that must be uprooted and replaced by truth. The questionnaires mentioned above bring up many of the areas that become infected with lies under demonic influence.

Second, once the lay of the land is clear, the battle begins to root out and replace all lies with truth. All false concepts must be challenged and removed. Simply, this is a battle for the mind. He writes,

> Most people in spiritual conflict have a distorted concept of God. Mentally they may have embraced correct theology but emotionally they embrace something different... these false concepts must be replaced by truth in order for freedom to be realized. The grid he encourages below allows the helper to walk through line by line some key issues so the person can move the heart of his model.[13]

Again, at this point, he stops the reader to remind them that they will start to encounter the demonic within the person and must deal with the individual, not the demons. "If you feel comfortable and are finding success in a confrontational procedure, God bless you. But I always caution those who deal directly with demons not to believe anything they say. They are all liars (John 8:44)."[14] He teaches those in ministry to bypass all the demonic by shutting them down so the person can be and will be the only being dealt with in a direct fashion. He does this using the prayer below:

> Dear heavenly Father, I come to You in the name of the Lord Jesus Christ and by virtue of His shed blood. I acknowledge Your presence

in this room and in our lives. I declare my absolute dependence on You, for apart from Christ I can do nothing. I take my position with Christ, seated with Him in the heavenlies. Because all authority in heaven and on earth has been given to Him, I now claim that authority over all enemies of the Lord Jesus Christ in and around this room and especially in (name). You have told us that where two or three are gathered in Your name You are in our midst, and that whatever is bound on earth is bound in heaven. We agree that every evil spirit that is in or around (name) be bound to silence. They cannot inflict any pain, speak to (name's) mind, or prevent (name) from hearing, seeing, or speaking. Now in the name of the Lord Jesus Christ I command you, Satan, and all your hosts to release (name) and remain bound and gagged so that (name) will be able to obey God. In the name of Jesus I pray. Amen.[15]

Pastorally, he also gives several suggestions at this point. First, the person being supported is asked to be honest and speak about what is going on inside no matter the image, language, or thoughts. Second, he says you should never touch someone during this process because the kingdom of darkness will always react to a follower of Jesus. Third, he will never physically restrain someone, for the battle is spiritual. If the person being helped runs, he waits and prays until they return. Fourth, if things get very tough, he will take authority again and pray for wisdom through the whole experience since every person is different and thus the cases are different. He asks the person to be in control. He points out that if there is no ground being gained then you must go back to dealing with who they are in Christ, for belief in the truth is key.[16]

As the final act, Anderson takes them through the Steps to Freedom (which is implied in step three). These are a set of questions and prayers set out in a formulaic pattern, which deal with six experience areas. The first step deals with the counterfeit such as occultic practice, cults, rituals, and non-Christian religious experiences. The second step deals with deception in all forms, self-made, world-given, and demonically inspired lies, exaggerations, and misunderstandings. Also, he spends time here walking a person through baseline orthodox theology. Third, he addresses bitterness and encourages forgiveness. Fourth, he deals with rebellion and points to biblical submission with family, religious leaders, and the state.[17] The fifth step deals with pride. He notes that "Pride kills. Pride says, 'I don't need God or anyone else's help. I can handle it by myself.'" Lastly, he deals with bondage and points to Jesus and the freedom He gives. This step deals with moral doings, sexual actions, stealing, lying, hatred, cheating, addictions, and the like.

With each step there is confession and prayers to repent, to forgive, to be healed, and to cry for God to move and help them move forward. It is here that he would claim that the demonic leave, usually without manifestations or any need to deal with them directly. As the truth is embraced, they lose ground and the right, access, and privilege to stay and must leave. One could say squatter rights are removed. The power encounter is between the Word of God, the Spirit of God, and the demonic. As the process comes to an end, he reminds them of their need for fellowship:

> Be sure to exhort counselees that their freedom must be maintained. People who take advantage of their freedom through careless thoughts or behaviors soon lose it. Satan will attempt to regain his lost ground in the days, weeks and months ahead. But if you have instructed the counselees properly they will know how to take a stand against him with authority. If they return to their old sinful ways they will probably end up worse than before.[18]

Now this form of deliverance has many strong points. It is foundationally reliant on Holy Scripture, which is music to any evangelical Protestant's ears. Second, this process is not just a method to deal with a group of fallen angels, but also addresses the many emotional, mental, and familial issues such as trauma, forgiveness, past hurt, etc. It really follows the teaching in James 4 that personal responsibility is key, focusing on confession of sin, repentance, rejection of false practice, and belief. Implied here is that the person is important in the process, not just clergy, church, or other Christians.[19] At times, this seems to come across as a do-it-yourself exorcism that really requires no help from anyone other than God and discounts any significance to the role of community, leaving the individual as ultimately responsible for his or her own freedom. Yet there are no examples of self-exorcism/deliverance in Scripture. As John Ellenberger wrote in his evaluation, "Without his or her activity seeking to be free, without active participation in asking forgiveness, rejecting powers and affirming new allegiances, the whole process will not result in lasting freedom."[20]

Personally, in my first two encounters with the demonic, Anderson was basically the only resource I had, so I used his approach and it seemed to work, to a point. Yet after years of ministry and my own experience, we have noted some shortcomings in Anderson's process. This "Truth Encounter method" is a battle for one's own mind and could be described as self-deliverance. The outside assistance (by an individual or group) only facilitates an individual's own affirmation, repentance, confession, and renunciation. Below are a few observations and concerns we have about a "Truth Only" model. But let me add up front, that within our experience, this model is the best place to start the healing process, but it is still incomplete. In terms of the three-fold emphasis I mentioned earlier, this approach deals strongly with allegiance to Christ and with truth, but falls short in recognizing the significance of power—God's power brought to bear in demonic encounters to replace or expel unholy power, parallel to right allegiance replacing false allegiance and truth replacing lies.

The first concern is that it comes across as better or more effective, or even more biblical than any other approach. This is only a method, however, and no matter what approach is taken, the same theological framework and power of the Holy Spirit must be present to overcome the evil one. The power of Christ is present in the Word of God, within the person or persons assisting, and within the person themselves. As John Ellenberger said, "I am not convinced by the presentation…that this methodology can effect a higher retention rate or maybe we should say expulsion rate."[21]

Second, this model by itself has no parallel in the full sense within Holy Scriptures. The Scriptures contain confrontational and power-encounter experiences where the person in bondage is not the catalyst, rather the person serving God brings freedom through applied heavenly power. Jesus, the disciples, Paul, Philip, and others are confrontational in their approach. Jesus challenged lies with truth; He insisted on allegiance in the face of false allegiances; and he confronted unholy power with God's power. I reject Anderson's claim that Acts and the Synoptic Gospels cannot fully inform our practices within this ministry. In actuality, we must read the Epistles through the Gospels, not the reverse. Making the Gospels secondary is a terrible mistake, which is unfortunate but found in the hermeneutics and the ecclesiastical fabric of most post-reformation evangelical churches.

I find it interesting that Anderson quotes Matthew 28 and Colossians 2 as a reason for *not* using the Gospels. But he then quickly turns around and says he knows that the principalities and powers now have been mocked and stripped of authority, and that all authority has now been given to Jesus. But we should still look to Philip in Acts 8 and Paul in Acts 13, 16, and 19 as the theological foundation for deliverance, as he does. Those cases are post-cross, post-resurrection, post-accession, and as mentioned in my last chapters, not just acts performed by Apostles but by others. It is inconsistent, and again involves reading the letters backwards, not seeing the letters like Ephesians through the lens of Acts 19.

Third, Neil Anderson's understanding of "truth" versus "power" is incorrect. He pits them against each other, inferring one is safe and heavenly, while the other is tainted, dangerous, and not the heart of God. At this point he betrays an extremely Western view that ignores the significance of experience (the Hebraic biblical component) and focuses almost exclusively on cognitive issues (Greek rationalism), based on the assumption that if we think right we will act right. But right thinking isn't the full picture of the human struggle. We can get our heads right and still do wrong. Kraft's work gives a much fuller understanding to this limited view. Understanding and undertaking deliverance is not about a truth encounter versus a power encounter; it is both, found within a new allegiance. We must address all three issues of allegiance, truth, and power to see someone set free.

We can't fight a wrong primary allegiance by restricting ourselves to either knowledge or power. We can only fight one allegiance with another allegiance. Likewise we cannot fight error or ignorance with either allegiance or with power. These must be fought by knowledge and truth. So also with power, we cannot fight power with knowledge or truth only with power. In other words, we fight allegiance with allegiance, truth with truth, and power with power.[22]

Now Neil Anderson starts here in his process, making sure that those participating in deliverance have a relationship with Jesus Christ. Kraft writes that this is the most important of the three dimensions. It is about conversion to God through Jesus Christ and its goal is to remove, replace, or supersede all other relationships and allegiances.[23]

Second is the truth/knowledge/understanding dimension. While Kraft agrees with the power of the truth of God found within Scriptures, he expands on the definitions so as to broaden the limitation of Neil Anderson's practice. Kraft gives a fuller understanding, which in the end adds more power to the above model. In his book, *Confronting Powerless Christianity,* he writes,

> Sometimes we have used the word truth as a label of the knowledge/understanding dimension, as in the phrase truth encounters. This usage makes sense to Westerners since we often associate truth with information, facts, explanations, and the like. But scripturally, truth—like knowledge—is something experienced, not merely something thought. It is not a theoretical thing, it is an experiential thing. When Jesus says, 'I am the way, the truth, and the life' (John 14:6) I believe he was saying 'I am the One who will be true to you as you follow me, the Way, and participate in My Life.' There are at least three kinds of knowledge in human experience: observational knowledge, intellectual knowledge and experiential knowledge. It is the third kind, experiential knowledge, that is usually in view in the Scriptures.[24]

Kraft continues by outlining some key definitions to support such a view.

> Scripturally both truth and knowledge are experiential, not simply cognitive, assuming obedience to what is known. Truth and knowledge are learned by doing them, not simply thinking them. Truth provides antidotes for ignorance and error. Though spiritual truth is pervasively relational and experiential (John 8:32), it also has a cognitive and informational dimension. Theology is primarily experiential with an important cognitive component.[25]

Now this is where Neil does very well. The model is not just words or ideas, but is expressed in prayer through relationship and is applied within everyday life. Truth is to be embraced, beloved, and acted on. Yet as mentioned, there still must be a power from heaven to deal with any power from the air, thus the power encounter is needed in some form to fulfill the process of freedom. The pattern that extends beyond Anderson's ideas is found in the life of Jesus. The power is not a political, institutional, or personal thing. It is given, delegated power to see others meet the Son of God and be free in Him. Kraft writes, "Jesus did all this to demonstrate God's love (a relational thing), to teach us what God and the Christian life are all about (knowledge/truth things) and to free people from Satan (a power thing)."[26]

Again, John Ellenberger pointed out that this model tends to reduce itself to one narrow view, which does not address all the realities of the "excluded middle." He writes, "I am trying to figure out why it is so important to set this power-level encounter into such a highly rational package. Could it be the pressure of our own worldview."[27]

As a church, our early forays into deliverance ministry were based almost exclusively on Anderson's model. And we found that those who came, confessed Christ, repented, confessed sin, submitted to the Holy Spirit's word, and the detailed prayers suggested by Anderson reported remarkable deliverance during the sessions. But six months later, they usually admitted that what they felt was "almost free" instead of delivered. Their descriptions sounded like a medical case in which the symptoms have been dealt with, but some of the underlying disease continues to hang on. In analyzing these cases, we discovered that the sessions had never involved any of us telling anyone or anything to leave. There had been no authoritative command spoken directly to the demonic, because we were practicing the truth model that prevented us from addressing the demonic. We realized we had a problem. We went back to the Bible and saw that Jesus repeatedly spoke directly to the demonic and commanded them to leave. He did not pray and ask God to expel the demon; He instructed the demon to leave. We had been overlooking this component of the deliverance process. We had to move beyond Anderson's approach, without losing the core that we had learned from him.

This reminds me of a vivid experience with a fellow pastor who was being led, like myself, into deliverance as a part of his overall ministry. He brought to me a young man from his church who was presenting evidence of demonization. He wanted me to intervene. He was open to the biblical practice of deliverance but didn't feel competent himself. My initial response was to inform him that as the young man's pastor, it was his role to take the lead in this intervention. When he and our team met with the young man, the demon made itself known in the context of our gathering. I looked at my friend and noticed the now familiar look on his face of someone who has believed theoretically and biblically, but is now face to face with reality. I said, "Don't worry, Jesus is real! And the Holy Spirit is here." After walking through the preliminary steps, I turned to my friend and said, "All right, it's time to tell it to leave." My friend instinctively began to pray, asking God to expel the demon. I interrupted and reminded him to command the demon to depart. He again started to pray. I again broke in and said, "You have the authority to speak directly, in Jesus' name, and order this demon to leave." The light came on in his eyes, and he instructed the demonic to vacate the premises. Immediately the young man was free. And my friend had learned a valuable lesson.

A couple of years ago, during the week I happened to be teaching my course on deliverance ministry, my then eight-year-old daughter and I had an amazing conversation. She is not aware of the content of my course, but we do have regular spiritual conversations. That morning, she said, "Dad, I think Jesus has been in my dreams."

She immediately had my attention. I answered, "Well that's great, honey. Tell me a little more about it."

To which she replied, "He shows up when I have bad dreams and evil things show up. And every time something like that happens I'm pretty sure Jesus is in my dreams."

I said, "That's great! So tell me what happens."

With her own precocious eight-year-old look, she said, "Well, it's interesting. It's like Jesus gives me His power, and I use His power and the bad goes away."

"That's very insightful and biblical, honey," I say as I'm about to give her a mini-lecture on the application of Christ's authority. But she interrupts me.

"Here's how I understand it, Dad. It's like a library book. When I check out a library book, I don't own it, but I have permission to read it and use it. And then I give the book back. And that's what Jesus does with me— He lets me use His power." Oh that we would learn to be like children in trusting Jesus to provide us with what we need, in every way.

From our experience, we have gradually discovered that when we have had to deal with very strong, entrenched demons, the truth of Jesus' decisive victory on the cross and their defeat may expose and remove demonic rights, but most times they themselves are not removed. The Holy Catholic Church, the people of God with its delegated authority must step in as a shepherd to remove the danger. Sometimes a person cannot do it on their own; it takes power from heaven, delegated to the church to deal with the demonic. I am also sad that Anderson does not emphasize more of a team approach. God has given so many different gifts that can both help directly and also build the faith of the person and those present. Prayer, discernment, wisdom, teaching, encouragement, and administration are all gifts used within our ministry. A corporate emphasis leads to an all-church effort to help in conversion, pastoral care, and sanctification of a person.

Two other thoughts of concern that I have already mentioned in passing: Anderson contends that we should never talk to demons and he exhibits a Western lens in dealing with the biblical material that is written from a Hebraic perspective. Now I do not make this a practice in order to get information, but I have been led at times to have demons confess Jesus' defeat of them, that they have no real power to stay, or confess where they must go and when. Yes, they are liars and they will try to pervert the truth, but I will never forget Kraft reminding us in class that every time demons spoke in the Synoptic Gospels during a power encounter they never lied; they always spoke truth. They tried to use it to their own end, but lying they did not do.

Second, our church is planted in one of the most multicultural cities in the world. My culture has become more pagan, more violent and cruel, and is going back not to holy history but to pagan roots found not only in Europe but wherever our various immigrants come from. A cross-section of the world has immigrated to Canada, and all of us have brought the spiritual baggage of our history with us. We as the church are increasingly in a minority position at the fringe of culture. As people come to Sanctus Church and become Christians, we often have to deal with their demonic baggage. Anderson's method has been helpful to include when dealing with a Western mindset, but that outlook represents only one type of person we minister to. The question was posed by one this way,

> While the truth encounter model seems to have worked well enough for Neil in cognitively-oriented North America, can we assume this approach would have equivalent impact in the power-conscious areas of the rest of the world? Often it is a demonstration of God's power that leads us to a new understanding of the truth, and a new step of allegiance to Christ.[28]

We have concluded that we do need much of the above model, but it remains incomplete. We appreciate the way Anderson includes personal responsibility, the role of standing in our God-given power (James 4:7), the confession of sin in community (James 5:16), the importance of background, clarifying interviews with afflicted people, emphasizes care for the person, and doesn't make the demonic the main event. He reminds us of the authority of Scripture and the fact that the person matters. He builds on the allegiance component that is prevalent in the Gospel model and adds the powerful component of truth to the process, but he stops there. This is why Kraft's three-legged stool (allegiance, truth, and power) expands the parameters of the Anderson model to support a multi-level approach to a diverse crowd, not just the typical naturalistic North American Christian.

THE POWER ENCOUNTER MODEL

What images and ideas most classically come to mind when we hear the terms *exorcism, deliverance,* and *dealing with Satan?* It is the power encounter—a full on battle between two forces. It's a clash with a violent reaction. There are many examples of power encounters. Many use an almost cowboy approach to deliverance, which tends not to respect the person's dignity, and will do this ministry no matter the cost to people. Yes, there is an emphasis on salvation, confession, repentance, and the significance of personal responsibility, but they depart from Anderson in several significant ways. Chief among them is seeing the act of deliverance as a face to face encounter with the demonic, applying Jesus' name and power with authority, and expecting to see visible and potentially violent responses on the part of the demons. This is warfare. It is wrestling with the demonic and the battles may take a long time. Not only the victim but also those intervening in Jesus' name are directly involved in the conflict and in taking authority over the demonic. They anticipate that very Gospel-like manifestations will occur, such as physical responses like groaning, shouting, vomiting, and being thrown to the floor.

The approach is based on acknowledging allegiance and truth, but focuses on the fact that holy power must be applied to expel unholy power. In other words, almost the direct opposite of Anderson's model. The results, while often dramatic, seem overly experience-based and often lacking in clear application of Scripture. But what we saw as an additional strength that we could include in our model was that the process includes commanding the demonic to leave.

For us, there was an author within this camp who represented a more helpful and balanced approach to a power encounter model—Derek Prince. In his book, *They Shall Expel Demons,* he outlines a power-only approach which is at least pastoral. He gives nine steps to set someone free or to set oneself free. "If you decide to claim the deliverance God has provided for you, you have two options: to seek ministry from your pastor or fellow Christians, or to turn directly to the Lord for help."[29]

With this simple yet accessible model, he gives one-line prayers to be said at every step. The first step is the call to "personally affirm one's faith in Jesus Christ." If you don't have a relationship with Jesus, you cannot call upon the power of Jesus' work for deliverance and forgiveness.

> We proclaim the victory of Jesus in a bold and personal way on our own behalf. When we do so, we invoke His ministry as our High Priest to bring our need before God the Father, thus releasing the whole authority of heaven on our behalf.[30]

Second, after making sure they have the needed relationship with Jesus—the only One who has conquered the kingdom of darkness—Prince calls those seeking deliverance to humble themselves before God (1 Peter 5:5-6), to cry out and say "I need you." Since he follows a power model in which manifestations are expected, he gives this advice. "When we seek deliverance from demons, there may come a point when we have to choose between dignity and deliverance. If dignity becomes more important than deliverance, we have not really repented of our pride."[31]

Third, there is a call to confess all known sin. He calls the person to relax, to let the Spirit bring to mind any sin, and to call it out loudly by its name (lust, greed, pride, etc.). He pastorally cautions against "self-analysis" and reminds the reader that the Holy Spirit really is a Helper, ready to do the work needed to help expose the sin.[32] The person is called to claim the truth of 1 John 1:9.

Step four is to repent of all the sins confessed, to forsake sin, and to take a stand against sin as God does. Prince urges, "Hate it as God hates it! The sin will have no more power over you."[33] He says that God will only deliver us from our enemies, not our friends. This step is a time to call out to God to learn to hate what He hates.[34]

The fifth step is a call to forgive all others (Mark 11:25-26). God has done this for us and so we must do this for others. Unforgiveness—with its companion, anger—keep a door open for the devil (see Ephesians 4:25-32). Forgiveness is foundational for the freedom we want from the kingdom of darkness.

> Remember that forgiving another person is not primarily an emotion. It is a decision of the will. First you must make a firm decision. Then you must verbalize it. 'I forgive so and so of all the wrong he or she did to me. I lay down all bitterness, all resentment, all hatred'.[35]

The sixth step is to renounce all occultic involvements and renounce all false religions. This call to revoke all other spiritual loyalties is key. This includes items like books, charms, objects of art, etc. As we have already seen, religious artifacts are not harmless. Worship to the only true God will undermine the power of the demonic beings that may use these items to control and influence.[36]

The seventh step is about a call to be prepared to see if there are any curses on you and the breaking of all of them. To this author, curses function like "a dark shadow," which in everyday life "shuts out part (at least) of God's blessings"[37] toward us. He outlines seven patterns that would point to the presence of a curse: breakdowns (emotional or mental), chronic sickness, fertility issues (like barrenness or miscarriages), breakdown in family or marriage, financial insufficiency, being accident prone and lastly, history within a family of suicides or deaths which are unnatural or untimely in nature.[38]

The eighth step is the call to take a stand with God's help. Those seeking deliverance are urged to declare their allegiance to God out loud, give all that they are to Him, and then stand publicly against "every kind of demon."[39]

During this act, you may already suspect or know a name or names of the demonic, or the Holy Spirit will bring a name to mind. Prince teaches that if we know their name, this will weaken the demon during the ensuing encounter, so it's important to stand and order it by name to leave. James 4:7 is the verse Prince uses for this next step. Lastly, the final act is to expel the demon or demons. After reading the prayer given, the person must agree with God and tell them to go, to expel them.

> The word for spirit in both Hebrew and Greek is the word for wind and also the word for breath. So how do you get rid of breath? You expel it, usually through your mouth….Begin to expel. That is a decision of your will, followed by an action by your muscles.[40]

After each time a demon leaves, the person should thank God and affirm Jesus as Lord over that area so that the demonic will not come back to fill the hole with many worse than itself.[41] Now it should be noted that Prince takes time to talk through what those present may see and/or personally experience during deliverance. Below is a summary of the manifestations he says should be expected when following the Power Encounter model.

> There may be different manifestations as a demon emerges. It may be scarcely perceptible, just a little sigh or yawn. Or it may come with sobbing, groaning, coughing, screaming or roaring. Remember, in the ministry of Philip, the demons came out with loud cries. One woman delivered from a demon of nicotine yawned so widely that she thought she was going to dislocate her jaw! But when she closed her mouth, she was free from nicotine. Set no predetermined limit as to how long you will go on expelling. Keep on as long as there are any demons to come out. When a demon is coming out, some people - usually women - may go on screaming without receiving any release. This indicates that the demon has stopped in the narrow section of the throat and is holding on there to avoid being expelled. In such cases, a deliberate, forceful cough will usually dislodge the demon and force it out. In a deliverance service, sometimes a demon's screaming will distract others seeking deliverance, hindering them and even making them afraid. This is when workers need to act quickly and help the person screaming to get released.[42]

Now for us, this model has proven to have some real strengths and has helped us move forward. Simply put, it allowed us to see that power used in humility and under the permission of the Father is good and needed, and truly follows the New Testament model. Many times, when we used just the Truth Encounter model, we were able to go only so far but could tell freedom had not been fully given. We were unsure and afraid of using commands or confrontation, but learned that delegated authority is the very heart of deliverance ministry. Power was given to be used by the Church and must be used. The demonic must be, to use Prince's language, expelled. For this basic knowledge we are very grateful.

Second, his dealing with curses was helpful. Now we still don't understand everything—why they are present and why sometimes they are not. And we can't always tell the difference between curses and influence caused by family of origin. But we do pray and look for curse-like patterns, which in some cases has been key to somebody's freedom.

Lastly, as in other models (Truth, Liturgical), when one gives an order and accompanying prayers but allows personal expression and flexibility, we sense we are being obedient while still giving God's Spirit room to work. Prince wrote, "do not feel bound to stick rigidly to this pattern of prayer. If the Holy Spirit prompts you to add words from your heart, do not hesitate to do so."[43] This almost mini-liturgical prayer guiding, acting as a promoter with permission for flexibility, is a great help and we use this formal and personal expression all the time.

Yet in actually applying this approach, we have experienced many concerns and weaknesses in a power-only model that we find hinders the process of deliverance. First, there is no calling all the demonic to the one in charge, which lessens the battle and quells manifestations. Second, we command the manifestation be shut down, where in this model they almost seem needed. Third, there is no outline of sins, or guidelines on emotional and mental history. Though Prince touches on some areas (occultic practice and such), too many people don't even know what actions are right or wrong. There is no reference to inner healing and no reference to clinical and medical support. This is most concerning for us because it overlooks a significant area of life that may bring a lot of clarity to what the victim is actually experiencing and how the demonic are using those matters to their advantage.

I've often used Kraft's language to describe the problem with the power encounter as a tendency to go after the rats before cleaning out the garbage that was sustaining them. We see this as ignoring or downplaying an area of truth which must be present in a holistic view of deliverance. Yes, power encounters are needed if all the preliminary work has been done, but not before. Again this goes back to Kraft's "garbage and rats" idea. A power-only approach may remove a little garbage, but does not address most of it. Without a more balanced model that includes the insights of power-only, the whole person will not receive all the help needed. Often, matters which may well be physical or mental health issues become overly spiritualized (the demon of ADHD or demon of over-eating) and the person isn't given needed help in other real areas.

Lastly, though Prince does speak approvingly of church or team support, it seems to me he sees this aspect of deliverance as optional. We disagree. Deliverance is a church act, the body of Christ using gifts to support, encourage, and exhort a person or family. I firmly believe we should always seek help from the Body of Christ unless it is not available. I am concerned here that both Anderson and Prince's models leave the door open to becoming too individualistic, too isolated, too self-help, too North American. Baptism, communion, preaching, fellowship, prayer, miracles, etc. in the book of Acts were communal first and individualistic second. This corporate environment should set the pattern for deliverance ministry.

At this point we had three models contributing aspects to the practice we were using at Sanctus Church. We understood and appreciated the strengths of each model: 1) Recent Evangelical emphasis on allegiance by relying on the importance of salvation/conversion in bringing the Holy Spirit to bear in a person's life; 2) Anderson's truth model adding the emphasis on the need to meet demonic lies with God's truth through confession of sin and standing in positional authority; 3) Prince and other charismatics' focus on the power encounter which downplayed or overlooked the importance of truth while seeking direct authority over the demonic. We were moving forward by attempting to balance all of these because we saw that each one left out something that the others brought to the deliverance setting. Further, we saw that all of these left out what we realized were other biblical aspects of deliverance. One of these, as I mentioned above, was the role of community.

As you are reading this, you may be experiencing at this point what usually happens when I am teaching a seminary class on deliverance: a rising tide of fear. Fear that you may be called to participate in something as overtly supernatural as we've just been describing. Fear that you may have misread a number of situations in ministry. Fear of the demonic. Fear of your own inadequacy to engage in ministry like this. Well, welcome to reality. All of us who confront the demonic rightly fear. And we fear most rightly when we fear God who has ultimate control over whatever we may face. God is sovereign, for real, and life, including confrontations with evil, creates opportunities for us to experience at every level the truth of God's awesome character and power. But there is also a natural, human, fearful side of this which highlights the potential dangers of the models we have just been reviewing with their tendency to individualize the process of deliverance. Even as we struggled to develop an effective and consistent model of our own for setting people free, we were repeatedly thankful we were not trying to do this alone.

This moved us to look at another model that we first assumed was universes distant from the classic charismatic power encounter, but after we read and learned about it, were shocked to see how close the models actually were—cousins in the world of dealing with demons.

Jon Thompson

CHAPTER 12
THE LITURGICAL POWER ENCOUNTER MODEL

Historically, the Roman Catholic Church has been open about the existence of the demonic and the need for the act of exorcism. Even the recent *Cate-chism of the Catholic Church* deals with both the baptismal rite and the pastoral care aspects of exorcism, while making sure to account for the differences between the spiritual and emotional. When the Church asks publicly and authoritatively in the name of Jesus Christ that a person or object be protected against the power of the Evil One and withdraw from his dominion, it is called *exorcism*:

> [Jesus] performed exorcisms and from him the Church has received the power and office of exorcizing. In a simple form, exorcism is performed at the celebration of Baptism. The solemn exorcism, called "a major exorcism," can be performed only by a priest and with the permission of the bishop. The priest must proceed with prudence, strictly observing the rules established by the Church. Exorcism is directed at the expulsion of demons or to the liberation from demonic possession through the spiritual authority, which Jesus entrusted to his Church. Illness, especially psychological illness, is a very different matter; treating this is the concern of medical science. Therefore, before an exorcism is performed, it is important to ascertain that one is dealing with the presence of the Evil One, and not an illness.[1]

Now for our present purposes, I have identified the model found within this tradition as a Liturgical-Power model. It is a confrontational model done through historic ritual and rite. The guidelines are found within the *Roman Book of Rites*. There are 21 guidelines given to those who might have to use this model. They lay the foundation for this structured form of power encounter. Let me summarize the broad commands and recommendations. First and most importantly, is that this act must be done by a priest, under the authority of a Bishop. This should not be overlooked, for they believe that spiritual authority is expressed and passed down from Christ to the Pope through Bishops to local priests, and since deliverance is connected to spiritual authority the below is key to this model.

The college or body of bishops has no authority unless united with the Roman Pontiff, Peter's successor, as its head. As such, this college has "supreme and full authority over the universal Church; but this power cannot be exercised without the agreement of the Roman Pontiff...The individual bishops are the visible source and foundation of unity in their own particular Churches." As such, they "exercise their pastoral office over the portion of the People of God assigned to them," assisted by priests and deacons. But, as a member of the Episcopal college, each bishop shares in the concern for all the Churches. The bishops exercise this care first "by ruling well their own Churches as portions of the universal Church," and so contributing "to the welfare of the whole Mystical Body, which, from another point of view, is a corporate body of Churches.[2]

Second, there is a call for great personal holiness, maturity, and study on the subject. Fasting, prayer, and humility are also expected and called on. They take a lot of time to help a priest understand what might happen, from demons lying, to them leaving during an encounter so things look okay but are not, to manifestations from sleep to violence. They also point out, like Kraft does, that the demonic might make claims about rights, ground accesses, and privileges, which need to be evaluated and carefully used.

Interestingly, in describing the realities of demon possession, they agree with many of the practices in other Evangelical and Charismatic models. Priests are told not to ask questions out of curiosity, but are commanded to find out from the demonic the names of spirits and the number of the demonic. They are to shut down and/or ignore all manifestations (laughing, yelling, etc.). The instructions emphasize the importance of discerning between the physical, emotional, and spiritual needs that might be present in the person. Priests are never allowed to give medicine. They say the way to see the difference between the psychological versus the presence of the demonic can be seen in the manifestations below.

> Signs of possession may be the following: ability to speak with some facility in a strange tongue or to understand it when spoken by another; the faculty of divulging future and hidden events; display of powers which are beyond the subject's age and natural condition; and various other indications which, when taken together as a whole, build up the evidence.[3]

Lastly, there is an element of the truth encounter and Kraft's call for information found here. The last general outline is that the priest is told the following:

He shall, moreover, command the devil to tell whether he is detained in that body by necromancy, by evil signs or amulets; and if the one possessed has taken the latter by mouth, he should be made to vomit them; if he has them concealed on his person, he should expose them; and when discovered they must be burned. Moreover, the person should be exhorted to reveal all his temptations to the exorcist.[4]

Instructions are given about identifying temptations, about how and why the demonic could have been given access, and also activities and items in the demonized person's life that could continue to give a foothold to the demonic. Like in the book of Acts, the person must renounce these and, when possible, destroy them by fire.

Now the actual application of this model is in the form of a liturgical prayer service, which is a well thought out pattern. Now again, as an evangelical, liturgy strikes me as some grouping of formal prayers, so I had to stop and ask where spiritual authority is given within this tradition. Is it just a group of prayers or is there specific authority to certain prayers given by the church? As mentioned, the priesthood, in their view, has a higher level of authority than laity. Yet to my surprise, liturgy also has implied spiritual power and authority. In Peter Kreeft's book, *Catholic Christianity*, he helps define the power found within a sanctioned Rite:

> The Spirit completes the liturgy as he completes and performs the Trinitarian 'economy (plan) of salvation.' The Spirit reveals Christ, and Christ reveals the Father. The Father sends the Son, and the Son sends the Spirit. In the liturgy of the Church, God the Father is blessed and adored as the source of all the blessing of creation and salvation with which he has blessed us in his Son, in order to give us his Spirit.[5]

And so, like preaching in the Protestant world, the liturgy in all forms brings to bear the very message, presence, and power of the Holy Trinity, which is the only power to overcome the kingdom of darkness. The process of exorcism in the Roman church is actually placed within a worship service, and the expectation is that not only the authorized priest will be present, but also lay members of the church.

The sanctioned Roman Catholic process of deliverance begins with a prayer called the "Litany of the Saints." This prayer is a general and grand prayer of intercession within the Roman tradition. When prayed, the Father, Son, and Spirit are invoked and then the people ask for the prayers of the whole church, Mary, angels, prophets, martyrs, saints—the great cloud of witnesses. It is a call on the whole body of Christ and all those who have the ability to pray to the only One who can overcome evil, the triune God. This prayer is used during Communion, Baptism, church entrance, Ordination, and

Easter celebrations. And so it is used here because of the significance of this act. From that starting point, a pattern is followed again and again—the reading of Scripture, prayer and then confrontation. In fact, the liturgy of deliverance is a tour de force of every relevant Scripture passage related to dealing with the demonic. One reads Psalm 53 and reads a liturgical prayer for courage, anointing, power, and mercy for all present and demonized persons. Then the priest commands the demonic with these words,

> I command you, unclean spirit, whoever you are, along with all your minions now attacking this servant of God, by the mysteries of the incarnation, passion, resurrection, and ascension of our Lord Jesus Christ, by the descent of the Holy Spirit, by the coming of our Lord for judgment, that you tell me by some sign your name, and the day and hour of your departure. I command you, moreover, to obey me to the letter, I who am a minister of God despite my unworthiness; nor shall you be emboldened to harm in any way this creature of God, or the bystanders, or any of their possessions. The priest lays his hand on the head of the sick person, saying: They shall lay their hands upon the sick and all will be well with them. May Jesus, Son of Mary, Lord and Savior of the world, through the merits and intercession of His holy apostles Peter and Paul and all His saints, show you favor and mercy. All: Amen.[6]

Next they read John 1:1-14, Mark 16:15-18, Luke 10:17-20, and Luke 11:14-22, which outline the supremacy of Jesus Christ and the power of Jesus and His followers over the demonic. Then the prayer focuses on personal holiness and the needed power of God. As you will see, the signs of the cross are printed throughout the document, placed to tell the priest when to cross himself or the subject. Then, with the support of a team, he makes the sign of the cross over himself and the one possessed, places the end of the stole on the latter's neck, and, putting his right hand on the latter's head, he says the following in accents filled with confidence and faith:

> P: See the cross of the Lord; begone, you hostile powers!

> All: The stem of David, the lion of Judah's tribe has conquered.

> P: Lord, heed my prayer.

> All: And let my cry be heard by you.

> P: The Lord be with you.

> All: May He also be with you.

Let us pray. God and Father of our Lord Jesus Christ, I appeal to your holy name, humbly begging your kindness, that you graciously grant me help against this and every unclean spirit now tormenting this creature of yours; through Christ our Lord. All: Amen. I cast you out, unclean spirit, along with every Satanic power of the enemy, every spectre from hell, and all your fell companions; in the name of our Lord Jesus ✝Christ. Begone and stay far from this creature of God. ✝For it is He who commands you, He who flung you headlong from the heights of heaven into the depths of hell. It is He who commands you, He who once stilled the sea and the wind and the storm. Hearken, therefore, and tremble in fear, Satan, you enemy of the faith, you foe of the human race, you begetter of death, you robber of life, you corrupter of justice, you root of all evil and vice; seducer of men, betrayer of the nations, instigator of envy, font of avarice, fomentor of discord, author of pain and sorrow. Why, then, do you stand and resist, knowing as you must that Christ the Lord brings your plans to nothing? Fear Him, who in Isaac was offered in sacrifice, in Joseph sold into bondage, slain as the paschal lamb, crucified as man, yet triumphed over the powers of hell (The three signs of the cross, which follow, are traced on the brow of the possessed person). Begone, then, in the name of the Father, ✝and of the Son, ✝ and of the Holy ✝Spirit. Give place to the Holy Spirit by this sign of the holy ✝cross of our Lord Jesus Christ, who lives and reigns with the Father and the Holy Spirit, God, forever and ever.[7]

Now the prayer turns and is a cry, an intercession over the inflicted person. Note how the liturgy provides reminders to insert the name of the person receiving this sacrament. The prayer asks God to heal and set the person free in their mind, emotions, and will. But unlike the truth-only patterns, they do not simply read Scripture but directly confront the demonic once again.

I adjure you, ancient serpent, by the judge of the living and the dead, by your Creator, by the Creator of the whole universe, by Him who has the power to consign you to hell, to depart forthwith in fear, along with your savage minions, from this servant of God, (name), who seeks refuge in the fold of the Church. I adjure you again, ✝ (on the brow) not by my weakness but by the might of the Holy Spirit, to depart from this servant of God, (name), whom almighty God has made in His image. Yield, therefore, yield not to my own person but to the minister of Christ. For it is the power of Christ that compels you, who brought you low by His cross. Tremble before that mighty arm that broke asunder the dark prison walls and led souls forth to light. May the trembling that afflicts this human frame, ✝ (on the breast) the fear that afflicts this image ✚ (on the brow) of God, descend on you. Make no resistance, nor delay in departing from this man, for it has pleased Christ to dwell in man. Do not think of despising my command because you know me to be a great sinner. It is God ✚Himself who commands you; the majestic Christ ✚who commands you. God the Father✚ commands you; God the Son ✚commands you; God the Holy ✚Spirit commands you. The mystery of the cross commands ✚you. The faith of the holy apostles Peter and Paul and of all the saints commands ✚you. The blood of the martyrs commands ✚you. The continence of the confessors commands ✚you. The devout prayers of all holy men and women ✚command you. The saving mysteries of our Christian faith ✚command you. Depart, then, transgressor. Depart, seducer, full of lies and cunning, foe of virtue, persecutor of the innocent. Give place, abominable creature, give way, you monster, give way to Christ, in whom you found none of your works. For He has already stripped you of your powers and laid waste your kingdom, bound you prisoner and plundered your weapons. He has cast you forth into the outer darkness, where everlasting ruin awaits you and your abettors. To what purpose do you insolently resist? To what purpose do you brazenly refuse? For you are guilty before almighty God, whose laws you have transgressed. You are guilty before His Son, our Lord Jesus Christ, whom you presumed to tempt, whom you dared to nail to the cross. You are guilty before the whole human race, to whom you proferred by your enticements the poisoned cup of death.

Therefore, I adjure you, profligate dragon, in the name of the spotless Lamb, who has trodden down the asp and the basilisk, and overcome the lion and the dragon, to depart from this man (woman) ✚(on the brow), to depart from the Church of God ✚ (signing the bystanders). Tremble and flee, as we call on the name of the Lord, before whom the denizens of hell cower, to whom the heavenly Virtues and Powers and Dominations are subject, whom the Cherubim and Seraphim praise with unending cries as they sing: Holy, holy, holy, Lord God of Sabaoth. The Word made flesh ✚commands you; the Virgin's Son ✚commands you; Jesus ✚of Nazareth commands you, who once, when you despised His disciples, forced you to flee in shameful defeat from a man; and when He had cast you out you did not even dare, except by His leave, to enter into a herd of swine. And now as I adjure you in His ✚name, begone from this man (woman) who is His creature. It is futile to resist His ✚will. It is hard for you to kick against the goad. The longer you delay, the heavier your punishment shall be; for it is not men you are condemning, but rather Him who rules the living and the dead, who is coming to judge both the living and the dead and the world by fire. All: Amen.[8]

This style of liturgical prayer and command is done in the model one more time. The content of the prayer includes God being uplifted and worshipped, and then again there is a cry for freedom. This is followed by another direct address to the demonic, a power encounter to drive the demonic out. The priest says with divine authority,

Therefore, I adjure you every unclean spirit, every spectre from hell, every satanic power, in the name of Jesus ✝Christ of Nazareth, who was led into the desert after His baptism by John to vanquish you in your citadel, to cease your assaults against the creature whom He has, formed from the slime of the earth for His own honor and glory; to quail before wretched man, seeing in him the image of almighty God, rather than his state of human frailty. Yield then to God, ✝who by His servant, Moses, cast you and your malice, in the person of Pharaoh and his army, into the depths of the sea. Yield to God, ✝who, by the singing of holy canticles on the part of David, His faithful servant, banished you from the heart of King Saul. Yield to God, ✝who condemned you in the person of Judas Iscariot, the traitor. For He now flails you with His divine scourges, ✝ He in whose sight you and your legions once cried out: "What have we to do with you, Jesus, Son of the Most High God? Have you come to torture us before the time?" Now He is driving you back into the everlasting fire, He who at the end of time will say to the wicked: "Depart from me, you accursed, into the everlasting fire which has been prepared for the devil and his angels." For you, O evil one, and for your followers, there will be worms that never die. An unquenchable fire stands ready for you and for your minions, you prince of accursed murderers, father of lechery, instigator of sacrileges, model of vileness, promoter of heresies, inventor of every obscenity. Depart, then, ✝impious one, depart, accursed one, depart with all your deceits, for God has willed that man should be His temple. Why do you still linger here? Give honor to God the Father ✝almighty, before whom every knee must bow. Give place to the Lord Jesus ✝Christ, who shed His most precious blood for man. Give place to the Holy ✝Spirit, who by His blessed apostle Peter openly struck you down in the person of Simon Magus; who cursed your lies in Annas and Saphira; who smote you in King Herod because he had not given honor to God; who by His apostle Paul afflicted you with the night of blindness in the magician Elyma, and by the mouth of the same apostle bade you to go out of Pythonissa, the soothsayer. Begone, ✝now! Begone, ✝seducer! Your place is in solitude; your abode is in the nest of serpents; get down and crawl with them. This matter brooks no delay; for see, the Lord, the ruler comes quickly, kindling fire before Him, and it will run on ahead of Him and encompass His enemies in flames. You might delude man, but God you cannot mock. It is He who casts you out, from whose sight nothing is hidden. It is He who repels you, to whose might all things are subject. It is He who expels you, He who has prepared everlasting hellfire for you and your angels, from whose mouth shall come a sharp sword, who is coming to judge both the living and the dead and the world by fire. All: Amen.[9]

This last prayer is the final part of the formal process. But as you read on there is an interesting instruction that if the battle is not won, you should start the process over again and repeat it until there is freedom. There is also a flexibility that should be noted. Participants are also encouraged to use the Hail Mary, the Athanasian Creed, and other songs from Scripture (Luke 1:46-55 and Luke 1:68-79; Ps 90, 67, 69, 53, 117, 34, 30, 21, 3, 19, and 12) to support the process.[10]

The only reference to follow-up after a deliverance is a formal prayer at the end of the whole process, and in the general guidelines, in which the one delivered is called to not fall back into sin or go back to practices that allowed evil to be present.[11]

Though the above was formal and very foreign to us as Free Church Evangelicals, it has become one of the most influential components of our process and especially for me. As evangelicals, we couldn't deny that the liturgy was saturated with Scripture and brought the truth of God's Word to bear in a very systematic way. There are five major lessons we have learned and adopted from this model. First, the process here, just like Neil Anderson's process, is formal and step-by-step. Especially in the early days, this idea tended to bring order in chaos and helped deal with the unexpected.

Second, one of most important lessons we have learned is the calling on the whole Holy Catholic Church. Now let me be clear, we reject the focus of the calling to the saints, patriarchs, prophets, and so on, all who have died and are in the presence of Christ. Yet it was that famed prayer used up front and its intention and pattern that led us to pray that the Holy Spirit would lead any and many living today in the Body of Christ to be led pray for us. This act of calling on the Lord Jesus to send His Spirit to move the "Holy Catholic Church" to pray, whether they know us or not, has had a positive effect and we have seen more freedom experienced. This is an application of the Protestant doctrine of the mystical Body of Christ, made up of all believers presently alive around the world. It moved us to see this ministry beyond a lone ranger action or even a local church ministry to an act for the kingdom, another place where God's reign and rule was established.

This practice was confirmed for me in part by an experience I had several years ago during a personal time of daily devotions. This was my usual round of Scripture reading, prayers, confession of sin, and commitment of my day to serving Christ. As I was finishing, I suddenly experienced something like a vision in which I saw an elderly Chinese man. I didn't recognize him nor had I been thinking about China that day. This was a spontaneous thought. I couldn't immediately think of anything that could have caused this to occur (I wasn't hungry, angry, lonely, or tired). But as I was contemplating this, I sensed the Spirit telling me, "You don't know this man, but he is a pastor in China about to be persecuted. Pray for him." The disconnect was obvious to me—I was on the other side of the world. But I felt compelled to obey the urging, so I prayed for him a while and then went about my day. I still haven't met him, nor do I know how his situation turned out—I expect to hear the whole story in heaven. But the vividness of the moment made the disconnect meaningless. I realized he and I were part of the same Body of Christ, even though I probably won't meet him in this life.

While this hasn't happened often for me, I've discovered it is the frequent experience of those who have the gift of intercessory prayer. They are unexpectedly called to pray for situations they are aware of and sometimes ones they are completely unaware of. Sometimes they get to see the results of their praying, other times not. But this makes sense if we remember that Jesus is the Lord of His Church right now and He, by His Spirit can marshal His forces however He chooses. We may be pressed into duty in unexpected ways on behalf of parts of the Body that are far from us. What we have discovered in practice is that when we ask the Spirit to bring the prayers of the worldwide Body to bear on our situation, the struggle seems less intense.

Third, implied in this model is a working between clergy and lay leaders as seen in the cadence of the prayer, response, and command. There is the prayer and command, and then an agreed response. Any model that brings the Body of Christ together is stronger than an individual-only approach.

Fourth, we are blown away at the language and thought put into the prayers above, which is why I included them in the body of this book. They are Holy Scripture and holy history condensed into intercession and command. They are a helpful reminder to those of us who are "free" pray-ers, that not everyone thinks (or prays) comfortably on their feet and all of us can be helped by being informed in prayer, by the wisdom of the longer and broader Church. This truly guards against pride, ego, heresy and self-reliance. It truly models the way Jesus used Scripture in the temptation.

Lastly, as seen above, the Roman Catholic Church uses empowered objects and symbols, the gustier of the cross, holy objects, actual crosses, oil, a stole, and more. I learned that this tradition sees these as foundational to worship. There are four symbols used: acts, words, music, and images. They teach, "the liturgy of the Church presupposes, integrates and sanctifies elements from creation and human culture, conferring on them the dignity of signs of grace, of the new creation in Jesus Christ."[12]

At first I was against all of this because it seemed to be like magic, dead rituals, or even demonic. Growing up in South America, I was concerned about some forms of Christ-o-paganism. Now, unlike this model, we don't do or use something every three seconds. But we have learned that symbols of God and His work are important. The Charismatic Catholic writer, Francis MacNutt in his book, *Deliverance from Evil Spirits,* helped us transition into a greater use of symbols. He talks about oil, water, and salt. Now we were fine with oil because of James 5, but the other objects still seemed wrong. But when we were led to use them, the reaction of the demonic was astounding. In two cases we blessed water and the demonic reacted and were greatly weakened.[13] It all became clear when reading through Acts 5:15-16 and Acts 19:11-12 and then reading Kraft's articles in *Appropriate Christianity.* It is here that I regained my evangelical comfort and understood that there was biblical support for such action and symbols and that we were not inventing some syncretistic form of ministry.

> Cultural forms can also be empowered with spiritual power. Such things as material objects, buildings and rituals can be dedicated and thus convey the power of God (if dedicated to Him) or of Satan (if dedicated to him). In dedications, blessing and cursing words are used to convey that power. These words are empowered as they are used in obedience to either God or Satan. When cultural forms are thus empowered, they convey (not contain spiritual power.)...What the Bible teaches concerning spiritual power both recognized the validity of the power and the power techniques practiced by animists and teaches us to use similar techniques based on similar principles but with the true Source of power.[14]

And so we learned it was not about the action, but the source of power— Who we were plugged into. Kraft's teaching also helps me to see the other differences between Animism versus God-given authority. We now see that there is no power in the object at all, but God releases His Sovereign authority through people and objects dedicated and/or representing Him. Again, we are cautious to put any trust in the crosses we have or wear or the oil we use. But what we know now is that the kingdom of darkness is repelled by all things dedicated to the Father, the Son, and the Holy Spirit.

You may be reading this thinking that the Protestant Reformation is over within me. It is not. All the protestant issues regarding church authority, the saints, Mary, Scripture versus tradition, are still alive and well within me. This Rite of Exorcism is full of issues that are touchstone concerns for us and this book is not the place to debate Rome. We are simply humbly open to signs of the prevailing church Jesus claimed in Matthew 16 that comes to us unbroken, even if it has been distorted or misplaced. Second, as you will see, Roman Catholics actually work with more of a matrix than a sole model. So we use and have rewritten parts of the historic liturgy to help us in certain situations, thus moving us from blind faith in ritual and dead forms. We know it is because of our relationship with Jesus, His Spirit, and His will that these prayers are effective. As mentioned above, we do not trust in something God empowers but trust God Himself and what He said He would do, expressed through His written Word.

Yet one of the greatest critiques we have is this—it is an all or nothing model. There is no reference to mild or medium demonic influences. The model does not deal with level 1-5, mild to medium demonic presence or influence. The idea of "possession" has fully informed their theology and thus unless a person shows the worst forms of evil manifestations, the over-the-top expressions of the demonic, then other experiences are not explained or explored with the possibility of demonic explanations. I do like that they support medical and psychological help, but again, major issues like conversion, personal relationship with Christ, standing in one's relationship with Jesus, inner healing, and renewing one's mind are absent and thus this model is only helpful when supported by other biblical practices.

On the experience side, I must report an episode that occurred several years ago as we were wrestling through how much of this liturgical model we could biblically incorporate into our thinking. We had a delightful, successful, involved couple in our church who had immigrated from the Caribbean. At one point, the husband approached me, concerned that something was going on with his wife. I agreed and showed up at their house to pray with her, with my Bible and a bottle of water (because I was thirsty).

As we began to pray, out of this woman who I knew well came this voice with an odd accent that seemed from another time—think old, old English. Actually, it sounded something like Jack Sparrow from Pirates of the Caribbean. It sounded nothing like her at all. That distorted voice confronted me with claims that it owned this woman and I wasn't going to take her. I responded by affirming Jesus is Lord and this wasn't about me having her but her freedom in Christ. I was also praying for the Lord's intervention. The pitched battle had been going on for an hour when I realized I was thirsty and, glad I had brought a bottle of water with me, I reached for it. I stopped when I sensed the Holy Spirit instruct me, "Bless the water." It was the last thing I expected. In fact, the following unspoken dialogue went on between the Holy Spirit and me:

Jon – "Bless the water? No, I'm a Protestant and we don't do that."

Holy Spirit – "Do it."

Jon – "No, I don't believe you're the Holy Spirit because you're asking me to do something that's not right."

Holy Spirit – "I am the Holy Spirit. Do it now."

At this point, I was processing what was happening and feeling baffled by the setting—a nice middle class living room with all the signs of normality, carrying on a conversation with the demonic and with the Holy Spirit. And I realized in my own spirit that the guidance was coming from the Spirit of God, so I reached again for the water. The demonic immediately reacted—"Don't you dare bless that water!"

That confirmed my hunch and I thought: "Now I'm definitely blessing it!" I held the bottle in my hand and said, "This is simply water, but in Jesus' name, I bless it."

Now the demonic was screaming at me. I opened the bottle, wet my fingers from it, and sprinkled it on the woman. With another scream, the demon left her and she was free.

Although I was amazed, I was also confused. I didn't know what to do with the events that had just transpired. Had I departed orthodoxy? How could I fit this with what I understood of spiritual warfare? And because I couldn't make sense of it, the event became an unresolved mystery. Then I read all this Roman Catholic material while developing our understanding of their model of exorcism. Here was the presence of water again.

I was still honoring two ideas from my upbringing—that ritual was wrong and that experience shouldn't be trusted. On the one hand, God wasn't going to be forced into a set of formulaic actions; on the other, He wasn't going to participate in every experience. I kept wanting to see the Bible connection, afraid that incorporating any form of liturgy might pull me away from the Gospel. This struggle came to a head while I was working on my doctorate and one of my professors, who came from a missionary background in Africa, firmly challenged my assumptions. He asked me why I thought the ritual was wrong and I said, "Well, it's magic and it's a ritual."

He responded by inviting me to sit down for an extended Bible tour. I was confident I was on solid ground until he added, "Let's look at the passages many do not preach on." We looked at several passages regarding the high priest in the Old Testament, taking note of the fact that he wore on his chest a covering that featured twelve stones representing the tribes of Israel. And the text mentions that the Spirit of God shone from this part of the priest's costume. I had no idea of either the significance or the purpose of the arrangement.

Then we looked at passages regarding the Tabernacle and the way it served as God's guaranteed meeting place with the people. And before I could raise the "but that's Old Testament understanding" response, he continued, "What about the empowered handkerchiefs in the New Testament. And how do we explain the healing effects of Peter's shadow? Was all that magic?"

I was more than ready to admit my ignorance and ask him for help. He said, "First, recognize there is no power inherently in physical things. They are simply objects. We are not animists who personify and empower objects. But, when things are dedicated for certain use or purpose they take on authority." He went on to point out various ways in which objects take on special significance in our lives. For example, the cornerstone of a church building, that usually sets that structure apart for special use. When we "dedicate" a building to the glory of God, is that a significant action or just a quaint tradition? When we dedicate children, is something real happening or are we just going through motions without real meaning? Are we not acknowledging God's ownership and authority over that building or that child? And if we make room for this kind of positive dedication, what about things dedicated to evil?

Take for example a not-too-unusual experience: a young Christian high schooler reports that a friend in the neighborhood has been given a bag with special stones by another friend. It turns out the source of the gift is a wiccan witch. The purpose of the gift is supposed to be a blessing on the recipient. When the gift is given, the recipient mentions it to the young Christian and wonders if there's anything weird going on. He isn't sure, but suggests they take the stones and their question to his pastor who has been talking about these kinds of things. When they approach the pastor, they hand him the bag of stones as they are about to ask about them. No sooner does he touch them than there is an immediate reaction and he tells them, "The contents of this bag have been dedicated to evil." Now, is something going on here?

In my own experience, I was once in Spain on a mission trip that involved smuggling Bibles into Algeria. We were also doing evangelism among Muslims in Morocco. On a shopping trip, a member of our group bought some Muslim prayer beads in a market as a quaint artifact from the trip. But he almost immediately became violently ill and medical consultation gave us no answers. Three days later, in reviewing his recent visiting places and eating practices, the purchase of the beads was mentioned. We recommended he get rid of them. As soon as he disposed of the things, his condition improved and he was fine. I am convinced those beads had been dedicated to evil purposes.

Now, does this mean we are saying the devil is living in a bag of stones or Jesus is living in the building dedicated to Him? No. But these items become dedicated places for encounter. Setting them aside or designating them for special purpose, good or evil, has ramifications in the spiritual realm. So, the accounts in Acts of miraculous effects involving Peter's shadow or Paul's handkerchief, not to mention such objects as the Tabernacle or the Temple, become physical objects or places of spiritual encounter through dedication to certain power sources. The question, then, is: what power source are you dedicating things to? And working this out doesn't mean going crazy with dedicating everything in sight as a central spiritual practice. The point is to recognize that the Bible is full of examples of this dedication principle and it matters. We are revealing an overly materialistic bias when we dismiss the possibility of these links or connections between the physical and the spiritual.

This brings us back to the earlier encounter with the demonic and the water bottle that made a lasting impression on me. When I blessed it, did the water become magic, or superwater? Did the demon leave because of the holy water? By the way, if you are wondering about water in the first place, realize that the connection is baptism. Your visible and experiential connection with Christ is seen in baptism. The water in the bottle became a symbol present to lift up the sovereign work of Jesus, overcoming the demonic.

So, just because you wear a cross doesn't mean everything is going to be great. Public figures wear crosses as jewelry all the time without a thought about what those objects represent. There's nothing inherently spiritually effective about the shape of a cross, but I have been amazed at the results in confrontations with the demonic when I have pulled out a simple cross and commanded the demon to look at the symbol of Christ's victory over them, quoting Scripture. The object has no power; the truth and Person to whom it has been dedicated exercise the power. The demonic hates anything that reminds them of hope. In a deliverance session with a woman years ago, after we prayed for her and she was free, her first observation was that she could finally see color. When we asked what she meant, she explained, "Oh, I've always known there was color, but everything I've seen has been washed out and faded; now I see vibrant color!" The demonic are so offended by beauty that they will distort it for those whom they torment, even the normal, wonderful colors of Creation.

All this to say that our examination of Roman Catholic doctrine and practice taught us that the use of objects is not witchcraft. When dedicated symbols of the faith are used with awareness, they can focus God's power in deliverance situations. And for those who want to use Scripture in strict regulative ways, James 5 presents a challenge to the dismissal of the use of symbols, for the instruction for dealing with sickness in verse 14 stipulates not only prayer but also anointing with oil. Is the oil magical? Should it be first press/extra virgin oil? Does it have to come from Israel? Is it a question of the source of the oil or the specific type? Neither of those discussions really deals with the order to use oil. What was James advocating? He was taking for granted the wider biblical understanding that oil was symbolic of the Holy Spirit. It represents the healing, presence, and power of God. And the Bible is instructing us to use an inanimate object as part of the healing process with people. Is it just symbolic and somewhat optional or is there more involved? Well, it's similar to what we realize about communion even if we are honest holders of the farthest-from-transubstantiation position. Yes, the elements remain just bread and cup, but something does happen of a spiritual nature in the sharing of rightly administered elements. As Calvin put it, Jesus isn't in the elements, but He is standing at the table. The term I have learned to use in preaching to help people grasp the occasional special access to God is *palpable*. The Gospels describe just how far God went to put Himself within reach as Jesus; God's Word gives us many glimpses of His willingness to touch earth with heaven.

We are attempting to acknowledge the difference between believing in the omnipresence of God everywhere and always, and believing in His promise to be especially manifestly present at certain times and under certain conditions. Those who know and trust God also know there is a difference. All the times He is there, but sometimes He is really *there*! And we are ignoring some significant parts of Scripture if we say that God is not interested in using objects in His dealing with us. This is part of a larger conversation about objects and their spiritual uses and misuses.

One of the clearest examples of this tension is found in the book of Numbers when God punishes His people with fiery serpents (21:4-9). When they begin to repent, He had Moses cast a bronze serpent and raise it on a pole: *"So Moses made a bronze snake and put it up on a pole. Then when anyone was bitten by a snake and looked at the bronze snake, they lived"* (v.9). But many years later, during Hezekiah's reign in Israel, the king had to have that serpent destroyed because it had become an idol (2 Kings 18:4). While dedicated to repentance, the serpent was useful; when it was rededicated to pagan worship it became scrap metal.

We have found there can be significant effectiveness in including liturgical aspects to our plan and tool bag as we seek to faithfully bring the Holy Spirit's power to bear on the demonic that are crushing people's lives. But it has its limitations and can never substitute for God's actual power at work by whatever means He chooses.

Jon Thompson

CHAPTER 13
THE DEEP HEALING AND DELIVERANCE MODEL

The last deliverance model we gave a lot of attention to is championed by Charles Kraft. When I went to Fuller Seminary, well over a decade ago, to study what was usually called Spiritual Dynamics (the catch-all phrase for the weird stuff in Christianity few talk about), Dr. Kraft was my professor. He is widely recognized as a world-class anthropologist. By the time I met him at Fuller, he was showing the effects of a lengthy career as a missionary, anthropologist, and pioneer in deliverance ministry. Personally, he struck me as a humble, broken man, seeking to do a lot of things right in the final days of his active work.

As a missionary, he had experienced conflict when he urged converts in indigenous peoples to write their own worship music rather than adopting Western tunes or expressions. He also got in trouble because after years of attempting to avoid the instances of open spiritual conflict that faced him among the people he worked with, he finally engaged biblically with their needs. For both these reasons, he was removed from his missionary position, victim of the closing expressions of colonial mission understanding. This embarked him on thirty years of solitary thinking about spiritual conflict when most of his peers rejected even the possibility of matters that were becoming increasingly apparent to him.

Working alone, he remains a great example of courage and independent thinking, and a healthy reminder that developing thoughts outside of community often includes some unintentional errors along the way. He gradually developed a methodology that combines inner healing, Christian counseling, and "power encounter" deliverance, with little or no acknowledgment of spiritual gifts. He affirms the truth-only model as helpful, but not able to deal with all forms of the demonic. On the other hand, he rejects the use of the power-only model for three simple reasons. First, the power-only model deals with the demonic, strength to strength, which will lead to the second concern. Without them being weakened, the battle is fiercer and thus takes an unneeded toll on both the demonized person and on the person or persons who are praying for the individual. Third, and most important, is the idea that the rights, grounds, access, and privileges the demonic may have because of sin, family history, or personal history are not dealt with in the power-only approach, so the person remains vulnerable to the demonic. That is, demons could use the unresolved situations to their advantage and resist expulsion or return after deliverance.[1]

And so, rejecting power-only and reminding the faith community that deliverance is about healing and not just casting out demons, the starting point for Kraft is to deal with all the "deep level hurts" that break and disrupt a person's relationship with God, self, and other people.[2]

Inner healing, in Kraft's model, is the foundation to freedom, like confession and the embracing of truth was for Anderson. It is asking Jesus and His healing power to be released to deal with the roots of any struggle being faced, which all other issues a person has (such as unforgiveness, bitterness, anger, sexual misconduct, fear, worry, self-esteem, and so on) spring from.[3] And the roots, he thinks, are actually pain. All the external stuff that must be changed and fixed remains tentative if healing at the core has not happened. Too often, he believes, we address the results and symptoms without getting to the causes, which are pain. He does not want to ignore the reality that all kinds of behaviors are repetitions and reactions to what we have ourselves experienced, such as the fact that most abusers turn out to have been abused themselves. He uses two definitions from authors, which round out his understanding of Christian inner healing:

> Inner healing is the healing of the inner person: the mind, the emotions, the painful memories, the dreams. It is the process whereby we are set free from feelings of resentment, rejection, self-pity, depression, guilt, fear, sorrow, hatred, inferiority, condemnation or worthlessness, etc. Romans 12:2 (KJV) says *'And be not conformed to this world, but be ye transformed by the renewing of your mind.'* Inner healing is the renewing of your mind.[4]
>
> Inner Healing is a form of Christian counseling and prayer which focus the healing power of the Spirit on certain types of emotions/spiritual problems.[5]

This process is all about honesty, transparency, dealing with truth, removing lies, and asking Jesus to heal and transform what are, much of the time, impossible situations. Kraft writes,

> With Jesus, we can go back to the experiences in which we were hurt, both those we can recall and those our brain has recorded but doesn't allow us to recall. We can re-experience them with Jesus there, enabling us to forgive those who hurt us and to give our pain to him. The result is freedom from the bondage to the past that has crippled us and, if demons are there, one must deal with the garbage they have been feeding on.[6]

Before any demon is dealt with, whether one or many are present, the process of inner healing must be included. Kraft says time and time again, if you remove the garbage then you can deal with the rats. The session begins with prayer, asking the Holy Spirit to take charge and lead the full session of inner healing. He also takes time to pray that the demonic would not attack anyone helping or any family member. Then the inner healing begins by reminding the person that the team or person assisting does not know why God allowed the issues they are facing or have faced to happen. Second, Satan does want to kill and destroy but as Christians, they have not been overcome by him. And so, someone more powerful, more sovereign, more all-knowing was and is involved in protecting them. He continues saying,

> We then invite the person to forgive all who have hurt them and to picture Jesus in the situation in which the abuse happened. We point out that Jesus was indeed present and protecting them (otherwise the Evil One would have been able to destroy them) but that they were not able to see him when the event happened. They are usually able to see or feel Jesus presence in the reliving and feel heartened as they are released from the pain of loneliness they have lived with for many years.[7]

This takes the person visually and emotionally back to the moment of injury and they are encouraged to feel it all over again, but the difference is that now the presence of Jesus is invited and visualized. Over a period of time and prayer, many experiences, hurts, and sins can be uncovered, prayed over, forgiven, and healed. Now this may appear to parallel a Christian counseling approach, but Kraft expects all of this to occur in a compressed time frame, and he questions the effectiveness of the "managed healing" pursued in most counseling, compared to the deep healing he envisions the Spirit can do. In his practice, he invites Jesus not only to reveal the deepest hurts but to heal them immediately, as only He can do.

It should be noted that Kraft will encourage a person to deal with all sinful sexual acts because those acts can create a bond between human beings.

> I first make sure all sin has been confessed and forgiven. Then I ask the person to picture the person(s) bonded with sexually and join me in saying something like 'I break my bonding with so and so and renounce any and all ties with that person that are empowered by satanic power.'[8]

In explaining his model, Kraft also holds to the fact that much of the time inner healing must go back to even before birth. This idea is based on some psychological theories that the baby is affected both by the mother's feelings and thinking and also by the desire of the kingdom of darkness to attack those made in the image of God, even before birth. He systematically prays over each month of gestation and also breaks any "generational curses, dedications, spells, emotional problems, diseases, and any other satanic influence that may have been introduced into a person's inheritance."[9]

This process allows the participant to forgive anyone that they think may have hurt them and to surrender even the unknown emotional causes and issues to Jesus Himself. He then proceeds to pray through the birth and early years, asking if anything must be prayed over or resolved. Kraft now makes it clear that the demonic, if they are present, will be dealt with at an appropriate time. He presumes the demonic will be present in some form, but does include a specific discernment process in his model. In fact, one of my earliest experiences with Kraft involved a deliverance exercise in our classroom with one of the members. As he began to work with the woman, it became very clear to me that while he assumed there was a demonic presence to be addressed, I could actually see it. He was proceeding from experience and confidence in Scripture. I moved closer to him and began to inform him of what I could spiritually discern in the moment. He was somewhat shocked, but later thanked me for helping him. He was so used to practicing alone that the experience of community involvement in deliverance was a longing for him. He simply had not made the connection between effective deliverance and corporate exercise of gifts.

Kraft freely admits he himself does not have the gift of discernment but over the years, through experience, he has learned to see patterns and manifestations that reveal the presence of the demonic.

> These are some of the things that can be discerned naturally either by observation or by asking questions. In addition, God does reveal things to people supernaturally, though usually in combination with the observation of natural phenomena. As you develop more experience you will find your ability to discern sharpened. You will also notice that demons make a lot of mistakes that give them away. Learning to look for these mistakes and to take advantage of them is an important part of the game.[10]

Now during inner healing, if a demon or demons begin to interfere or outright manifest in the person before the inner healing work is done, you must shut them down and bind them until the garbage they use as rights, grounds, accesses, or privileges is removed. Yet Kraft does admit there is no discernible pattern.

> Once you are reasonably sure that a demon might be present and inner healing has been brought to a satisfactory point, it is time to challenge the demon(s). By 'a satisfactory point' I mean to indicate that at some point in the ministry it becomes a higher priority to deal with

the rats that are stirring up the garage than to deal with the garbage. Usually not all the inner healing the person needs can be done before it is advisable to get rid of the demons. Seldom is it necessary to prolong the inner healing beyond dealing with the most basic issues, since most of the remainder needs to be done independently by the person.[11]

After the inner healing is done, Kraft then follows a power model of deliverance. First, he takes authority over the environment, the people, and the time of the session, during which he calls for protection, wisdom, authority, and power. He uses simple prayers similar to the following:

> I speak in Jesus' name against any emissaries of the Evil One who may be here. I command you to leave. I claim this place, this time, these people for the Lord Jesus and forbid any activity by any satanic being except what I specifically command...I claim protection in the name of Jesus Christ for each one of us, our families, our friends, our work associates, our property, our finances, our health and everything else that pertains to us from any revenge or other dirty tricks from the Enemy.[12]

The key, at this point, is to cut off all demons present from any other demonic force outside or inside the person, thus weakening those spirits even more. Finally, at this time, all manifestations are forbidden; then and only then is one ready to challenge the demonic.[13]

Next, Kraft makes clear in this model that the demonic must be challenged directly. They don't like to be exposed and so they must be forcefully addressed "even if I'm not sure one is there."[14] Again, since he usually works alone, he will use names of whatever spiritual or emotional problems have been prayed for to see if they are demonic. He also calls for the chief or head spirit to come to attention, and again forbids them to take any form of control. He also requests Jesus to send powerful angels to help in this battle.[15]

The key here then, is to find out who really is in local control of the kingdom of darkness and what the hierarchy is of the demonic forces within the person. He will command whatever spirit is present to tell him who is over them until the chief demon is identified. Then all other demons are bound to him so that when he leaves, they will all leave.

> I then make sure this binding together has actually happened by quizzing the head demon about whether or not all of them are bound to him. Often he will indicate that some are not. I command him to give me the reason. 'Do they still have anything on so and so?' I will frequently ask. Either the head demon or one of those that are not bound will then, when commanded, tell me what still needs work.

Dealing with the remaining issues usually weakens the wandering demons to the point where they join the bound ones.[16]

Next, he commands the demons to reveal if there are any intergenerational curses or rights, and he records that if they do admit them he will deal with it. If nothing comes forward or no words of knowledge are given, by the Spirit then he will pray a general prayer for them.

In the name of Jesus, I take authority over the intergenerational spirit of _____ coming through the father's bloodline and break your power in Jesus' name. I forbid you to have any more power over (person's name).[17]

After this work following the inner healing, most demonic powers should be expelled. If they refuse to leave, command what rights they hold on to and deal with those through commands or more inner healing. Near the end, in force with power, authority, and patience, he deals with them. Kraft summarizes this act in a few different ways. The first is to command them to leave and go to the feet of Jesus the Christ.

If they leave, well and good. Usually, however, this is not enough. If the head demon refuses, command it to tell you what right/ground it still has to live in the person. Command it in the name of Jesus to tell you the complete truth. You may find it useful to remind the demon again who he is and his kingdom has been defeated. Remind him of the cross and the empty tomb. Demons don't like to hear about the blood shed on the cross or the tomb from which Jesus escaped. What seems to work best for me in sealing the deal is to ask Jesus if he will have the angels lower a box or bag over the tied-together demons and lock them in...I then check with the head demon to see if all are locked in. When they are, I ask the angels to take them to Jesus...then I ask Jesus to dispose of the box/bag and separate the demons from the person forever.[18]

At the end of the sessions' inner healing and deliverance, he blesses the person in the areas in which inner healing has occurred and the demonic have been removed.[19] Over and over again in his writings, Kraft argues that inner healing, deliverance, professional counseling, and other acts of mercy and healing are needed. Post-deliverance, he says a person should join some form of support group and continue to see a professional Christian counselor.[20] Kraft was also one of the first to advocate for blending the strengths of various models in pursuing deliverance.

Before I describe the strengths and weaknesses of Kraft's model, I need to note that there are three foundational ideas that ground his method. First, is the idea of talking to demons. This controversial act is key for his outlook. He first uses Mark 5:1-20 to prove that this activity is acceptable, allowed, and needed. The other verses where Jesus told demons not to speak (Luke 4:1-13; Matt 4:1-11) are provided not to discourage that act, but to prevent them from revealing who He was for a time and thus showing again that He (and we) are in control in dealing with the demonic.[21] Kraft gives four reasons why he uses this act. First, he has found that information can be used against them. Second, the demonic giving up information can speed up the healing process which will lead to deliverance because when God gives information through words of knowledge and forces the demonic to reveal information, He shows the rights, doors, and accesses still being held on to. Third, the forcing of information from the demonic weakens them in the battle.

> As we demonstrate their weakness by forcing them to obey Jesus, they get upset and discouraged. Many don't seem to have had to face God's power before and seem to think they are invincible. Demons often speak very arrogantly until they begin to feel the power of God directly against them.[22]

Lastly, the demonic speaking can help the sufferer see the difference between themselves and the spirits present, and also helps their faith when they see and hear the demonic cry out and leave by the power of God.[23] It should be noted that Kraft says again and again that there is "no substitute for listening to God," but that the demonic speaking is a secondary place of needed information. Kraft also directly responds to Neil Anderson's above criticism that the demonic are all liars and cannot be trusted. He writes,

> Deceit is not the same as lying. The myth is abroad that demons always lie. That is definitely not true. Remember that in the temptations of Jesus it was not lies but the misuse of truth that Satan used (Lk 4:1-13). And remember that the reason Jesus silenced the demons so often was that they recognized him and told the truth concerning who he was (Mk 1:24, 34; 3:11; Lk 4:41)…Deceit is a deliberate attempt to mislead. It is one of the satanic kingdom's primary devices. Watch out for it, even when what the demons are saying is true.[24]

Second, one of the best insights he brings that acts like a lens for evaluating what is taking place during a session is his "attachment scale." As already seen, other models tend to treat all the demonic the same (power model), only deal with the most violent and obvious (liturgical-power model), or simply deal with the weaker spirits (truth model). Yet Kraft shows us that not all demons are the same nor should any act of healing be approached in the same way. His scale uses three categories—weak, medium, and strong. Weak is 1-3 Medium is 4-6 and Strong is 7-10.[25]

177

On pages 133-135 in *Defeating Dark Angels*, Kraft outlines patterns of what the demonic will tend to do during sessions and what should be done in response. It is his contention that demonic who exhibit four or less on the strength scale will probably leave under almost any prayerful approach. Those who are five or more will stick around for a fight. With them we can expect resistance and plan accordingly. It is a great grid to use because you can see what is going to happen based on interviews and history. It can also be used in the middle of sessions to show their level of resistance. This acts like a bridge between the truth-only and power-only models, allowing needed flexibility in very difficult spiritual situations.

Lastly, he does give some great pastoral insights to watch out for in any ministry session you are doing. He really stresses the need to maintain dignity at all times, which is done by forbidding the demonic to manifest. It is also important to not share with the sufferer all words of knowledge because they could be misunderstood. Second, it is important to make sure you pray and that there is a team of people praying during the session. Third, cleanse the room of any evil spirits. Fourth, keep people encouraged during and after the session to help them know that Christ is with them, and also to get them into a support group, post-session.[26] I end this section with Kraft's words calling for a holistic view of healing.

> We advocate a combination of inner healing, deliverance and solid Christian counseling for most people, but especially for those who have experienced extreme trauma...we need to be open to God working through many vehicles of healing. Both inner healing and counseling offers a positive step toward resolving a deep level of emotional pain.[27]

What we found really good about this model was that it began to fill in some missing pieces. First, he connects to inner healing, the act of listening, and what he calls words of knowledge. This pattern of hearing and acting is foundational to our discernment process and acts like a check and balance for our team. Studying his book, *I Give You Authority*, really crystallized certain understandings for us. Jesus was with the Father in prayer, would align His purpose with the Father, and then act. This is now our pattern.

> Jesus prayed before He did His deeds. But what He did during them should not be called prayer....We are to imitate Jesus and take authority as He did. When Jesus said that whoever believes in Him will do what he did, I believe He meant to include the way He did things in the what of that verse. Like Him, we are not to ask God to do the works, but to line up our wills with His and talk not to the Father but on his behalf, speak authoritatively to correct the situation.[28]

The call for inner healing, which was different from clinical help and a different form of confession, was really affirming for us. We had also been using inner healing in different forms, but this helped us see it was one of the central pieces in deliverance. On a personal note, it was Kraft's writings that moved me to see that the whole ministry is healing in the broadest sense. Truly it is power wrapped in love, not confrontation—a balance that is needed—thus giving glory to God and support to the person.

The model also gave us another way to see power in context. When reading his model, his practice of binding the demonic and then coming back to deal with them later was something we had been doing for a while. It was good to see the same pattern. There could be much more to talk about, but let me focus on two last things. As mentioned, Kraft's scale gave us a grid to explain, explore, and quantify our encounters. We had used different types of spirits, names, and roles, but this approach gave us a simple language to communicate. The other item, though so simple, is his phrase "rats and garbage." This has allowed us to explain this ministry to so many others, and even some counseling centers use this description to help people see the need for all forms of healing, including deliverance.

Yet, there are a few concerns to mention. We like the flexibility of inner healing and the structure of the truth model. We found that the latter was lacking here. Second, we are not sure about the "back through the womb" prayers. We have talked about it, but are just not sure. We would need to understand the physiological model that he bases this on. So far this has not been successful or helpful for us in our ministry. We are also somewhat cautious about "remembered" wounds or pain, because there is a growing body of research indicating that humans can vividly "recall" events from the past that didn't actually happen. This is now formally called false memory syndrome. We don't want to ignore the power of suppressed memories, but we don't want to treat every reported memory as self-authenticating. We recognize that the demonic are fully capable of suggesting past events that did not occur as a way of maintaining control. This requires us to recognize the tension between the Spirit's work in helping us remember, the human capacity for imaginary invention or expressing an agenda, or active demonic suggestions.

Another concern worth mentioning is the lack of clear instances of inner healing in the Bible. Judged by regulative standards, the Scriptures do not specify an internal or deep healing. But normative standards keep the door open for aspects of deliverance that may not have been specifically noted but may have occurred. In practice, I have observed that inclusion of inner healing directed prayer in our deliverance matrix has in fact had profound, positive results. I think of the son of a life-long motorcycle gang member. He became a Christian and during his early days in the church that was discipling him, he continually struggled with baggage left from his upbringing. He eventually attended a youth program at our church and had the opportunity not only to re-dedicate his life to Christ, but also to talk with someone who treated seriously his reports of ongoing demonization. We welcomed him into our deliverance process and discovered along the way that he had previously invited Satan into his life at around age 14. We walked him through all the steps we use: personal history, renouncing prayer, detailed prayer addressing the demonic. The last thing to be confronted was this invitation to Satan, which provoked determined resistance from within him. We stopped making headway and were stuck for a while, exhausted. Then I remembered that his memory of allowing Satan's influence might hold the key to deliverance. After praying quietly for a while, I asked him to close his eyes and go back in his mind to the very moment where he had opened his life to the satanic.

He was able to see the moment and describe his circumstances vividly. He was in a bathroom stall taking shelter from yet another beating he had received in school. He remembered the fear, humiliation, and helplessness. Based on his father's expressed allegiance to Satan, he asked the darkness to help him and he felt filled with an angry power. From then on, he aggressively responded to anyone who gave him a hard time, beating up those who had tormented him. He sensed an evil energy that filled him with confidence but scared him at the same time.

I asked him, "Are you willing to give up your power and trust God?" This took several minutes of soul-searching on his part. Then, for the first time, I employed an approach I had observed Kraft use. I asked him to return to that bathroom stall in his mind, but this time, invite Jesus to join him in that moment in the past. He said he would and audibly did so. I asked him, "Can you see him?" He said, "Yes. He's right here!" "What is Jesus doing and saying?" I asked. He responded after a moment, "He's forgiving me for what I did." This biblical answer was not scripted or suggested by anyone in the room. He was experiencing this visit by Jesus into his memory. When I asked what else Jesus was saying, he added, "Jesus is telling me and this thing that it has to go…and it's leaving me." At this point I felt like a spectator to the work Jesus was doing directly in someone's life. Those on the team with the gift of discernment immediately noted that the demonic was, in fact, leaving him. At this point, the young man said, "He's gone." And we were done.

Now, despite that deep healing of the root of much chaos in his life, this man wasn't simply a happily-ever-after story. He did take up a lot of normal living among us, participating in community and eventually getting married. But there was still a lot of residual baggage from his past and some clinical mental health issues that he refused to address, though help was offered. Eventually he walked away from his family and the church. He didn't let the real victory in his life continue to guide him in the ongoing struggles with life. His problem was no longer so much Satan as his own issues. Like the Israelites who were given an amazing freedom from slavery in Egypt yet continually reverted to bitterness and sin in the desert, the deliverance God gives in one area doesn't automatically transfer to all of life. In our efforts to follow up with this young man we found no evidence of his previous demonization; his struggle was his own. Sanctification is an ongoing work that must continue even after the most amazing works of God in our lives.

Lastly, an issue he freely admits and that I talked to Kraft about personally, is the lack of community and team. If there are gifts present, then calling on demons that may or may not be there is not needed. As mentioned, however, the desire for a team and the availability of ministry partners are not always the same. Also, he does believe that his model can be used by anyone—it is not calling, gift, or personality based. This presumption violates the nature of Paul's view of gifts. I think some of his practice—both written and that I have seen—is based on a one person model evolving over years, and now we would see it as a significantly limited practice. Our experience has led me to believe in having groups in the room and outside of the room to support, pray, and be involved. This is not just for their gifts alone, but also prevents burnout for those in this type of ministry.

Jon Thompson

CHAPTER 14
BEFORE OUR MODEL –
THE DISCOVERY OF CONVERGENCE

Although I have mentioned this a few times in passing as we have surveyed the primary models for deliverance, let me highlight the major difference between all five of them that we have incorporated in what we have developed at Sanctus Church. Each of these approaches by and large ignores the crucial role of spiritual gifts or limits the crucial role of community in the process of deliverance. We're saying that deliverance is the unique ministry of the spiritually gifted community called the body of Christ. The proponents of several of our models are actually opposed to the use of spiritual gifts. This difference inadvertently places the weight of each model on to the already taxed shoulders of the local pastor. If you are reading this as a pastor or church leader, you are most likely asking the question at this moment (if you haven't been asking it already), "How does this work of deliverance fit with all my other duties in ministry?" For someone already overloaded with responsibilities and expectations from a congregation, responding to the need for deliverance may seem more daunting than you can even consider. And if you are considering what it would mean to embark on deliverance ministry on your own, stop. You will need to address the reality of spiritual gifts and assess the presence of spiritual gifts, particularly ones you do not have at all, in your ministry setting. You will need a team before you take the field. Let me put it the way I do with my eager seminary students who can't wait to do battle with the demonic: "A team approach to deliverance is not optional; it is a requirement based on Scripture, experience, tradition, and reason."

In my book *Convergence,* I spend a good deal of time on spiritual gifts and the various lessons we have learned as a church (far beyond deliverance ministry) that come with the employment of giftings in the body of Christ. Some of what you are about to read covers that ground as it relates to this specific ministry, and it really matters!

Jesus is not only our model in the things He taught and did; *He is our model in the way He lived,* particularly as it relates to His relationship with His Father and the Holy Spirit during His time on earth. Hebrews 13:8 says, *"Jesus Christ is the same yesterday and today and forever."* This verse does more than shut down the ongoing deluge of newly discovered modern versions of Jesus that regularly appear in books and magazines. Of greater importance is the way we actually apply it and think about Jesus' sameness. If you think this verse in Hebrews is an isolated statement, think for a bit about what he said in John 8:58, *"'Very truly I tell you,' Jesus answered, 'before Abraham was born, I am!'"* We need to take into account the unchanging sameness of Jesus in our thinking about the church and our efforts to obey Him as Lord.

JESUS AS GOD *AND* MAN

Serious thinking about the claims and character of Jesus leads us to think about God. In particular, the revelation of God as the three Persons-in-One God—Father, Son, and Holy Spirit—whom we call the Trinity. I am thoroughly Trinitarian and would gladly submit that everything in this book is true to the way God has revealed Himself to us. As Karl Barth said, "The doctrine of the Trinity is what basically distinguished the Christian doctrine of God as Christian."[1] Marshall Shelley wrote, "Within his own mysterious being God is Father, Son, and Holy Spirit. The designations are just ways in which God is God. Within the Godhead there are three 'persons' who are neither three Gods nor three parts of God, but co-equally and co-eternally God."[2]

Think about it. Outside of time and space, God the Father, the Son, and the Holy Spirit coexist equally. But when God Himself enters time and space, in creation, in salvation, the unity of the Trinity never changes but the persons take on different roles, and it is here where so much insight and freedom is available but sometimes missed in our churches. Let's consider the familiar words of John 1:1-14.

> *In the beginning was the Word, and the Word was with God, and the Word was God. He was with God in the beginning. Through him all things were made; without him nothing was made that has been made. In him was life, and that life was the light of all mankind. The light shines in the darkness, and the darkness has not overcome it. There was a man sent from God whose name was John. He came as a witness to testify concerning that light, so that through him all might believe. He himself was not the light; he came only as a witness to the light. The true light that gives light to everyone was coming into the world. He was in the world, and though the world was made through him, the world did not recognize him. He came to that which was his own, but his own did not receive him. Yet to all who did receive him, to those who believed in his name, he gave the right to become children of God—children born not of natural descent, nor of human decision or a husband's will, but born of God. The Word became flesh and made his dwelling among us. We have seen his glory, the glory of the one and only Son, who came from the Father, full of grace and truth.* (John 1:1-14)

This passage introduces us to God and the Word, and identifies them further as God the Father and God the Son in verse 14. The passage not only claims that the Word is/was God, it also demonstrates that the Word did many things (like making everything that was made) that only God can do. John's short phrases manage to convey with clarity the mystery that is one God who is also three. Although this passage is not overtly Trinitarian, there's no particular reason to exclude God the Holy Spirit from verse 13 as the divine person directly instrumental in making us children of God, born of God (see John 3:5). Verse one speaks of the Word's constant, eternal existence that leads to His temporal experience of becoming flesh and living among us (v.14). Yet as verse 14 concludes, Jesus' dwelling among us in flesh did not diminish His glory or His Sonship.

That little phrase, *"The Word became flesh"* (v.14) is both the foundation of our salvation and a stumbling block for all who fail to understand the unique and awesome role of Jesus Christ, God's Son. The phrase summarizes the results of *kenosis*, a word Paul uses in Philippians 2:7 to describe the way the Son of God transformed Himself into one of us, never ceasing to be God but setting aside His privilege and power as God to fully take on the limitations of being truly human. Paul wrote, *"He made himself nothing by taking the very nature of a servant, being made in human likeness"* (Philippians 2:7). Jesus became flesh and is now physically resurrected, and in that state we will meet Him face to face and spend eternity with Him.

That word *kenosis* (translated *"made himself nothing"* above) has been the foundation for orthodoxy and the spark for heresy since New Testament times. In English, the word has been translated *to empty, to pour out,* and *to make oneself nothing.* The Church has held councils in which the exact meaning and implications of this term were thoroughly debated. In particular, the Council of Nicaea in 325 (which settled the full deity of Christ) and the Council of Chalcedon in 451 (which settled the full humanity of Christ) are the prime examples of our forbearers painstakingly working through all that God's Word reveals to us about God the Word, who became flesh.

Understanding Jesus, His relationship with the Holy Spirit, and their (the Son and Spirit) ongoing relationship with us is the key to spiritual power for thriving churches. Let's be clear from the outset that speaking in the present age about a relationship with God through Jesus Christ that deliberately or accidentally leaves out the immediate, essential, and unavoidable participation of the Holy Spirit is to ignore a significant body of clear teaching by Jesus Himself during the Last Supper (John 13-17) about His coming physical absence and the role the Holy Spirit would carry forward into the future (where we come in).

As God came in the flesh, Jesus is at one and the same time our savior, our Lord, our judge, our model, our shepherd, our teacher, and our friend—to name a few of His roles. But to understand the roots of convergence, we need to look at the context of *kenosis* in Philippians 2:5-11. Paul is writing about how our lives should imitate Jesus, but his foundation for this is the key to understanding the significance of the way Jesus lived when He was on earth:

> *"Your attitude should be the same as that of Christ Jesus: Who, being in very nature God, did not consider equality with God something to be grasped,"* (Philippians 2:5-6).

Being in very nature God: these five words are ground breaking. Paul starts with Christ's pre-existence before the manger. He was the form (*morphe*), the very nature of God Himself, which means Jesus was God. You cannot have the nature of God and not *be* God for there is only one who has the nature, the DNA, the personhood of God, and that's God Himself. This is *not* to say He was *like* God but not really God; it *is* to say that Jesus of Nazareth, born more than 2,000 years ago who walked this earth for 33 years, was the Creator, God in flesh! Both John 1:3 and Colossians 1:16 emphasize the role of Jesus as the agent of Creation.

Then Paul wrote that Jesus *"did not consider equality with God something to be grasped"* (Philippians 2:6). This is really central to understanding Jesus and the idea of spiritual power. This phrase tells us that Jesus, though He was fully God, chose not to grasp, to be selfish, or to hold on to the reality of who He was. He rejected the common and popular view of power and instead deliberately chose to pour Himself out, to be humble, and to be submissive. He didn't stop being God or become something other than God. He simply and firmly chose not to seize or take advantage of what was His by divine nature. As Gordon Fee commented, "Jesus did not empty himself of anything but simply emptied himself, poured himself out."[3] The *Message* paraphrase got it right: *"Jesus had equal status with God but didn't think so much of himself that he had to cling to the advantages of that status no matter what. Not at all"* (Philippians 2:6).[4]

How did Jesus do this? This ancient song gives us the answer: *"but made himself nothing, taking the very nature of a servant, being made in human likeness. And being found in appearance as a man, he humbled himself and became obedient to death—even death on a cross!"* (v.7-8). God took on flesh, the incarnation we celebrate at Christmas, and then lived a perfect life, died a death we all deserved, and ultimately overcame the grave. The point Paul emphasizes here is that Jesus' life was one of humility. As N.T. Wright wrote, "The real humiliation of the incarnation and the cross is that one who himself is God and never during the whole process stopped being God, could embrace such a vocation."[5] The result is what has given the world and many of us the personal hope we have in our Christian faith.

Paul assumes the resurrection and moves directly to the eternal results of Jesus' actions: *"Therefore God exalted him to the highest place and gave him the name that is above every name, that at the name of Jesus every knee should bow, in heaven and on earth and under the earth, and every tongue confess that Jesus Christ is Lord, to the glory of God the Father"* (vv. 9-11). Notice this is a full picture of Jesus: His pre-existence, His incarnation, His death on a cross, and His exaltation, not only from the grave but also to the pinnacle of heaven for all eternity.

What happened during Jesus' thirty-three years and *how* it happened matters. It might come as a shock to many of us to realize that we often speak of Jesus as if we were actually Apollinarians, who believed Jesus was not fully human—having a human body, but a divine mind. We too can treat Jesus' life as extraordinary, but not as a human life, rather, a human life that relied on His own power as God to perform activities like miracles and unrivaled teaching. We will come back to this because it shapes in a fundamental way our understanding of everything that it means to follow Jesus.

At the heart and start of Jesus' ministry life was His baptism at the hands of John, described in the first three Gospels (Matthew 3:13-17; Mark 1:9-11; Luke 3:21-22) and implied in John 1:6-8. We accept the fact of Jesus' baptism, but are somewhat uncomfortable with the implications. John preached and practiced a baptism of repentance and we wonder, but often don't ask, *why would God need to repent and be baptized? What was the sinless God doing in the water? And how does the response of the Trinity factor into our understanding of everything about Jesus?*

There are three reasons why Jesus wanted to be baptized. First, as R.T. France wrote, "Jesus intended to identify himself with John's message and with the revival movement it had created to enroll as a member of the purified and prepared people for God, it is this rather than forgiveness."[6]

Second, and even more importantly, Jesus wanted to be connected to us fallen sinful humans. He wanted to show solidarity with all of us who are separated from Him. It's the first glimpse of the gospel that says, though Jesus was perfect, He came to take on our sin and alter us through God's power. Later Paul would write these history-changing words in 2 Corinthians 5:21, *"God made Jesus who had no sin to be sin for us, so that in him we might become the righteousness of God."*

But third, only when we pair Philippians 2:5-11 and Jesus' baptism do we start to get a clear picture of His divine power at work in the human context. At this point we see how Jesus continued not to grasp His deity even between His baptism and His death. The *kenosis* wasn't a momentary choice that allowed Him to become flesh; it was a continual choice that allowed Him to live life as we live it, with limitations. The gospels fill in the blanks between Christmas and Easter with the account of Jesus, fully human while remaining God, accepting the limitations of humanity in order to show us how we could truly follow in His footsteps and rely on the power He relied on every moment of every day.

We need to get to the place where we actually believe Jesus when He said, *"I tell you the truth, anyone who has faith in me will do what I have been doing. He will do even greater things than these, because I am going to the Father"* (John 14:12). And we won't believe it if we harbor a secret assumption that Jesus was able to do everything He did simply because He was God. Resolving this dilemma takes us back to His baptism:

> *"When all the people were being baptized, Jesus was baptized too. And as he was praying, heaven was opened and the Holy Spirit descended on him in bodily form like a dove. And a voice came from heaven: 'You are my Son, whom I love; with you I am well pleased'"* (Luke 3:21-22).

"Heaven was opened": It was immediate, it was straightaway, and His coming up out of the water was answered by a coming down from heaven itself. Heaven now speaks; heaven's will is now being done on earth, and the words spoken over 740 years earlier by Isaiah finally happen, *"O that you would tear open the heavens and come down"* (Isaiah 64:1).

Don't miss that in almost every image and actual historical occurrence, these words and signs all point to the life, ministry, murder, death, resurrection, and ascension of Jesus. In Mark's account, he reports that Jesus *"saw heaven being torn open and the Spirit descending"* (Mark 1:10). Some three years later, when Jesus died, the huge carpet-like curtain that prevented people from going into the Holy of Holies, the very presence of God within the Temple, was torn in two. The beginning and conclusion of Jesus' ministry are bookends of a great tearing that would change the fabric of human existence and allow messed up, alienated people like us to know God again in a face-to-face relationship. The writer of Hebrews spells this out in Hebrews 9 as part of an explanation of Jesus' unique ministry as our eternal high priest.

Out of the torn heavens comes the *"Spirit descending on him like a dove."* This is of huge significance when you remember the historic acts of God in the Old Testament. The Spirit of God was first seen at the beginning of creation. *"Now the earth was formless and empty, darkness was over the surface of the deep, and the Spirit of God was hovering over the waters"* (Genesis 1:2). The image of the dove over water was also seen in the days of Noah. As Alan Cole commented, "The Spirit is seen here in two lights. He is the gentle dove hovering over the waters of baptism as Noah's dove had hovered over the ark of salvation and the waters of judgment, but he is also the mighty Spirit of creation, hovering over the baptismal waters out of which God will call his new creation, in terms of new-made men and women."[7]

The Spirit alights on Jesus for two reasons. The first is seen in what heaven declares, *"And a voice came from heaven: "You are my Son, whom I love; with you I am well pleased"* (v.11). The Spirit is present/sent to affirm Jesus' identity so His ministry, death, resurrection, and ascension would be valid. Here we see God in His fullness: the Father's voice, the Son of God in flesh, and the Spirit in the form of a dove. Father and Spirit authenticate the divine nature of the Son. In this we see the reality of the Trinity.

The second reason reveals convergence. Not only did the Spirit's appearance confirm Jesus' identity, but the Holy Spirit was also given to empower Jesus. His reliance on His Father was real, not pretended. His emptying left Him in our same position of need for God's power and direction. One of the clearest statements of this is Hebrews 4:15, *"For we do not have a high priest who is unable to empathize with our weaknesses, but we have one who has been tempted in every way, just as we are—yet he did not sin."* The God/man remains a mystery to us, but always to our benefit, since both these aspects of His incarnation were for our good and God's glory. Think about it; in all of Jesus' life to this point, He never healed, never cast out demons, and He did not teach in public. Only once, at age 12, did He speak at the Temple, yet no one followed after Him. It was only after the Holy Spirit came on Him at His baptism that His ministry began.

The third person of the Trinity empowered Jesus, who was sent by the Father. Without the power of the Spirit, Jesus, out of choice alone, would not have been able to bring the good news. In this way He did not grasp the power or privilege of deity; He did only what the Father wanted by the power of the Holy Spirit. Jesus did not perform ministry out of His deity, but only under the power of the Holy Spirit.

Charles Kraft wrote:

We read in Philippians 2:5-8 that Jesus laid aside the use of his divinity and worked totally as a human being in the power of the Holy Spirit while he was on earth. He did nothing to indicate to the world, including the people of his hometown, Nazareth, that he was, in fact, God incarnate until after his baptism. Then, functioning wholly as a human being under the leading of the Father (Jn. 5:19) and the power of the Holy Spirit (Lk. 4:14), he began to set people free from captivity to the enemy as evidenced by sickness, lameness, blindness, demonization and the like. Jesus worked in the authority and power given him by the Father, never once using his own divinity while on earth.

Jesus did all this to demonstrate God's love (a relational thing), to teach us what God and the Christian life are all about (knowledge/truth things), to free people from Satan (a power thing). Thus he showed us how we should go about our lives as participants in the Kingdom of God that Jesus planted in the middle of Satan's kingdom. He gave to us the same Holy Spirit under whom he worked, saying that whoever has faith in him will do the same things he did, and more (Jn. 14.12). Since today, as in Jesus' day, the enemy is doing power things, Jesus gave us his authority and power (Lk. 9.1) to carry on the freedom-giving activities of Kingdom builders.[8]

You could miss a crucial detail if you read this too quickly. It says in Mark 1:12, *"At once the Spirit sent him out into the wilderness."* Jesus, fully God, was now sent out by the Spirit. But the word *sent* means *driven,* or *pushed.* Jesus' expulsion by the Holy Spirit is real and it matters to you and your church.

So the heavens tear open, the Spirit comes down, a heavenly voice announces, John points, the crowd wonders, and we who are reading in amazement think things will now get better and easier. The stage is set and the star of the show has been revealed. There should be a great big victory party. Instead, Jesus is led into battle in a hostile place. As Luke writes, *"Jesus, full of the Holy Spirit, returned from the Jordan and was led by the Spirit in the desert, where for forty days he was tempted by the devil"* (Luke 4:1-2).

Why would Luke include the "forty days" detail here? Does it matter? Yes, because it parallels a pattern we see in the Old Testament. Moses fasted for 40 days and nights when he received the Ten Commandments (Ex. 34:28); Elijah, running for his life, wandered for 40 days and nights to meet God (1 Kings 19:8); and Israel wandered for 40 years in the desert before they were let into the Promised Land. Why should we pay attention to all these historic precedents? Luke wants us to know that Jesus is God who came as a servant, greater than Moses, greater than Elijah, and unlike Israel—who wandered, disobeyed, and failed God. As the ultimate servant, He is acting on God's orders. He will travel and suffer in the wilderness but will not give in to Satan. He will successfully live the life and witness that Israel was supposed to give to the world.

There is further significance to Jesus' desert experience. Right after His identity is given and exactly when He is empowered for ministry, the first thing that happens is a clash between the leader of the kingdom of darkness and the leader of the kingdom of light (Colossians 1:12-14) who was coming to destroy it. There's a pattern here. As we saw in the book of Acts and other places in Scripture, when God moves, there is a demonic attempt to stop God and His people every time. The slaughter of the children in Bethlehem following Jesus' birth was not only about an earthly ruler threatened by a new king; this was the kingdom of darkness realizing it had been invaded. We run the risk of being blindsided in our world today if we overlook the power behind Jesus' ministry and the resisting, evil context in which He moved.

After Jesus was baptized, affirmed, empowered, and overcame Satan, He started His public ministry under the power of the Holy Spirit by declaring that freedom through godly power was about to come!

Jesus returned to Galilee in the power of the Spirit, and news about him spread through the whole countryside. He taught in their synagogues, and everyone praised him. He went to Nazareth, where he had been brought up, and on the Sabbath day he went into the synagogue, as was his custom. And he stood up to read. The scroll of the prophet Isaiah was handed to him. Unrolling it, he found the place where it is written: "The Spirit of the Lord is on me, because he has anointed me to preach good news to the poor. He has sent me to proclaim freedom for the prisoners and recovery of sight for the blind, to release the oppressed, to proclaim the year of the Lord's favor" (Luke 4:14-19).

There is so much to unpack in this powerful summary of why God entered the world to win us back to Himself. Never forget that the poor not only include those in bondage caused by lack of education, gender, family, religious purity, vocation, or economics, but also the heart of every single person sentenced to the poverty of sin, and of death, and the poverty of living under the dominion of the Satan. We are called to love, to help, and to advocate for the widow and orphan, but the fundamental issue remains a poverty of spirit that can only be dealt with by the person, truth, and power of Jesus the Christ.

When Luke concludes his summary with the words, *"Jesus returned to Galilee in the power of the Spirit"* (v.14), he is making clear that Jesus would not use His own power or carry out His own plans. Luke's phrase is not just a transition statement to bridge Jesus' time in the wilderness and the launch of His ministry. Everything Jesus said and did He did in surrender and under the power of the Holy Spirit.

JESUS OUR EXAMPLE

Our view of Jesus' ministry changes significantly when we ask the question: If Jesus didn't teach, or cast out demons, or heal because He was God, but did all these amazing things under the Holy Spirit's power and direction, what does that look like today? How does His way of life and ministry intersect with ours? Jesus operated under the Holy Spirit's power, not His own (which He had set aside). Jesus used spiritual gifts to serve and He clearly had the gifts of teaching, miracles, healing, and discernment—to name a few. The Holy Spirit provided what He needed to carry out the Father's purposes on earth. Do you see the connection? If we have the same indwelling Holy Spirit Jesus had, and the church universal has the same spiritual gifts He used, together we can do what Jesus did.

We can and should give great attention to all the ways that Jesus is different from us and therefore worthy of our worship and obedience. He is and always was our Savior and Lord, the second person of the Trinity. But He chose to become one *of* us and one *with* us, for very important reasons that go beyond His priceless act of substitution on the cross. He not only made our eternal life possible; He made our life *now* possible by demonstrating as a human being how to live as people empowered by the Holy Spirit. In fact, since the time of Jesus, every generation of believers has had to re-learn this truth— that the authentic life of a Christ-follower must be a Spirit-filled life. The Holy Spirit whom Jesus promised and described during the Last Supper (John 13-17) isn't a useful add-on to the spiritual life, but the driving force behind everything God wants to accomplish in us and through us. Where Jesus went first, we the Church go now.

Jesus provides a pattern for us both personally and together. Remember that the Bible calls the church the Body of Christ— corporately, we are Jesus on earth. Everything He did in His earthly life and ministry, we are able to do together as His representatives on earth. We are called into His life by using the practices He used and we are called together to use the gifts He used to serve the Church and the world. Watch this—our walk with God is just like Jesus' walk:

- We are all baptized in the Spirit when we become Christians and enter the relationship with the Father that Jesus had: *"So it is with Christ. For we were all baptized by one Spirit into one body—whether Jews or Greeks, slave or free—and we were all given the one Spirit to drink."* (1 Corinthians 12:12-13).

- We are all spiritually marked or sealed by the Holy Spirit at the time of our conversion: *"And you also were included in Christ when you heard the message of truth, the gospel of your salvation. When you believed, you were marked in him with a seal, the promised Holy Spirit, who is a deposit guaranteeing our inheritance until the redemption of those who are God's possession—to the praise of his glory"* (Ephesians 1:13-14).

- We are all called to ask God to produce in us the same character that Jesus had, which was the fruit of the Spirit: *"But the fruit of the Spirit is love, joy, peace, patience, kindness, goodness, faithfulness, gentleness and self-control"* (Galatians 5:22-23).

- We are all called to walk in the spiritual practices that Jesus walked in. It is here we are transformed, learn to hear God's voice, and are challenged to move to the deeper places in our walk personally and together. Notice that each practice is open to all of us. Every Christian is invited into these practices to be truly transformed, and as we move in them over a long period of time we will continually become more like Jesus.

- We are all called to walk in the power of the Holy Spirit by using the gifts of the Holy Spirit. As a church we will have all the gifts, while personally we may only have one or more. You, personally, will not have all 21! That's the difference between the practices and the gifts. The practices are open to all; God gives the gifts as He wills. The result is that we can never say, "Well, we will never see all that Jesus did again, because He was God and we are not." No, like Jesus, the Spirit is given to affirm that we are children of God and to empower us.

Jesus laid aside the privilege of deity and was filled by the Spirit and perfectly did the will of the Father. So when we are baptized in the Spirit and filled by the Spirit, and when we follow Jesus in His practices and recognize our spiritual gifts as undergirded by the fruit of the Spirit, we, like Jesus, can and will do greater things.

We have the same access to the Father that Jesus had. We have the same Holy Spirit living in each one of us that Jesus had. We have the same power that He had and the same character traits offered to us that He had. We have the same gifts He had and we have the same practices He followed. If spiritual gifts are a guaranteed source of power, then spiritual practices for the believer are a guaranteed source of transformation!

The spiritual practices and spiritual gifts were the inner and outer life of Jesus and they ought to be the inner and outer life of each of His devoted followers. They are the glue in our relationship with God and others. Jesus used spiritual disciplines to hear and walk with the Father, because these holy habits are guaranteed places of personal change. Jesus used spiritual gifts to demonstrate submission and service because they are the only heaven-guaranteed place of power. They are the sanctioned and empowered means God has provided to us to accomplish His purposes and bring Him glory.

With Jesus as our model, let me emphasize a key verse that puts Jesus firmly where we live each day: *"Jesus gave them this answer: 'Very truly I tell you, the Son can do nothing by himself; he can do only what he sees his Father doing, because whatever the Father does the Son also does'"* (John 5:19). The Gospel of John presents in Jesus the pattern of submissive empowerment and permission-based action that should characterize our lives. This obliterates the assumption we often make that Jesus' actions can only be explained because He was the Son of God. We therefore conclude that we couldn't be part of such a demonstration of God's power because we're *not* the Son of God. But throughout His life here among us, Jesus, as He said above, could *"do nothing by himself."* In His humanity, He was completely dependent on His Father and the Holy Spirit for permission, direction, and empowerment. That Jesus expects us to imitate Him is a foundational idea introduced in John 5:19 and repeated in John 14:12, *"I tell you the truth, anyone who has faith in me will do what I have been doing. He will do even greater things than these, because I am going to the Father."* It comes as no surprise then that Jesus is the original Spirit-baptized, Spirit-filled, Spirit-empowered person in every sense of the term. And He wants each of us to follow in His steps in all ministries, including dealing with evil.

SUMMARY OF DELIVERANCE MODELS

With all the background of agreement and disagreement we finally come to our current practices. Again our approach truly is a matrix, a blend of the above, which has helped us deal with the diversity of people, gifts, and cases we have and will face. The following summarizes our take-aways and cautions regarding each of the models we have been taught by:

- From the "Gospel Model" we took the idea that one must truly come to the Lord Jesus Christ in a personal conversion. We love their strong biblical stands and hard work in systematic theology. They are strong on understanding who God is and what God has done for us. The more Reformed teachers are amazing at working out our God-given identity. But unlike that model, we reject the idea that a Christian cannot be demonized.

- From the "Truth Model" we took the principles of being led by the Holy Spirit, and submitting under and using Holy Scripture throughout this whole process. Second, this model helped us to see we must address not just evil spirits but the many emotional, mental, and familial issues like trauma, forgiveness, and past hurt. The ideas expressed in James 4:7 and James 5:16 show us that personal responsibility is key—confession of sin and repentance, along with rejection of false practices and beliefs, is now foundational for us. Also, the implication that the person is important in the process, not just clergy, church, or other Christians has strongly influenced our views.

- From the "Power Model" we understood that power is needed and must be used alongside truth. A call for meekness while still using power gave us a new freedom to see people set free.

- Though the "Liturgical Power Encounter Model" was foreign to us and fraught with the deep disagreements and presuppositions many of us would have with traditional Roman Catholic teaching, it did allow us to see many things we had not encountered before. A step-by-step process helps both a team and the person being ministered to. The calling on heaven to mobilize prayer beyond those directly involved was invaluable, but still our take on this is far from the Tiber River. The work and mutual reliance between clergy and laity was a great example of shared responsibility. Lastly, some of the liturgical prayers are the most biblically informed and best-written prayers, and we do use them sometimes in our sessions.

- Lastly, the "Deep Healing and Deliverance Model" is where we began to see the need to use inner healing and then the power encounter. The image of removing the garbage so the rats have no place to live and eat has crystallized much of our ministry experience.

We now have a foundation for the model we have developed at Sanctus Church, which is not only a matrix of useful parts from the models above but also a return to Scripture to find in Philippians 2:5-11 what we might call the Jesus Model. Here we unpack the limited understanding of the purposes of Jesus' Incarnation. He came not only to be our Savior and Lord, but also to be our Model. He was the original Spirit-filled Spirit-directed man who intends that we follow in His steps.

All of the factors above have had a significant impact in shaping our current deliverance ministry at Sanctus Church, which continues to develop today. The next chapter is an overview of our current practices. We continue to seek to be open to God's leading in necessary changes and we are aware that there are still unresolved issues in our ministry. Our list of things to improve or address continues to be a matter of prayer and a motive for humility. We have made many mistakes along the way and God continues to show us that He can always do *"immeasurably more than all we ask or imagine, according to his power that is at work within us, to him be glory in the church and in Christ Jesus throughout all generations, for ever and ever! Amen!"* (Ephesians 3:20-21).

Jon Thompson

CHAPTER 15
APPLIED CONVERGENCE

THE BACKGROUND OF SANCTUS CHURCH'S CURRENT MODEL

In my book *Convergence,* I identified the three most significant components that must be present within a local church in order for revival to occur and to endure. Those three components are: 1) Emphasis and encouragement of spiritual disciplines; 2) Recognition, identification, and use of spiritual gifts; and 3) Expectation that God does work, is working, and will work in and through His Church. If any of these components is ignored or only given lip service, what God is doing will be missed or quickly fade. While God is the undisputed Author of revival, or accelerated spiritual growth, and actually determines when it will occur among His people, our study of Church history has confirmed to us over and over that when remarkable spiritual events occur, they invariably accompany the three components I just mentioned above. *Convergence* provides an important background for the specific ministry we are looking at in this book and will be described in detail in the pages to come.

In the larger picture, here is the way the three streams of convergence impact spiritual deliverance ministry. Spiritual disciplines (fasting, prayer, Bible study, solitude, silence, etc.) are the guaranteed places of walking with God in our process of sanctification. Jesus used spiritual disciplines. Our reading of the Gospels is transformed when we begin to note how clearly Jesus used spiritual practices every day as the lifestyle that kept His relationship with the Father up to the moment. The intentionality with which Jesus went about His ministry was not because He knew He was the Son of God (as we tried to show in the last chapter) but because He was carrying out His Father's instructions in the power of the Holy Spirit. And those instructions flowed out of the time Jesus spent in silence, prayer, and attentiveness each day. As they did for Jesus our model, disciplines allow us to walk with God and hear from God. They are the eating, breathing, exercising aspects of our life in Christ. This distinguishes them from spiritual gifts, which allow us to serve God.

Spiritual disciplines can (and should) be done by any Christian. They are open to the whole church and should be used by the whole church. These disciplines are how you walk post-conversion. These holy habits are not an end in themselves; they are an effective means to make continual progress in sanctification. They are not works leading to salvation but the kind of living that flows out of salvation. The recovery of spiritual disciplines is needed in the Protestant church.

Spiritual gifts, in contrast to the disciplines that form us, are how we *serve* post-conversion. They are the guaranteed means of spiritual power. How Jesus served the Father wasn't through the disciplines; it was through spiritual gifts. Notice, however, how often Jesus intentionally made the exercise of His gifts a corporate effort by enlisting others in the process: He called out the faith of many of those He healed; He involved others in opening Lazarus' tomb and un-wrapping His resurrected friend; He had the disciples organize the multitude and then serve them by delivering the multiplied bread and fish. He was modeling a team approach even before He asked the Father to give us the indwelling Holy Spirit.

Jesus as our model showed us how to use the disciplines as well as the gifts. How did He hear what He was supposed to do as He moved through the world? By practicing the disciplines. This helps us understand the parallel work of sanctification (discipline) and serving with power (gifts).

All 21 gifts are open to the whole church (Romans 12; 1 Corinthians 12; 1 Peter 4; Ephesians 4—all are about spiritual gifts, but two of those passages explicitly say the Spirit of God decides which gift to give you). Not everyone gets the same gifts and no one gets all of them.

In order to study how the gifts interact, we can divide them into three categories of gifts: LOVE, WORD, and POWER. There are 21 gifts mentioned in the Scriptures and they fall into these areas.

- *Love gifts* demonstrate the mercy or love of God: administration, helps, mercy, and giving.

- *Word gifts* continually clarify who God is and what He is doing: teaching, exhortation/encouragement, apostleship, leadership / ruling, shepherding/pastoring, and evangelism.

- *Power gifts* demonstrate that God is in the room right now / He is an interventionist all the time: prophecy, tongues, interpretation, miracles, intercession, faith, discernment of spirits, words of wisdom/knowledge, and healing.[1]

If you are missing, ignoring, or rejecting one of these three elements in your church, it will be unbalanced. We as Christians believe in boundary-set love, it is holy love. God is perpetual love and also perpetually holy.

When the Spirit's generosity comes to the matter of deliverance ministry, there are particular gifts that are very helpful. This is also a great ministry in which to discover what gifts the Holy Spirit has given. In a deliverance ministry we use the gifts of administration, discernment, knowledge, wisdom, intercession, faith, miracles, prophecy, and sometimes tongues/translation. I will highlight the way these gifts inform and energize deliverance. The more of these that are present, the greater the effectiveness of the ministry.

Gift of Administration[2]

This gift shows you care and gives both the demonized and the ministers a system with a beginning, middle, and end, which creates a structure of safety. It brings order and helpful logistics to what might otherwise be a chaotic situation. This gift, whether in combination with others or in someone as a primary gift, creates a structure where other gifts can be more effective by taking care of a multitude of seemingly unimportant details that can increase the effectiveness of the ministry.

We discovered through practical experience that we were "losing" people who approached us for help and were "put on the list" but were then essentially forgotten because none of us at the time were gifted with "list management." When your team is made up of people who are low on the process end and high on the encounter end, you are likely to create frustration among those whose needs get forgotten. And on the other side, the gift of administration will care about follow-up—what happens *after* the encounter.

This gift is not a spotlight gift, but it often keeps the power supply for the spotlight connected. As a parallel, I often point out that the effectiveness and longevity of a worship ministry within a church doesn't rest with the creativity of the artists or the level of musical talent; rather, it relies heavily on the presence of someone with administrative gifts who keeps all that creativity moving in harmony.

Gift of Discernment[3]

This gifting is about source, not information. Discernment identifies the power or influence that is present. There are areas of discernment: God's presence, human factors (something can be off, motive), or satanic presence. For example, a preacher can preach a great sermon, and a person with the gift of discernment in the audience can pick up that there's a background issue that is not apparent to anyone else. I may have inserted two lines in the sermon that targeted someone, all with the purest intentions of course, but betraying human, fleshly thought rather than pastoral care. This is discernment at the interpersonal level and it notes that something is off.

Other discernment-gifted people can tell that Jesus is present; He has shown up. This kind of discernment is easy to covet; it's the fun one. You are specially attuned to the manifest presence of Jesus in a setting and encourage others to recognize His ministry.

A third kind of discernment is awareness of the satanic. Whether the circumstances superficially appear right or wrong, a discerner can tell if the source is satanic, even under the cover of an angel of light (2 Corinthians

11:14). In individuals, the gift of discernment rarely covers all three of these areas, but often focuses on two of them.

The gift of discernment also functions differently than the gift of prophecy. Discernment has to do with seeing or perceiving the source; it's not information. It's not prophecy or even a word of knowledge. With this gift, you can discern in three ways:

1. Sensing: You may sense a presence externally. This is a rational, clear knowing or awareness of a particular source: human, evil, or divine in the circumstance.

2. Feeling: You may feel a movement inside of yourself and know where the demonic is in another person (eg: a back pain). This "feely feely" kind of discernment can also be reported as a frigid extreme cold, because the evil is walking death.

3. Seeing: Actually seeing the demons; God reveals them and (in some cases) their names.

Let me hasten to add that these descriptions often provoke comments like, "This sounds like a psychic encounter." I'm not a psychic or a witch; I'm a follower of Jesus Christ and the exercise of this gift is an example of the Spirit of God empowering a believer to do His work. This is not proprietary knowledge I possess and can exercise randomly, which would inevitably lead to significant struggles with pride. Those with this gift must employ it humbly and without projecting superiority over those who need help. In other areas, I'm the one who needs help! But in certain circumstances, I have the privilege of being used by God, as do you if you are open to His guidance in the use of your particular gifting. In a session I may become aware of the number of demons involved and can even hear them interacting. If I reveal this to the person we are helping, I must also add, "This is not my power; it's discernment given by the Holy Spirit. God is allowing me to see and hear these things." And if we see or feel a presence, we must stop and ask "Why did you show me that Jesus?" We are not necessarily supposed to confront everything we see. Our dependence on God's Spirit for guidance, even as we exercise the gifts, is crucial.

One of the issues for us has been that without the spiritual gift of discernment present during a deliverance session, you can misdiagnose the problem, concluding it's demonic when it's not, clinical when it's not, etc. This doesn't mean those with the gift of discernment are an elite group in the body of Christ, but in this particular ministry, discernment is a significant component to effectiveness. The fact is that in the broad life of the church there are places in which every spiritual gift can shine and make an important contribution to the work God is doing. Paul's somewhat humorous description in 1 Corinthians 14 of certain members of the body feeling put out or desiring the roles of other members of the body makes the point that there's no room for pride when all are serving in the role they were designed for and gifted to serve in.

Remember, spiritual gifts are given to us by God. If Jesus reveals a specific way of discernment, it's always ultimately about the edification of the body. It's always about humility, not humiliation. Jesus uses His gifts (through us) any time He wants to in any given ministry or circumstance.

Every particular ministry must be about practicing mutual submission while using our gifts. For example, for compassion ministry, you look for people with gifts of helps and mercy.

The vast majority of the time, God may just want us to pray. We only confront with permission from God. Our system ensures that those who approach us for deliverance have also given permission. We make it a practice that any time we are about to exercise a gift, we clear our intention with the party in question. Our question is often, "Do you really want to do this?" So, if someone approaches us for prayer after a worship service and we discern there's a lot going on, we will check for their permission and speak cautiously about what we discern. We realize we can be mistaken. But we are actually most intentional about seeking God's permission before we take action to confront the demonic. Again, the question is, "Why have you shown us this, Jesus?"

I illustrate this with something that happened to me while on a date with my wife, a special occasion. We had young kids at the time and going out by ourselves was a big deal. We went to a restaurant in Toronto that specializes in Thai food, one of our favorites! As we were standing in line to order, I glanced around the restaurant and noticed the typical shrine that looks like part of the décor in those places. Usually there is some kind of figure that might be an idol surrounded by smoking incense sticks, fruit, and flowers. They are often lost in the background. Except that I could see a demon hovering behind this one. This was, after all, an altar of sorts, with demonic spiritual implications. I didn't, however, spring into action to deliver that restaurant of the demonic. We were there for spring rolls and some fun together. Being aware of the demonic doesn't necessarily mean a call to action at every moment.

As Christians, we are free to live normal lives. Jesus can show us things to remind us of the pervasiveness of evil without calling us to take up arms immediately. Frankly, I'm not sure why Jesus allowed me to see the demon on this occasion. There's a little more to the story. I had been observing the demon for several minutes when I realized it had finally noticed me and knew I could see it. It got angry and left its hiding place to move toward me.

When I excused myself to visit the restroom, my wife knew something was up, but she was more focused on her spring roll order. I moved to the restroom, followed by that harassing presence, and confronted it in Jesus' name between the sinks and the stalls. When I rejoined my wife in line, the demon returned to its perch and remained scowling at a distance throughout the meal. This was a classic blend of weird and normal that ought to characterize more of our lives if the biblical description of reality is accurate.

God will show us what He wants when He wants. And He will tell us what to do about it. Sovereign timing and permission really matter. Part of the boundaries in spiritual ministry is to trust in God's sovereign timing.

Remember, as a discerner, it's not about us. Our instinct is to focus on power; the Spirit's instinct is about submission and humility.

Also, we must work in pairs or teams. If you start every ministry situation from gift orientation and a mutuality model, the ministry will be far more effective. The parable of the talents is about accountability of the gifts, but the talents (gifts / life) aren't taken away until the Master returns.

Be careful of using discernment language too liberally and loosely. We are talking about a spiritual gift; not hunches. The Holy Spirit gifts some of us with a special capacity to see the source of power and to know the timing God wants to follow. I talk about this so much more in Convergence.

Gift of Knowledge[4]

Words of Knowledge are evident when the Holy Spirit gives a person information that they otherwise would have no access to. This is always for the purpose of healing or humility, never humiliation. These are not the product of a seminary degree or a demonstrated ability in preaching/teaching, which are often put forth as evidence of this gift. This is not the result of diligent Bible memorization or study that allows one to know a lot. The knowledge of which we are speaking is not acquired through effort but provided by the Holy Spirit and not accessible to the giftee in any other way. Words of knowledge are always best expressed from the point of humility and caution: "I'm not sure if this is right, but…I think Jesus wants me to tell you…" always remember this, because you are being given supernatural information. Permission is sought. How you say it matters.

In deliverance, someone with this gift may be fed by the Holy Spirit the knowledge of where the grounds or rights of the demonic came from. This may be completely new information to the demonized person or suddenly allow them to understand a past experience or circumstance as spiritually significant in a way they have not previously understood.

As an example, I have permission to use the story of a young married woman who ended up at our church after experiencing not only significant abuse by her husband, but also a failure on the part of the church to which they belonged to intervene and support her. Without knowing much of her story, I originally simply felt led to pray for her. I approached her after a service and asked permission to pray with her, leaving the decision in her court, not assuming my role as pastor automatically gave me that permission. I also asked if others could join us, and she readily agreed. As we began to pray, a very clear picture of her sprang into my mind. She was sitting in her bed, a safe place, reading her Bible and singing to Jesus. Note that this isn't discernment; it's knowledge I didn't previously know about details of her life, along with the sense that I was supposed to tell her what I was seeing. So what I actually said to her was, "I'm not sure if this is right, but I sense the Lord is showing me a picture I'm supposed to describe to you, so here it is." I described the picture along with the impression that I was supposed to assure her that when she was reading and singing to Jesus, He was in the room with her, listening intently to her. She responded by beginning to weep deeply. At first, I thought I might have told her something hurtful, but after a few moments she managed to whisper, "I just didn't think He heard me anymore."

That word of knowledge reminded her Jesus was with her, affirmed her faith, built up her devotional life, and offered her a desperately needed sovereign moment of intimate confirmation over her efforts to draw near to God by letting her hear from Jesus.

On another occasion, we met with a pastor/missionary who had been serving God for more than three decades. He came seeking deliverance. Nothing in the questionnaire he filled out gave us any indication of how he might have become demonized. But as we prepared for our time with him, I got a picture of a young boy playing in a barn who was traumatized by seeing someone do something very inappropriate with an animal. When we met with the man, I said to him, "I'm not sure of this, but have you ever been in a situation like …" and I described what I had seen. He said after a stunned silence, "Yes. I had completely forgotten that happened to me." Later, in the time of deliverance, when a demon proved stubborn, it was that event that turned out to be the point in his background where the demonic had gained access and that door was closed. That crucial information, no longer remembered by the man, was brought to light by the Holy Spirit as a word of knowledge.

Gift of Wisdom[5]

Words of wisdom differ from words of knowledge in that they provide very specific information about what a person is to do next. Wisdom is knowledge in effective action. Wisdom only becomes wisdom when knowledge is acted upon. This gift isn't about being smart or measurably intelligent; it's about wise choices coming from the Spirit. Someone with this gift has a strong sense when they are with another person of what that person should do next in their walk with Jesus. This information functions in harmony with other streams of guidance that the person can act on. It is not manipulative nor does it approach the person in an overruling manner. A word of wisdom may in fact seem like a small suggestion that proves its divine origin by the way it affects the life of the one who receives it.

Notice that discernment, words of knowledge, and words of wisdom are all situational. They are not static; they're dynamic. They happen all over, all the time when the Spirit gives insight in the moment and the one delivering it is often not even aware of the implications or importance of what they are passing along. All of these have significant roles to play in a deliverance setting, providing vehicles by which the Holy Spirit speaks directly in various ways to the person being delivered, identifying sources, filling in missing pieces, and providing direction for the future.

Gift of Intercession (Standing in the Gap)[6]

While this does not appear overtly among any of the gift lists in Scripture, observation and experience has led me to believe this is a gift or a clear expression of one of the gifts, like faith. Every great move of God has intercessors at the core. Every intercessory movement has an element of deliverance.

In practice, the centre of gravity for this gift is someone else, not us. It is an ongoing, prompting gift orientation. We see it when Abraham interceded for Sodom and Gomorrah and when Moses went to the Mount and pleaded with God. As is the case with the practice of most of the gifts, there is a sense in which we all engage in intercessory prayer. We are told of a crisis or need in someone's life and we pray earnestly before God about that need. This, for most of us, is intercessory prayer as a spiritual discipline. There are those among us, however, for whom interceding is a spiritual gift.

I have found that those with this gift often don't realize it. But if we listen, there are clues that emerge in conversation. We note that they seem a little off, so we ask them, "How has your day been?" And they respond with something like, "I'm feeling a little low right now because I only got to talk with Jesus for two hours this morning." While we are commiserating with them, we are desperately trying to remember when and if we have *ever* spent two hours talking to Jesus! They continue, "Yeah, I usually start my day with three or four hours of prayer to cover all the things I need to talk to Jesus about. Don't you?"

At this point, there is some danger created by what I call "gift tension." Whatever our gifting, we have a tendency to assume others look at, do, or feel the same things we look at, do, and feel. But what our gifting allows us to do "naturally" others frequently can't do, while they do "naturally" things we couldn't imagine doing. The danger comes if we allow a feeling of superiority to creep in when we discover we are doing something not that usual. Spiritual maturity brings us to the place where we take seriously the call that comes with our gifting because God's Spirit hasn't gifted everyone the same way, while at the same time humbly appreciating the gifting of others that is unlike ours. All the gifts are needed and contribute to the building up of the body.

Intercession is a specific form of prayer with several expressions. In fact, this problem of gift tension can actually show up between different expressions of intercessory prayer. There are at least three types of intercessors:

1) Phone book intercessors: Give them a list and they are in heaven. They will gladly and faithfully pray through the entire membership list. If they gather with others for prayer, they tend to expect an agenda to pray through. These are methodical pray-ers with a long view of God's faithfulness and they pray continually.

2) Prompting intercessors: This gifting promotes spontaneous suggestions for prayer that require immediate action–"I need to pray for that need or that person right now." Those with this gift report patterns of unexpected urges to pray for situations or people that often occur at unusual times. They are accustomed to being awakened during the night with an urgent desire to pray that is sometimes confirmed by reports of what was happening somewhere in the world at the time they were called to prayer. These are the intense, laboring pray-ers with the expectation that God answers immediately what He specifically urges us to pray about.

3) Assigned intercessors: Sovereignly assigned by Jesus for a season or a lifetime to an area, church, people group, or person. This is profoundly biblical. People like Moses needed input from people like Jethro, Joshua, and Aaron to carry out their ministry. Jesus asked His disciples to pray for Him. Paul made it a practice in most of his letters not only to report his prayers for those he was writing to, but also to earnestly ask them to pray for him. Leaders need people to intercede for them. These are task-oriented pray-ers who see their role behind the scenes as a significant contribution to God's work that may never be seen by others.

There is an amazing woman in my church who has been called to pray for me, and she does so in and out of season. When I speak or teach somewhere else within reasonable distance, she makes it a point to be present in the room, praying. My seminary classes are blessed to have her sitting in the back each day, asking for God's presence to fill the room and particularly to guide my words. She has been doing this for almost two decades. She is not my accountability person, nor do I go out of my way to share specific requests with her; she has been assigned to pray for me without needing to know details.

We meet on a weekly basis for prayer and she knows my schedule in order to structure her prayers.

There are stories from the life of both Moody and Spurgeon that illustrate the role of intercessors. Moody was confronted by two women who insisted they had been assigned to pray for him. It took him time to realize they were serious. Under Spurgeon's pulpit in London was the boiler room of the church, which was also filled by people in prayer each time he preached.

In a deliverance setting, the presence of an intercessor can be crucial in keeping those in leadership focused on the task at hand, knowing that their personal weaknesses are being covered by prayer. This illustrates the importance of mutual submission in ministry, when those leading the charge are thankfully aware that other believers have their back.

Assuming that you may be wondering about your own gifting as we continue to unfold the relationship between these gifts and deliverance, always remember the "dot theory" regarding your gift identification. If it happens once, fine; twice, that's interesting, but if it keeps on happening this is likely one of your gifts. If prayer functions like a default setting in your life, you're not weird; the impulse to pray is part of your gifting.

It's also important to remember that we are looking at the gift of intercession, not the overall discipline of prayer in the life of a believer. I know people who have developed a rich prayer life who are not intercessors. This gift is designed by the Holy Spirit for those He calls to "stand in the gap" in some way for the kingdom of God.

When it comes to being the recipient of prayer, my experience has been that it's important to accept prayer from others, but be careful about submitting under it. An example for me is prayer with laying on of hands. 1 Timothy 5:22 cautions people in ministry about hastiness in laying on hands. It goes both ways. Prayers can be used as a weapon—a prayer of manipulation. If someone lays a hand on you, it is symbolic of being "over" someone authoritatively. I readily accept the offer of individuals or groups to pray for me, but unless I know them and am in a subordinate relationship with them, I draw a line at accepting this additional gesture.

Motives in the exercise of gifts are a big deal. The "cool factor" can be a problem if the prestige of the gift overshadows the purpose of the gift. Do I love God or what He gives me? The gifts are not about ownership or entitlement; they are about stewardship, service, and building up the body. Hold it all lightly. This also applies to the core of leadership. We don't own the church. I make it a practice to regularly pray for my successor. All of this falls under the significant point that in deliverance ministry, as in all authentic ministries, humility empowers proper gift practices.

Asking God for permission/direction in using gifts should be applied primarily to power gifts. This is strictly about when you are going to deal with a demon or a healing issue or such. Speaking into someone else's life by word of knowledge or wisdom is best done by permission, particularly in cases where the person might not be open to the message. If they have agreed to at least listen to a word offered in humility, the setting is more likely to yield agreement to the message.

Gift of Faith[7]
If you find you believe that when God says He's going to do something, He's going to do it, you may well have this gift. In deliverance ministry, those with the gift of faith pump oxygen into the room. Because they are so focused on what God is doing and confidently anticipating what God will do, they help keep the practitioners of other gifts from the detours and distractions that the demonic will try to create. When discouragement and fatigue become factors, those with the gift of faith spur the rest of us to keep going.

Gift of Miracles[8]
A miracle is an exercise of authority over the demonic and authority over nature. The gift of miracles is the ability to cast out demons on a regular, ongoing spiritual gift basis, and must be part of your deliverance ministry.

This gift is not the gift of healing. Paul separates them in 1 Corinthians 12. Healing refers to physical healing (and "inner healing" according to Charles Kraft—more on healing a little later). But the gift of miracles includes altering natural laws or overruling the demonic.

Gift of Prophecy[9]
With regard to this gift, I recommend you read Wayne Grudem's *Systematic Theology* and his section on why prophecy is *not* teaching. Conservative churches have often claimed that teaching and prophecy are the same. Grudem unpacks the biblical basis for seeing prophecy as exceptional and different from teaching/preaching. Some (not all) Old Testament prophets were also inspired by God to record Scripture. A New Testament prophet is the one who gives an utterance for the community or an individual. It is a foretelling, but must be tested. It is presented as a word from God that must conform to the Word of God. So, in the book of Acts, Agabus the prophet warned Paul about what would happen if he went to Jerusalem and others urged him not to go. The prophecy was true; their interpretation of its significance wasn't. Between the Old and New Testaments, the equivalent "Thus says the Lord" authority passed from prophets to the apostles. The gifting of prophecy took on a more immediate, practical, limited role in the early church. But it was there and an important aspect of life in the body.

Hearing from God in this way can have a significant impact on a local church. It emphasizes the reality of God's interest, involvement, and direction in the immediate situation. This kind of prophetic input is part of the larger spiritual view that takes all the gifts of the Holy Spirit seriously. When you make the supernatural a normal part of church life, people can handle prophecy and the other gifts much better.

The question of logistics immediately shows up when we start talking about releasing and exercising the gifts in the local church. Conservative believers have often assumed that the danger with gifts is the loss of order. Paul seems to indicate this in 1 Corinthians 14 when he lays down some guidelines for gifts used in a congregational setting. Note that the biblical handling of gift exercise is not to worry about their misuse as a reason to forbid them, but concern for disorder as a reason to exercise them wisely. But can a gift like prophecy be exercised in a large church setting such as what we have at Sanctus Church? We didn't base our approach on the assumption that if it seems difficult or complicated we shouldn't do it, but rather on the confidence that God would show us ways to do it that would overcome the complications while allowing the gifts to have their intended effect.

In the case of prophecy, we have employed a cell phone. We call it the prophecy phone. Those with the gift of prophecy don't interrupt the sermon or teaching; they text the word they have received from the Lord to the dedicated prophecy phone number. We invite people to do this in each service, encouraging those who think they have received a picture or word from the Lord to text it in. Those texts will be "tested" by discernment and shared with the congregation if they are judged appropriate. We are not assuming that anyone who claims to have this gift or any prophecy that is submitted is automatically from the Lord. Those with the gift of discernment are evaluating on behalf of the church. One of the amazing things that happens (this is when the hair on the back of your neck rises just a little) is when several texts come in from various parts of the congregation and they have an uncanny way of being almost identical or in close harmony with one another when there has been no collusion or awareness ahead of time of the way the word would confirm the message of the day or encourage the particular direction being discussed in the teaching. Scriptures are sometimes texted in that have a direct comment on something that happens later in the service, as God affirms what He is doing by His Word ahead of time.

When this becomes normative in worship, the supernatural nature of the supernatural takes on a worship-encouraging tone rather than a fear-inducing effect. The God who could write on the wall of pagan banquet hall or thunder His Word from a mountaintop can easily inspire two or three of His gifted servants to share an immediate thought via text. God draws near in this way and His people welcome and worship Him.

One of the ways we have discovered that the gift of prophecy contributes to deliverance ministry is in seeing and describing the positive outcome of God's freeing work in someone's life. We prepare a letter of encouragement in advance of the session with a person and give it to them afterward. Those with the gift of prophecy and discernment exercise their gifting when writing that letter. Then, during the session, words or pictures of encouragement often come through prophetic gifting that speak powerfully and uniquely into the lives of those who have come for deliverance.

Gifts of Tongues/Interpretation[10]

Some of us on the deliverance teams have this gift as part of our overall gifting, and when it has been used we have generally found it very effective as long as there's a translation. When an interpretation is given, it is often a direct rebuke to the demonic causing it to go.

We recognize that Paul was a practitioner of private speaking and singing in tongues, so we encourage that exercise of the gift. But if this gift is used in public and there's no translator it must be shut down. The body is not edified if it's not interpreted because we don't know what the Spirit is saying. We base our practice per Paul, allowing two or three tongues to be spoken and then asking the question: "Is there a translator/interpreter among the people?" If not, we simply move on.

Conservative people need to learn grace when it comes to the more "out there" gifts. We have to provide environments where people can use their gifts. We have simply not found the deliverance setting to be such an environment. But we have welcomed the ordered use of interpreted tongues in worship.

Our early efforts at gift inclusion did not immediately include tongues. But we knew we needed to address the presence of this gift publicly. Plus, we were very aware that the question or availability of interpretation is often not answered until after the message in tongues is spoken. There may be several people with the interpretive gift in the room but not all of them necessarily understand a tongue that is spoken. With these challenges in mind, we not only taught about this particular gift, but during a young adult service (which was more attitudinal than age specific), I felt a strong sense that someone in the congregation was supposed to speak in tongues. As the service was ending I spoke to the group and asked if there was someone who felt they might have an expression of the gift of tongues. A young woman sheepishly raised her hand. I instructed her to stand and speak nice and loud so everyone could hear. We were about to do something for the first time and not everyone in the room was entirely sure this was a good idea. But she stood and spoke for about 20 seconds, then sat down. I then asked if there was anyone in the congregation that found they understood what had been said. Several raised their hands. They were as amazed as the rest of us! They represented a range of ages and both genders.

But rather than ask them to say what they had heard, we instead invited them to take a moment to write down the message they understood or the picture they had seen described. We then collected those notes and read them at the front. Another somewhat hair-raising moment occurred when we realized that these separated people had heard the same message though they had not conferred before writing them down. On top of this, the message was clearly something we as a church needed to hear from the Lord at that moment.

We were able to confirm in this way that this gift could be exercised effectively in our setting. Our concern was to avoid the situation found in many churches where tongues are regularly heard yet seldom interpreted, causing almost inevitable confusion and even sense of spiritual superiority on the part of those who speak and those who can't understand, though we are convinced the public use of this gift, like all the gifts, is for the edification of the body at large.

If programs aren't the place of authority and office isn't the only place of authority and the power of the Holy Spirit is most demonstrated in gifts, this is what we need to reach a post-Christian country. In the meantime, we need to step up the practice of grace among ourselves as we discover the usage of gifts. We see this in abundance with some gifts and lacking with others. If I preach a poor sermon, my gifting in the area of teaching isn't immediately called into question. But if a tongue is spoken and not interpreted, the speaker can easily be treated as an instrument of Satan rather than a brother or sister who had a bad day. Let's make sure to distribute grace all around when it comes to the practice of the spiritual gifts.

This grace can begin with teaching from the pulpit on all the gifts, acknowledging they are present in the room even if some of those who have them don't realize it yet. The challenge in the church is to do this kind of ministry and experiment while also being safe and healthy. You will need to gently call out gifts. What do you think would happen if next Sunday at your church the pastor said, during his message, "By the way, I need to meet with all of you who regularly see demons. No, you're not in any trouble. But I need to have a conversation with you in my office later today." Don't you think it would have some kind of effect if ten or twelve people showed up? We find that new believers and even some who have been following Jesus for years have been led to think the evidence of their gifts is a weird problem or weakness rather than a clue about God's special purposes in their lives.

The evidence of gifts is not just fruit, it's also faithfulness. Your use of the gifts will deepen your relationship with God and it will be evidenced.

CHAPTER 16
THE CHALLENGE OF DEMONIC ACCESS

While we are discussing the complex nature of the symptoms of demonization and parallel but perhaps unrelated physical or mental issues, we need to also discuss what we have discovered about demonic access to someone's life. How does it enter a human being or an environment? Whether the demonic is wanted or the suffering fair is often irrelevant to the reality of the demonic presence. According to the Scriptures and our observed experiences, there are five ways the demonic gain entrance into someone's life:[1]

1) Occultism (this can take on many variations depending on culture), whether formal or informal. If you participate directly in occultic practices, you are opening yourself (and perhaps others) to demonic influence. Dabbling in satanic rituals, studies, and activities swings wide a door for evil in your life. Practicing divination (accessing information from a source other than God) imprints a demonic foothold. Ouija boards, tarot cards, and similar items—though advertised as harmless games—invite demonic influence. Seeking knowledge or exercising power that does not come from Scripture or from Jesus comes from a source that seeks to ultimately enslave and destroy you. More recently, the internet has vastly enlarged the contact points between "surfers" and demonic forces.

2) False faith and false religion. If you worship other gods, you are worshipping the demonic. Our movement is exclusive. There is no path to heaven other than Jesus Christ. The Biblical warnings against idolatry not only cover the confused worship of the creature rather than the Creator, they also reveal that behind the mute, deaf, and lifeless idols are often demonic powers at work. The same is true of false religious leaders, who may insist their system isn't religious because it is humanistic or atheistic, but the power they exhibit isn't from God. Secret societies, even ones that claim superficial allegiance to Christianity, include deeper evidence that they are exposing members to the demonic.

3) Sexual encounters. In the Greek version of the Old Testament, one phrase in Genesis 2:24 *"and the two shall become one flesh"* reads they will share one psyche. There is a bonding to others. Our soul gets torn when we do something sexually that God forbids. Paul says that when you sin sexually, you sin against your own body. Every time you mess around outside of marriage you are creating openings and opportunities for the demonic to act or invade.

4) Trauma. Although it's not scripturally referred to, when someone has gone through extreme trauma, it might be a door. When you are dealing with people who have been really hurt, they're trying to work out their trauma. It's like a cut that, if not treated, can be infested with bacteria (demonic). Trauma can also affect a person like the loss or lowering of immune systems to the point of danger to health, including spiritual health. The demonic have no reason to fight fair, and the reality of spiritual warfare is that a wounded soldier is vulnerable to further injury in other ways. Again, you must be gentle and careful. Much of the time the people we are praying with are the victims and yet the demonic have used this unwanted situation to gain access. This is not fair, this is not just, this is not right, but this is a real war and fairness and rules are out the window. The great news is that Jesus is the Good Shepherd, God is the good Father, the Holy Spirit is the Comforter and can take evil and replace it with good.

5) Habitual sin. Paul talks about the way we handle anger and the danger of "giving the devil a foothold" in us. Established patterns of sin are an open door for the demonic to wreak havoc in other areas (again, read Ephesians 4).

The inclusion of forgiveness is essential in deliverance. Note how many of the "doorways" above involve others. Forgiveness is not about forgetting; it's about showing mercy toward someone who deserves not to be forgiven. It's the deliberate and costly choice to not use someone's sin against them. It's saying to Jesus, "I am not able to forgive the person right now, but I am willing to start the process toward it."

The process of confession, repentance, healing, and forgiveness is how we stand when the day of evil comes. Spiritual conflict causes us to wade deeply into the brokenness of the human condition.

GENERATIONAL CURSES

The matter of generational curses or influences can often be seen in a deliverance setting. We are not islands. We often assume a disconnect between generations and claim a personal autonomy unaffected by what others in our family may have done. This makes us even more vulnerable to previous demonic access. Sins of parents are visited on succeeding generations. As an example, we have found instances in which a grandmother was a witch who welcomed the demonic into her own life and into her family, who are experiencing the ongoing effects years after she died. The Bible is written to communities first and individuals second. The principles are always communal. You can and should choose to pray for the doorways and strongholds of the demonic to close if you are a first generation Christian in your family.

In the early days of exploring deliverance ministry in our church, I received a call from an elder who asked me to come to his house because there were weird things going on that he suspected were demonic. I was still the youth pastor at the time, but eager to engage. As we toured the house, praying, the wife—who happened to be from Burma—became increasingly distraught and finally collapsed. I realized the problem wasn't with the house; it was with the wife. I had known her for years as a baptized believer with a radical conversion, and I had had no indication of demonization, yet at the name of Jesus in her home she reacted strongly. Here she was, an elder's wife, in community, active in ministry in the church. The team returned to the church with her and we began the deliverance process as we had developed it then. It wasn't long before her face changed and a demon manifested itself and said, "I own her! And you can't have her!"

We continued to pray. I quoted Ephesians 1 and inserted her name to personalize that Scripture. The demon argued forcefully: "I'm the household god. I've been in her family for a thousand generations. I have been invited by this family. I have a right to be here."

I responded with, "You may have rights to the rest of her family, but this woman is now owned by Jesus Christ. So, who wins? You or Jesus?" With an angry admission of defeat, the demon left. She was free.

On another occasion, when there was no ethnic background involved, we were praying with a woman in whose life there was a pattern of sin. As we prayed, this thing altered her face as it also said, "I own her!" Our preparations with her had revealed the sin patterns, so I said, "You might still have rights to the rest of the family (who were not believers), but you no longer have rights to this woman. She belongs to Jesus." It left. Unfortunately, it remained in evidence among her family. Her story illustrates a point we made earlier that possession (ownership) is positional; demonization is not. It may claim ownership, but its claims have been made null and void by Jesus. Her story also points out that in many cases when the gospel impacts a family, there is a spiritual turf war for the first generation.

All five inception points listed above can provide entry into family systems, not just individuals. In our deliverance model, one of the consistent components addresses the issue of generational sin and asks Jesus to shut that down, giving the person language to pray a break with that past and closing of all doors, known or unknown that would allow that demonic influence to continue. When we are dealing directly with the demonic, we insist they look back to their point of arrival and admit that Jesus is shutting down whatever rights they have had to that life.

As a church, we know we are playing catch-up with a number of people whose backgrounds have perhaps made them (and therefore the church at large) vulnerable to demonic influence from the past. We are actively encouraging people to address these rights and influences in community, taking authority over them through Jesus and the power of the Spirit.

TERRITORIAL SPIRITS

Over the last few years, a significant international mission movement called Lausanne has brought to light a much needed spiritual warfare component to the modern missions tactics and philosophy. Launched by Billy Graham and John R.W. Stott, the association produces the latest, clearest thinking on a wide range of issues from a biblical, evangelical perspective, demonstrating the mind of the global church intent on carrying out the Great Commission. In 2000, their scheduled gathering focused on the topic of spiritual conflict. Here were evangelicals from all over the world meeting to hear and discuss biblical studies and research done to address this major ongoing challenge to the spread of the Gospel. In many ways, this was a watershed moment regarding a discussion within the global church for almost half a century about the subject of territorial spirits.

What emerged was a fierce debate over the existence of these beings. Some say there is no scriptural basis for them and that it's unbiblical to suggest they exist. Others say it's absolutely true and biblically demonstrable.

So, what is meant by the term *territorial spirits*? These are described as evil beings that have authority or permission to function geographically. For example, a spirit may be over Thailand—that is, it owns or exerts some kind of spiritual control over Thailand. The domain of these spirits may be limited to families, clans, and small people groups or large geographical locations. Among the reasons given for this kind of demonic control are such matters as rights, grounds, acts, privileges, or worship. Any of these ways of ceding may be traced to the distant or recent past or even present choices.

The recurring issue for missionaries and missiologists is the troubling observation that some areas and some ethnic groups seem very open to the Gospel while other groups or areas seem hardened, resistant, and even hostile to the Gospel. What can explain this persistent phenomenon? Are we seeing glimpses or evidence of a level of conflict and power above our pay grade or "up there" that we can only see and feel in part now?

As Christians, our answers to these questions must begin with the Bible rather than just experience. What, if any, evidence is there in the Scriptures for territorial spirits? And if they do exist, so what? How does their existence impact our lives and ministry? Those who are convinced of the biblically de-monstrable territorial spirits point to four primary passages in Scripture. The NIV version of Deuteronomy 32:8 says, *"When the Most High gave the nations their inheritance, when he divided all mankind, he set up boundaries for the peoples accord-ing to the number of the sons of Israel."* A text note mentions, however, that the Masoretic text ancient interpretation translates the inheritance as "for the sons of God," a term used in Genesis before the flood to report the mating be-tween human beings and these *"sons of God"* (Genesis 6:2) and early in Job (1:6 and 2:1) that includes Satan. The implication is that beings of great power ac-tually had an allotment or inheritance when God divided up humanity. The further implication is that even though fallen, these beings retained their in-heritance or sphere of influence here on earth.

In Daniel 10, we find Daniel praying and fasting and after twenty-one days the archangel Michael comes. Michael explains he was immediately dis-patched in answer to Daniel's prayers, but couldn't get to him because he was sidetracked by a thing called the Prince of Persia in the heavenlies and had to fight to get through. Then Michael said he had to go and fight the Prince of Greece. The terms used by Michael suggest territorial language assigned to beings. If those are spiritual beings, they do have an authority over a region, a movement, or a group.

The third text stream that seems to indicate territorial spirits are the references to the gods of the nations throughout the Old Testament. Idols and grotesque symbols were fashioned by craftsmen who produced lifeless forms but were quite possibly inspired by these demonic beings. The picture suggests a pattern of territorialism connected to nationality.

We find a fourth example in Legion, the name used by the demonic Jesus confronted and allowed to enter the herd of pigs (Matthew 8:28-34; Mark 5:1-20; Luke 8:26-39). He (they) begged to stay in the area. It likely "owned" the territory, but of course had to get permission from Jesus Christ.

These examples seem to indicate that a cosmic conflict is going on "up there," which affects us in various ways but over which we have little con-trol. Now, some scholars say that if there are territorial spirits, the local church should map out what the history of the city or territory is and repent on behalf of that community because they are part of it. This is called *identifica-tional repentance.*[2] Now, understanding the spiritual history of your neighbour-hood is a good idea, but you can't repent for someone else. And while the limited biblical passages do indicate conflict in spiritual realms, elaborate strat-egies for participating in that conflict are probably not a wise investment of effort when we have plenty of challenges in every area in our own realm. To use our own situation as an example, there are sincere and committed groups in the Toronto area who are convinced that territorial spirits are having a sig-nificant effect in preventing the spread of the Gospel. Their plan is to gather large groups of Christians to pray and command these spirits to leave Toronto. But there is little evidence that the Holy Spirit Himself is directing or encouraging these efforts.

These "spiritual military ventures" create needless casualties when all sorts of Christians are dealing with demons they don't have permission to deal with. This is an "above my pay grade" moment. Make very sure you have a "yes" from the Holy Spirit before proceeding to engage the demonic. Remember, Jesus shows us the pattern of using power gifts right: He only did what the Father told Him to do.

The way in which to weaken a territorial spirit is not through direct attack but through carrying out God's standing orders about evangelism, repentance (of God's people), and God-given revival. Faced with spiritual resistance, there must be redoubling of prayer for God's intervention and guidance rather than commanding the demonic to leave. Of course, Jesus can move pastors and leaders in a certain place to take direct spiritual action, but care should be taken that this is not merely a human plan of action. The biblical process to claim a city is modeled in Acts 19. It is through conversion. In our day, I think of the strategy plan by Tim Keller called "Tipping Point"[3] in which he aims to increase the convert rate in Manhattan to 15% of the population because he is convinced that is the point at which societal change becomes significant.

In 1 Thessalonians 2:18, Paul reported he was delayed by the enemy in getting to the people. The apostle's response to that satanic resistance is recorded in 1 Thessalonians 3:11, *"May God our Father and the Lord Jesus Christ clear the way for us to come to you."* He invoked the Trinity. When he faced a blockage "above his pay grade," he turned matters over to God. Many preach this passage without referencing the context for Paul's prayer, which was a direct blocking by Satan.

In our deliverance ministry, there have been multiple times where we have known what God wanted us to do, but we couldn't do it. Following Paul's example, when we have sensed Satan hindering the work, we have prayed 1 Thessalonians 3:11. Satan can and does block the work of God, but he is not stronger than God and ultimately can't stop God's will, as he also answers to God. This is not to say that humanly we won't face challenges or potential danger in carrying out the will of Christ. The account of Paul's ministry in Ephesus demonstrates the power of the Gospel to undermine existing spiritual resistance. So many were converted and the church grew at such a rate that people were getting rid of scrolls and other items related to pagan worship.

In the book of Jude, when Michael the archangel is fighting Satan, even he doesn't do it in his own strength; he calls upon the name of the Lord.

Given all that we have studied and experienced, our current stance when it comes to territorial spirits is to be open to acknowledging their insidious work, but cautious about seeking to confront them directly. We don't take a "name it and claim it" approach, but also don't sit in defeat, counting on God to clear a way for us.

On our list of things to regularly do in ministry, we have added another "check box" when we are trying to reach a neighbourhood. We ask God for revelation regarding what areas to focus on. For example, is this a geographical location where there's a lot of new age stuff or a lot of crime/murder? Part of the hostile environment may be due to a territorial spirit. We are seeking to have a regular, vigilant worldview—continually having people pray, asking for divine help. But we definitely recognize this as an area "where angels fear to tread," so we guard against any actions that would assume authority that doesn't come with God's permission. Roles and duties are challenging enough down here; up there, we are much more likely to be functioning "above our pay grade." Let's take our proper place in God's plans and purposes, willing to see His will done in and through our lives.

THE CRUCIAL ISSUE OF AUTHORITY

So, what is our "pay grade"? Where do we fit and what are our responsibilities in the kingdom of God? What about the large matter of authority, particularly as it applies to the ministry of deliverance? The kingdom of darkness is all about legalism, territory, and permission. Remember the sobering scene in the beginning of the book of Job when Satan basically dares God to give him permission to test Job. Within the overall absolute sovereignty of God there are delegated or allowed areas of authority that operate even when God Himself is not openly acknowledged. On our side, God has established four groupings of biblical authority:[4]

1) Common Authority (Ephesians 2): Given to all believers since we are seated with Christ in the heavenlies. We are forgiven, we can resist the devil and he will flee from us (James 4:7), and we have protection (Ephesians 6—armour of God) to resist temptation and sin. This authority is available to all Christians. So can any Christian command evil to leave a person and situation with this authority? Yes! But should they do this all the time in a ministry context? Most likely, no. And this is so important. Almost every model presumes this is the deal, but there is so much more.

    As Protestants, we believe that the priesthood of all believers means we all have access to God. When the writer of Hebrews says, *"Let us then approach God's throne of grace with confidence, so that we may receive mercy and find grace to help us in our time of need"* (Hebrews 4:16), he is basing his call to us to exercise authority of approach on the effective ministry of our high priest, Jesus. We all have equal access to the top, but we don't all have the same offices in the structure of the kingdom. We haven't listened to the whole counsel of God if our common authority is the sole means by which we function in obedience to God. This is not to take away from the position each of us has in Christ to resist the devil and to move with confidence in every area of our spiritual lives. But there is more.

2) Office Authority: Those who have been given offices of leadership in the church—elders, deacons, pastors—also have delegated spiritual authority from Jesus. A spiritual position is given by God. There is an authority in office that is beyond common authority. It's interesting that in spite of the renewed interest in organizing local churches on the elder model, there remains a significant doubt on the part of elders that they have genuine spiritual authority, even though the demonic certainly recognize it. In our early experiences with deliverance, I was still the youth pastor in our church and though the senior pastor was supportive of what we were doing, he did not usually participate directly. But when he was present and the demonic manifested itself, it clearly recognized the senior pastor held the highest office authority in the room and was compelled to address him, though the rest of us were more directly involved in the effort.

3) Gift Authority (Romans 12): The Spirit of Christ gives you spiritual gifts. This includes guaranteed ongoing power in your gift area that other people (who do not have that gift) will not have. There will be a stronger spiritual "umph" when you do because the Holy Spirit will be present. When you work in your spiritual gifts, the well you draw from is not you. This helps with burnout and lack of joy. That is why all ministries should be led primarily out of gifts. It's as if your gift orientation is a river, but God determines the "bank size" of the river—He determines how much of the "river" He's giving you. Like a stream or a raging river, your gift has a volume to it. These are your "divine limits" or "anointing." The age of *The Prayer of Jabez* has affirmed our insatiable hunger for wider and bigger ministry when what we ought to be praying for is God's help in deepening the ministry He has actually intended for us, whatever its size. The only time the "umph" weakens is when you grieve the Spirit by ignoring or rejecting your gifting.

There is a correlation between the effectiveness of your gifts and your character. The priority in churches needs to be character first, not gifts. For example, humility is a necessary character trait in those who exercise their office authority and their gift authority well. Ripening of the fruit of the Spirit has a huge impact on the effectiveness of authority in every way. In *Convergence*, I spent an entire chapter teaching the core truth that spiritual character development is an essential component in the healthy use of gifts and authentic practice of the disciplines.

Let me also add a note here about the significance of balancing office and gift authority within the wider context of a churchwide ministry in which various gift combinations are put to use in the Spirit's work. I can give you a good example of the problems that can develop when the balance is off. As Sanctus Church moved into deliverance ministry, we were all discovering our gifting and realizing the demonic treat office authority seriously. It didn't take long for us to reach a point where my own gifting and role was actually creating a serious bottleneck and obstacle to the expansion of the ministry. First, I'm a Christian, so I have common authority with others. I'm also an elder, so I have been assigned office authority by other believers. Further, the Holy Spirit, in order to glorify the Father and Jesus, has gifted me in the areas of miracles, discernment, and words of knowledge (the lighter side of my Reformed self would say I was predestined for deliverance ministry). But my use of these gifts (words of knowledge, discernment, and miracles) in the fledgling Sanctus Church efforts became a problem.

Yes, we had a team in place, but in practice, this is what would happen. We would meet with someone who reported being demonized. After the opening prayer, I would immediately verbally assess the situation. I could see the demons and I would name them off, noting their relative strengths. I often knew when and how they gained entrance to that person's life. As I made my report to the group, they would take notes for use in our releasing prayer time. When I was done, we prayed, dealt with the demons, and called the session done.

In one sense that was effective, and I was using the gifts God's Spirit gave me, although at the time I assumed I was primarily exercising one gift— discernment. But I was also functioning as a self-contained team. Others participated in prayer, but many others who had overlapping gift combinations with mine were not exercising their gifts. I was inadvertently disempowering others in our church. We weren't able to solve this problem until we began to shape multiple teams composed of giftings that did not require me to be present. We discovered that when I was present, the demons would only talk to me because I was the perceived authority. In our early efforts to remedy the situation, I had to keep reminding people on the team that they had authority to speak to the demons; they didn't have to speak through me. We had to learn how to recognize who was the designated authority in the room, because the demonic certainly knew.

We now recognize that there are different levels of authority that affect the course of deliverance. And bringing a team with various gifts into that authority setting sometimes takes more time to function effectively. But the results are the same—God's Spirit will use the gifts He has given, through the people to whom He has given them, to do His work in freeing people from the demonic. But again, the reality of authority differences has been a significant part of our learning curve. We had to work through our respectful disagreement with someone like Charles Kraft, who bases his system on common authority of the believer and resists acknowledging other types of authority or the significance of gift orientation in the process.

I'm summarizing a series of discoveries that actually took us the better part of two decades to figure out. We've had several complete re-starts along the way when things seemed to spiral out of control. All the setbacks, counterattacks, and false victories that are part of warfare we have experienced in this ministry, along with amazing, God-given effectiveness.

4) Marital Authority: As was established pre-fall, the created order has man serving as the spiritual protector of his wife. Again, there is so much to this and I know many reading this will hold very different views on women in ministry. No matter what theological view you hold on whether women can lead in the church, Scripture is clear that husbands have spiritual authority in the home and can take authority to stand and protect. There is a God given spiritual power for husbands to stand in the gap for their families—to pray for and over wife and kids if they have them. The demonic do recognize this and we should too. These prayers should be empowering, loving, and faithfully done.

CHAPTER 17
OUR UNFOLDING MODEL

From our collective almost two decades of experience together, with the significant influences covered in the last chapter, here now is the hybrid matrix we currently use. We call the ministry and process within Sanctus Church "Restoration Prayer." We chose this name to avoid the many pitfalls that come with words like exorcism, deliverance, dealing with demons, and the like. This form of crisis prayer can have up to four steps. These steps, especially the three types of prayer, create an environment where we have found a person is given a holistic answer to their inner battles, followed by significant support through clinical counseling.

The process (which, as you will see, doesn't necessarily happen in this order) is "Intake & Inventory," "Listening Prayer," "Renouncing Prayer," "Releasing Prayer," and follow-up support. This process can happen within a day, but is usually done over a few weeks. The reason I have included this step-by-step outline is simple. Not only is this our actual model, but these also represent the answers to questions I asked for years. And many with whom I have talked have echoed these same sentiments.

Below is a very pragmatic overview of how we do this ministry. This chapter is meant to flesh out Sanctus Church's experience and practice, and then make recommendations in a logical sequence so others might implement this within another context. But again, I would caution against any sense of "plug and play" as if our matrix could be lifted as a whole and dropped into another situation without a full understanding of how we arrived at each component and without a careful reason for including it and adjusting it for a different setting. In your setting, deliverance may take on significantly different aspects than we have discovered or practice in ours. We encourage you to adapt what you see in our systems, but more importantly to continually seek God's guidance while recognizing that you will make mistakes and have to learn as you go. Never forget you are stepping up to be a partner with God in His work of deliverance, not the other way around.

STEP ONE: STARTING THE PROCESS
How does one get on the deliverance team's radar? The people who think there could be an issue with the demonic tend to be referred to us by pastors,

those having gone through the process themselves, elders, local counseling centers, and other ministry leaders within the faith community. I should note here that we tend not to take people from other churches unless they are leaders within those faith communities, or accompanied by leaders within those faith communities. Our priority remains to minister to those within our own sphere of influence, and in the past our own wait times have precluded us from the ability to extend this ministry to others. These are two of the worst and most troubling parts of this ministry: the need for more churches to struggle with this type of kingdom work and the need for networking between these types of ministries.

Now when someone is referred and comes forward, the process follows the path outlined below. The person applies for the process by self-identifying to the administrator of the ministry, currently through our website. The coordinator contacts the participant for an initial intake interview to better understand the participant's expectations and goals, as well as to confirm that the candidate is in fact a Christian. This is an opportunity to emphasize that this is just one part of their greater discipleship journey. The coordinator gives him or her the comprehensive and confidential "Participant Inventory," which includes the consent form (a waiver they must sign recognizing they are willingly participating and that this is not a clinical process). They are asked to complete the two forms and encouraged to begin going through Neil Anderson's *The Bondage Breaker* video series while they wait. This is to help clarify their level of confidence in the process we are offering and their personal beliefs about the demonic. We do not chase the participants for their completed inventories, and they only get added to our active waiting list once they have submitted their forms.

This phase of the plan used to take as long as a year while our team had limited capacity. This often appeared to observers (and some participants) like a long timeline when people report they are desperate. But we had to make the hard decision to slow down the process in order to preserve several objectives: 1) to increase the likelihood that we were dealing with genuine needs (we westerners have a built-in bias toward quick answers, which rarely satisfy), 2) give the participants enough time to engage with their problems seriously, and 3) preserve the health and well-being of the team since we were being swamped by "emergency demands" that wore us out while too often producing "quick fixes" that didn't produce lasting results. It helps to remind people that while we usually have a pastor involved in this process, the bulk of the ministry is carried out by volunteers exercising their spiritual gifts.

Our handouts, the confidential Participant Inventory, and the consent form are a mishmash compiled from interviews, books, and seminars we have attended. We have produced several versions of these two forms over an eight year period. This is what we now consider the paper discernment process—understanding that rights, grounds, access, and privileges can come from history, sin, family, emotional experiences, etc. Therefore, we move the person through a series of questions to find where doors could have been opened. The consent form is devoid of clinical language and outlines what the goal of the ministry is, what will happen, and what they can expect in the broadest sense.

STEP TWO: LISTENING PRAYER

Once the coordinator collects the completed forms, the participant is added to the active waiting list. The prayer team meets once a month on a Saturday morning to discern over the upcoming participants and to take notes. This happens without the participants present. What we are actually doing on those Saturday mornings is an ancient practice called "Listening Prayer," which basically means an extended time of silence before God with the expectation that He will guide. Listening prayer for us has become our second act of discernment, which is more Spirit-led, more gift-oriented, and centers on listening rather than information gathering through an inventory or interview. It is one of the most important and critical tasks we do as a ministry. This second discernment process acts as a check and balance to ensure that we are really hearing from the Lord, and it allows us to see God at work. Fundamentally, this applies our view that gifts are needed to do the ministry, but it is spiritual disciplines (such as silence and solitude) that provide the environment for God to speak, just like Jesus modeled time and time again.

There are some key spiritual actions we do to prepare before we pray. We take time to confess sin to God. We pray the armour of God on each other. We pray over the space—asking for the Light of Christ, the presence of Jesus through His Spirit, and that angels would be released to assist us by bringing answered prayer, fighting on our behalf, and anything else that God would ordain. We take authority over the place, command the kingdom of darkness to leave, and forbid them to hear, listen, or interfere in this time. We also ask for the session, that the team be isolated and protected from any other fight over the church, the area, or our families. Prayers for the protection of our families and church are also included since our experience has taught us that the enemy tends to cause issues outside the group to distract or shut down this prayer time. We also take time to praise God, read Scripture, and ask for the filling of the Holy Spirit. Time and time again we give back our gifts to God, acknowledging they are from Him and praying that our unity, purity, and relationships would be supported. These sessions tend to last for an hour and a half to two hours.

At this point, the team only knows the gender of the participant (e.g. male #2, female #3). The heart of our praying is: "Jesus, what can you tell us about this person that will help us see them through this need." During the prayer time there is no talking, but team members take notes of what they are given during the silence. This might include Scriptures, pictures, and some might see the demonic influence. After this time, the team shares their notes with one another. Often there are distinct themes that emerge. For example, several team members might be given the word "abuse." All of this information is compiled. On occasion, a member will actually receive an extended, but quite pointed message of encouragement that is recorded in letter form to be given to the participant later as a demonstration of God's participation in the effort even in the preparation stages. The gift makeup of our teams and the checklists we use help us keep in mind that the presenting needs of the participant are not necessarily demonic. Part of the discernment process (and this also occurs even as the participant is filling out the forms) seeks to identify what other factors might be causing the problems.

I cannot stress enough the importance of listening prayer. For us, this becomes a key check and balance and teaches us that our reliance is on God and not ourselves. Though we have the person's sheets with all the information, we do not ever open or look at them at this time. The coordinator knows the person's name, but the team is only given their gender. The last prayer we say before becoming quiet is that nothing we hear would be from us, the demonic, or any other source but God's Spirit. After the above prayers are uttered and we have asked for God's help, we go silent and listen for the Lord. For several minutes each person reads Scripture, prays, and writes notes.

Now different people receive information through different means. Many will get Scriptures for the person or about the situation. Others get names of the demonic, sin, struggles, or experiences. The Lord tends to show me in detail the demonic, visually, with names or purposes, color, place, or attachments. Words, images, names, and statements are all considered and are tested by the group. At the end of the listening session, we will go around the circle, share all our notes, and see what common themes there are. These are all tracked and added by the coordinator to the participant's package (which already includes the inventory).

The inventory is still not consulted at this time in any way. Only those leading the prayer sessions with the participants compare the listening notes to the inventory, to really see if the issues brought forward are demonic in some form and to see where there might be issues with rights, grounds, access, and privileges in the person's life. Also, it acts to confirm what is in the inventory, but also what may have been left out knowingly or unknowingly and where the process needs to go. We have also found that this is a powerful way to help the person see God's hand at work. When appropriate, we will share with the participant—either fully or in part—the insights pre-session and post-session from both venues of discernment, so they can see that things are not manipulated or constructed to appear as something more than it is.

This activity tends to give us a road map into seeing what is to be renounced, what experiences need healing, and what demonic beings must be confronted in time. The Lord gives us simple pictures or words like "Pride" or "Rage," or as specific as an image of a boy in a barn watching sexual acts that have scarred him for life. This real life example was left off the inventory by the person but was given to the team in prayer, providing key knowledge needed in that person's deliverance.

We operate under the assumption that there is something to stand against—whether the world, their flesh, or the enemy. Even when we have found that the demonic are not present in them at all, we will still have them go through the process of renouncing prayer, and then take the time to pray with them to stand in authority against whatever they are battling. Depending on what other factors are at play, we refer them to clinical or medical help. Let me state here and now that we always tell people that have been medically diagnosed to stay on their medications and to listen to the medical community.

The people included in this process are the Restoration Prayer team members. This is a great environment for growth and development for the team, especially since participants are not present. Those who serve on this prayer team tend to be people who are gifted and attuned, and thus able to help in this particular act. We have discovered through the encouragement of spiritual gifts and disciplines that some are actually proficient and gifted in certain kinds of prayer. It is also a helpful environment for introducing people to the discipline of listening prayer in their own lives, as well as a soft-entry to serving on the prayer team in general. There are no participants present and no confrontation happening, therefore it is an easier place to start for those who are new to serving.

At the end of the session we pray again for ourselves, the church, our families, and the person or persons in question. Then we give the person's journey over to God and head out to the rest of our day.

STEP THREE: RENOUNCING PRAYER

After our listening time, we move to the first prayer time called Renouncing Prayer. The participant joins for this step. The thinking behind this third step is the truth encounter model, which as mentioned, has deeply helped us. We have found it to be one of the best face-to-face starting points for all those seeking this type of help. This step moves them from their initial request for some kind of help, through the step of recognizing "I need help," to the significant point of declaring, "I'm not going to hide anymore. Good, bad, and ugly—my life is open." This prayer process could simply be described as confessing, receiving forgiveness, renouncing a sinful act or acts, and replacing it with God's Word and truth. Really, this is James 4 and 5:13-19 in action. One image used by a team member is that this act is like sweeping a floor clean before washing it. Kraft would place inner healing as the main act before confrontation, where we place more emphasis here.

One way of describing what occurs here is as a straightforward closing of every recognized door in their past life that may have allowed the demonic permission or territory in their lives. The approach is almost mechanical, going systematically through their checklists of sin and verbally acknowledging the wrongdoing, asking Jesus for forgiveness, and formally declaring that gateway into their life no longer open. This third step involves meeting with two to three prayer team members. Before the person enters the room, we take time to pray for them specifically. We pray about the clarity of their mind, their ability to renounce, and for their faith to be strengthened. Simply, we cry out for Jesus and His mercy on behalf of the person.

One of the most common matters we had to work out and that we are asked about over and over again involves the sequence that happens when the person arrives. We first introduce the team and thank the participant for coming, encourage them to relax, and explain that the team will be taking notes. We remind them that what is occurring is not a "you and us" but a "we," since, as believers, they have a role on the team even while they sit in the focus chair.

One huge barrier we face is that many who come are hoping this will be the silver bullet (no pun intended). Because of these common expectations, we explain every time that this process is not a "quick fix" and that they have a responsibility to begin to make choices and to walk in truth in order to maintain freedom. God wants them to be whole physically, emotionally, and spiritually. We also remind them up front that we will be making some additional referrals for them at the end of the process that will continue to help them on this healing journey. Below is the checklist and verbal questions we use to prepare them and support them in this James 4:7 process, adapted from many different sources. Also, as our church has become more global, new items that exist in one culture and not another are added to help.[1]

- Ask them for their verbal permission to proceed and obtain their full name—including middle and maiden names.

- Ask them to remove any sharp objects, including keys and water bottles.

- Explain this is not a magical process. Give the description of a long hallway with doors open on both sides. The Renouncing process is walking the hallway and closing each of the doors that may have given the enemy rights and grounds. We will be asking Jesus to seal each of the doors with His blood once they have been closed.

- In Old Testament times the renouncing process meant a person wanted to publicly disconnect from a contract or agreement. They would stand and shake the dust off their garments as a symbolic act that they were ridding themselves of an agreement or contract. Sometimes we may not even realize we have made an agreement, especially if it was passed down through our ancestors. Explain how they could have allowed evil in—the Biblical notion of how the demonic can enter from either family or personal history of sin. It's like when we legally break a contract or agreement with someone. We can apologize and be sorry but we need to legally break the contract to show the contract is over—and the door is shut.

- Ask for a brief history of their spiritual journey.

- Ask them to offer up a clear verbal statement confessing Jesus as Lord and have them ask Jesus to help them. Also, have them verbally affirm their salvation and baptism.

- Encourage them to dialogue with the team about any thoughts, feelings, colors, smells, sights, etc. Nothing is too weird.

- Ask them if there is anything they feel they need to share with the team before commencing.

- We offer up a prayer to prepare the room (protection, profession, Holy Spirit's guidance, and so on).

- Begin the Renouncing Process, working systematically through the checklist.

- We always use the person's full legal name when working through the process.

Throughout the session, we tend to write notes for ourselves or to pass to each other. We do this so as not to share inappropriate information with the person or to ask clarifying questions between team members. We compare the notes gathered from the earlier listening prayer time as well as the initial renouncing prayer time. If there are inconsistencies or gaps in confession, we seek clarification. We share all of this up front so the participant doesn't feel like they are in grade school again with things being said about them in any negative way or that they are being unfairly challenged. We also take time to explain the confidentiality of the process and reassure the participant that they have been courageous to pursue freedom. We take as much time as needed to encourage them to be completely honest and not fear being judged. Also, we have found that it helps to reassure the participant that each of the team members have been in their position and realize it may be uncomfortable. We try to keep the session to around two hours. We have found that sometimes there can be more than one session required.[2]

Now again, we have learned over time that the reason a matrix works better is it provides a framework for flexibility. As Neil Anderson argued, this kind of truth encounter can remove the demonic. And in our many prayer times, we have found that this time does deal with the issues of sin and sometimes it also removes the demonic. Again, referring back to Kraft's attachment scale, when the demonic are weak, they tend to leave. Also, if the person's faith commitment is in question, then it is here that it is established and some of the time, when the person truly comes to Christ, the demonic leave fully and the inner doors are sealed. In most cases, however, we are praying with people who give every sign of being authentic believers and who are also struggling with the demonic.

We do not remove the demonic at this time, but we do command them to hear the affirmations and confession of faith by the person they inhabit or are trying to assault.

STEP FOUR: RELEASING PRAYER
DEALING WITH THE DEMONIC DIRECTLY

Once all the doors have been closed and the roots exposed or pulled up, then we deal with the demonic directly. By this time, some of the demonic might have left and been sent to Jesus, but the more powerful tend to stay for the wrestling match (Ephesians 6). This step is really a power encounter where Jesus, working along with the local church, confronts demons that try to stay. Again, following Jesus' lead, I and others will take the time to make sure we have permission to deal with the demonic (that is, both the person's permission as well as Christ-given freedom to act) and when we have that, we proceed.[3]

We usually enlist four to five people to help during this process. Because there are so many different team members and participants on a given ministry night, we do our best to shape the teams in a way that honours the participant. However, we are continually amazed at how often the composition of a particular team fits the need in ways that indicate supernatural planning.

During the session, the seating is in a semicircle with a chair in front for the person to sit in. The person who will do the confronting of the demonic is visually directly in line with the person in the chair. In our case, when I do the confronting, which is most of the time, my personal intercessor will sit beside me and pray for me through the whole session. The others are there to listen and pray, led by the Spirit to use whatever spiritual gifts they have.

The confronter, who really coordinates the session, should know the gifts and personalities on the team and decide where people sit. Don't take this as weird or some controlling leadership power trip. It really helps out the team.

For example, one woman on the team can see the demonic, like myself, and I tend to place her in my line of sight so we can confirm what we see and make sure things are not being invented or letting the demonic flee or hide. It is a fluid process but we have found it key to working together. We also invite the person's counselor to be present and to sit amongst us. Their presence is very helpful every time they come.

The preparation process for the team is very important for us. We have taken time to flesh out what spiritual actions and disciplines must be done by team members before the person even comes. These acts are the same ones we do before the Listening and Renouncing Prayer sessions but there are some additions. In this case, many times we are called to fast, which is another dimension of this type of ministry that Jesus clearly referenced when He said, *"But this kind (of spirit) never comes out except by prayer and fasting"* (Matthew 17:21). When we gather, the team will do an overall review of what has been discerned in previous sessions, and what demonic are present. We also take time to ask if there is anything new the Lord has revealed. Many from this team have not been with us at other points during the process, so we take time to see, confirm, and listen one last time. It is amazing how things are confirmed or what other insights are given that help the person in this healing journey. Before the person comes in the room we again pray for them, the church, and our families.

We also ask the Father and the Son to send the Holy Spirit throughout the body of Christ to mobilize the saints to be raised up in prayer anywhere around the world if He chooses. This has so much power and really is the reverse of the Catholic call for support. We do not go to heaven for the saints' prayers but ask those saints who are living (which is all Christians) to be led and prompted to pray for us and for the release of this person. We are also prompted sometimes to ask for this during the session.

Once the person has arrived, we tend to once again, in an overall fashion, reinforce what was said at the Renouncing prayer. We focus on reminding them that this is not the magic bullet, but Jesus is real and is ready to get rid of the evil power dynamic at work within their life. We take time to share that some of the sinful struggles will be gone, but others will continue. But we have found that the energy and strength for the struggle will be drastically different. We talk about the power of Jesus and also the power of His gathered church and emphasize that what we are doing together is what the church is called to do—to be the body, to be the hands and feet of Jesus to each other and the world. We remind them to tell us about any sounds, colors, smells, thoughts, voices, and pictures they see. We assure them that we have heard much of it before and that we recognize the difference between them and the demonic.

Many times, we have found that for a period during the session the participant may not be able to speak, so before the session we instruct them just to raise their hand to indicate their inability. We also tell them that they are in Christ and have the same power we do, so they will also have to take authority during the process. Time and time again when the situation is very heavy and the person does not seem to be present at all, we ask them to pray inside or take authority inside. We lead them in prayers and God's power breaks the power of the enemy from the inside out. In moments like these, we are truly standing in a day of evil. Up front we will sometimes reference what they will have to do before we begin. We lastly ask them if they submit to the authority of the church and the leadership to help them. We make sure the person removes anything that could be dangerous to the team or themselves.

The most asked question we hear is about how the act of confrontation is expressed. By this point, we know the spirits, the holes, and the strongman, and we bind all of them to the strongman. Then we tend to separate them out in groups, cut them off from each other and cut them all off from the kingdom of darkness. When there is more than one, we tend to deal with them in clusters. We ask to see the head of sub-groups or the spirits under the strongman and then deal with them one group at a time. We bind all other spirits that work underneath each sub-leader, confront them and expel them, working back towards the strongman. We continually cut the others off from each other and the strongman, and we almost always deal with the strongman in the end. We also pray and say that they may not work together, share power, or imitate another demonic being. We ask for the light of Christ to command the demonic to hear every confession of the person and every command from us. We forbid them to manifest and ask for angelic support not just before the session, but also during the session.

Almost every time we deal with one key spirit or a group, we ask God to send angels to bind or strike them. We also at points have felt led to ask God to restrain the person so the demonic will not be able to hurt them. Praise God we learned that in His mercy, angels will hold down those needing help. I know it sounds weird, but I have seen it time and time again.

Sometimes we know the person is connected to a cosmic level spirit because of family, history, or travel for example, and we ask Jesus to stand in and cut them and us out from that fight. Never have we directly confronted a cosmic level spirit. There is one other team member who tends to be able to discern when the outside is trying to get involved in the inside and that is another key expression of discernment for us that really protects us.

We command the demonic to go to Jesus Christ of Nazareth, who sits at the right hand of the Father, being specific so they will not leave to another false Jesus, which we have seen more than once. Though not always, we do sometimes command them to take the person's face and eyes so we are dealing with them face-to-face. This can result in some acting out behaviors, but may also be something as simple as the person not blinking for minutes on end. We will command them to tell us when there seems to be rights still left and command them to tell us if there are other demons still present. Most of the time, we will make them confess who owns the person, what heaven is telling them, and what they must do. We also make them confess to whom they are going to face. That tends to be the end of them every time, with a little or a lot of resistance. We tell them they must leave our church or other churches that the person has been involved in. This is so important because demonic presence changes the very nature of that local church. Again, we are always being stretched and moved away from approaching this with such an individualistic worldview.

During this act of confrontation, we use Scripture, musical worship, prayer, and authoritative commands. Now these components are not used in a structured way most of the time, but every one of them is present at every session. Many times we are given Scripture, not only for the person but also to speak to the demonic. We have been led to stop and sing, which tends to expose or break the power of the demonic. Prayer, as mentioned, is used throughout the whole process. It is usually done quietly unless the situation calls for communal prayer. Since by this time, we have authority to deal with the enemy, we do take authority over them and command them to leave.

Another small observation that must be clarified is the passing of notes between those praying and also given to the one doing the confrontation. It cuts down on confusion for the person leading the process and is also done to respect the participant by not exposing them to inappropriate information. We will also take breaks to talk about the unfolding situation without the person present in order to decide what must happen next.

Sometimes we bring anointing oil and a cross to use as led, and we have also brought water and even communion elements. We tend to use the cross and make the demonic look upon the symbol of their defeat. Colossians 2:13-15 is read or quoted during this time and it brings all of heaven's truth home very quickly and clearly. I have already walked through our reasoning for the use of symbols in Chapter 12.

When the session is done, we pray that the Holy Spirit would fill the person and occupy all the places where the demonic had been expelled. We tend to anoint them with oil and give them any verses or passages the Lord had spoken to them. We inform them they will hear from us within four days by phone or email to follow-up on their experience. Also, sometimes two of our members are given a letter from God to the person. This is given as a parting gift of encouragement. We remind them of their role in freedom and also invite them to call any of us to further process and ask any questions about their experience. We offer any suggestions we have regarding next steps

231

they might take by way of spiritual direction, clinical counseling, joining a connect group, etc. We give them a forty-day Bible study entitled "How to Walk in Freedom," so they can continually see the biblical foundations of their experience. The emphasis here is on their part in our community and the expectations that they will continue involvement.

Notes are taken throughout this process and when we are done, we give them to the participant. We want to help them remember what occurred and the process by which they have been freed. They are often amazed in reading the notes of the listening prayer session and what God revealed to those gathered who did not know their name or the specifics of their situation. God does speak and give direction. God does make a way by preparing us to help in ways we would not have planned in our own thinking.

As I've tried to make clear, the gift of administration plays a crucial role in this entire process. This was one of our serious errors in the early years. And it showed up primarily in our preparation and in the lack of follow-through with participants. The spiritual health of our team members has been another major challenge for us. Over the years we have had to undergo a significant overhaul of our systems when things spiraled out of control. But God has been gracious and demonstrated He is continuing to receive glory even as we demonstrate our frail nature as His servants. Each time the failures have resulted in a clearer and more consistent pattern of convergence between God's work, spiritual disciplines, and the exercise of spiritual gifts.

After the person has left, we pray for the team, our families, and our drive home, but we also take time to make sure the church and room/rooms we have used are safe and clean. Below is a prayer from Francis MacNutt's book, *Deliverance from Evil Spirits,* that has become foundational to our exit process.

> Lord Jesus, thank You for sharing with us Your wonderful ministry of healing. Thank You for the healing we have seen and experienced today. But we realize that the sickness and evil we've encountered is more than our humanity can bear. So cleanse us of any sadness, negativity or despair we may have picked up. If this ministry has tempted us to anger, impatience or lust, cleanse us of those temptations and replace them with love, joy and peace. If any evil spirits have attached themselves to us or try to oppress us in any way, I command you, spirits of the kingdom of darkness to depart now and go straight to Jesus Christ for Him to deal with as He will. Come Holy Spirit, renew us, fill us anew with Your power, life and joy. Strengthen us where we have felt weak and clothe us with Your light. Fill us with life. And Lord Jesus, please send Your Holy angels to minister to us and our families, to guard and protect us from all sickness, harm and accidents

– and guard us on a safe trip home. We praise you now and forever, Father, Son and Holy Spirit.[4]

Jon Thompson

CONCLUSION

What a process this has been. These last 20 years have been a gift. That is, they have given me the space to think, to evaluate, and to record what we have been through. Being in full-time ministry, running a church and its staff, being a dad, a husband, and a friend, there would have been no way to do this without this formal process. So what have I learned, what is the future? Well, in brief, our story so far can be summed up in six ideas. First, I think that Scripture, church tradition, reason, and experience provide ample support for this type of ministry. It should be grounded in calling and spiritual gifting and is best suited for local churches. Fear, non-reflection, and bad experience can never become the reasons we do not help those in bondage.

Second, this whole ministry is not about human power, ego, or theological positioning—it is about mercy. I read on Twitter that someone said "you cannot talk about spiritual warfare without love." People's freedom and people's healing matter most. Like Luke 13, we cannot miss the awe of freedom nor the danger of becoming the religious leader who misses God's work because mercy and love were overridden by secondary views of theology.

Third, this process has enforced the need for charity and linguistic mutual understanding. As noted in my work, there is honest disagreement between many of us who do this ministry and even those who do not. What is paramount is our unity in Jesus Christ and His work on earth. We must have space to honestly disagree, but we also must love and honor each other. Directly connected to this is that I find there is a reduction of suspicion and anger when there is an understanding of language. This process has enforced the idea that we must work hard to understand what others are saying theologically or in practice. We all use different words or categories for the same idea or experience. If we can learn each other's language, much of the debate and misunderstanding could be avoided. Like on a Sunday morning after I preach, the conservative at Sanctus Church says, "That was a strong word today." And the charismatically inclined says, "You were so anointed today." They mean the same thing, but use different language. In this type of ministry, not only is a common script needed for the team but knowledge of other scripts is also needed. This will help with unity, training, and cross-denominational work.

Fourth, I have learned beyond all the models, theology, and history that character matters most. That is the fruit of the Spirit—godliness. One author outlines in simple form what a leader or ministry must think on as a team expands. He says there are three C's: character, competence, and chemistry. For over ten years, these three have worked themselves out among us and that is why this ministry is so strong. And these three are still helpful as we look at creating a recruiting process for new team members. First and foremost, the character issue is massive. He says,

> By this I mean that I need to have confidence in a person's walk with Jesus Christ. I need to know that they are committed to spiritual disciplines. I need to see evidence of honesty, teachability, humility, reliability, a healthy work ethic and willingness to be entreated.[1]

My response to this is, "Yes to all of that and more." Again, since we are working with the pain and sin of a person's history and dealing with evil itself, character is paramount. That is why Gary McIntosh's book, *Overcoming the Dark Side of Leadership*, is also very important. The shadow sides of the people serving, if not addressed, will set up a sinful and toxic environment that could lead to sin and abuse of those supporting others. The greatest danger is for the team members to fall themselves.

Character is also a bridge for dialogue for those who are skeptical. Many times people inside and outside of Sanctus Church have said, "I trust you as a teacher and a pastor but this other stuff, I just don't know." But they do add, "I am willing to talk because I know you." Character allows one to speak with authority, to walk through issues, to see misunderstanding become understanding. If more people with maturity, public affirmation, and known faithfulness would think and engage in this type of ministry, many more skeptics and dissenters would at least listen and engage. Character—the fruit of the Spirit—is the bridge, the ever-growing place that will protect the team from itself and the demonic. A person of character will never become a militant evangelist for this type of ministry either. Trust is won over time and sometimes never won, but the process matters as much as the results.

Fifth, not only do I feel that we are in good biblical standing all these years later after this reflection, but I have now come to the conclusion that the sign or power gifts are a needed reality in each local church. They tend to round out the other gifts and are a necessity for this type of ministry. I cannot find evidence of a model within Scripture without the use of gifts or team. This process has allowed me to find theological categories for my team and my own experiences. We are definitely "small c" charismatics working within a mixed environment. Again, I love the charismatic view of gifts because it does not demand the experience for all. It has a high view of sovereignty of the Spirit, it allows and wants a diversity of gifts, and it removes the un-biblical burden for all to participate in power or sign gifts. This ministry, as an example, provides the environment for these gifts to be used. It is no better or worse than any other ministry found within the local church. Gift-based ministry is more important than program-based ministry any day.

Lastly, I have come to the conclusion that in a post-Christian, de-Christian, post-modern world, this ministry must be a standard for all church-es in the West. Why? Because the West has access to and is becoming the world. The devil is not under every bush, but he is under every third bush. The work of evil in peoples' lives is rampant throughout the church, let alone society. We need to include this as a normal part of holiness in our churches. Though I think our matrix is a stronger and more balanced approach than others, I also understand it reflects the culture, the theology, and the place of our church. To deal with the violence, sex, and power abuses within culture and their spiritual implications, we must reflect and act as the first faith com-munities did. We must see that this is not a non-Christian only ministry but a both/and. Many more in our communities would be free if we included this as a part of ministry that would strengthen the local church and then would al-low more to be reached. As Jesus said in the Sermon on the Mount, we are the light of the world and the salt of the earth. This salt and light would be much more effective in many cases if this type of ministry was working with the many among us and those to come. We cannot forget either that as we reflect on the kaleidoscope of implications stemming from the Atonement, one such outworking is the breaking of the power of evil (Col 2:15). The rea-son Jesus did appear was to destroy the work of the devil (1 John 3:5b). And if we are the body of Christ—that is, not just allegory or image, but truly His body, His very presence on earth—then this work must continue to take place because He did it.

FINAL THOUGHTS
There is much more to understand, to learn, and to experience. Do I cherish this task? Yes, some days, and on other days, no. It is a frightening, somewhat dangerous and draining form of ministry. It is fraught with controversy and misunderstanding. Yet, what I am reminded of again and again is that the church is the only hope for the world and we as the body of Christ have the only answer to this form of universal ailment. Religion, science, medicine, psychology, and other expressions of help, though needed and useful, cannot heal a ravaged soul inhabited, vexed or oppressed by a fallen angel that chose

to rebel against the God of the universe before the beginning of known time. Restoration like this can only come from above, never from below. In John 10:10, Jesus said that He had *"come to give life and life abundant"* and this is one expression of that future life given in the now—truly it is the kingdom of God and the will of God on earth as seen and experienced in heaven. It is the seeds of Eden before Genesis 3 given in part again. There is nothing more powerful than to see a person set free to know God and follow hard after Him and His will.

My challenge and prayer is not that more would be called, but that more would listen to the call already given and trust God with the rest. I close with the prayer of Jesus' cousin for myself, our team, and any who would read this and act upon heaven's calling, for this captures the very essence of this whole ministry. From the Old King James, John the Baptist declared:

> *He must increase, but I must decrease. He that cometh from above is above all: he that is of the earth is earthly, and speaketh of the earth: he that cometh from heaven is above all* (John 3:30).

END NOTES

Chapter 1

[1]Charles Kraft, *Appropriate Christianity* (Pasadena: William Carey Library, 2005), p. 100.

[2]Jon Thompson, *Convergence* (Ontario, Canada: Sanctus Church, 2018), pp.8-9.

[3]For a summary, see "The Wesleyan Quadrilateral—Not Equilateral", by Robert G. Tuttle in *Basic United Methodist Beliefs: An Evangelical View,* James V. Heidinger II, ed. (Wilmore, Kentucky: Bristol Books, 1986), pp. 19-25).

[4]James R. Payton Jr., *Getting the Reformation Wrong* (Downers Grove, IL: IVP Academic, 2010), pp. 157-159.

[5]Charles Kraft, *Confronting Powerless Christianity* (Grand Rapids: Baker Publishing Group, Chosen Books, 2002), pp. 121-122.

[6]Paul G. Hiebert and R. Daniel Shaw, et. al., *Understanding Folk Religion* (Grand Rapids: Baker Academic, 2000), pp. 46-49.

[7] My working definition is adapted from Alister McGrath, *Evangelicalism and the Future of Christianity* (Downers Grove: Intervarsity Press, 1995), p.51.

[8]These concepts rely heavily on unpublished lectures given by Roy Matheson in 2000 at Tyndale Seminary, Toronto, Ontario.

Chapter 2

[1]Gregory Boyd, *God at War* (Downers Grove, IL: InterVarsity Press, 1997).

[2]Boyd, p. 162.

[3]Boyd, pp. 162-163.

[4]Bob Becking, *Dictionary of Deities and Demons in the Bible.* Edited by B. B. et al. Grand Rapids, MI: Eerdmans, 1999), p.925.

[5]Boyd, p. 94.

[6] K. VanDer Toorn. *Dictionary of Deities and Demons in the Bible.* Edited by B. B. Etal. Grand Rapids, MI: Eerdmans, 1999), pp. 684-686.

[7]Toorn, p. 686.

[8]See Boyd, pp.73-113 and Charles H.H. Scobie, 2003. *The Ways of Our God* (Grand Rapids, MI: Eerdmans, 2003) pp.237-243.

[9]Boyd thoroughly explores this.

[10] Daniel G. Reid, *God as Warrior* (Grand Rapids, MI: Zondervan Publishing, 1995).

[11] Claus Westermann, *The Psalms, Structure, Content and Message* (Minneapolis: Ausburg Publishing House, 1980), p.59.

[12] Reid, p. 80.

[13] Reid, pp.80-81.

[14] Mitchell Dahood, *Psalms Vol 3 (1-50), The Anchor Bible,* (Granden City; NY: Doubleday and Company, 1965), p.251.

[15] Boyd, pp. 163-164.

[16] Boyd, p.164.

[17] Victor P. Hamilton, *The Book of Genesis Chapters 1-17, The New International Commentary on the Old Testament,* (Grand Rapids, MI: Eerdmans, 1990), p.187.

[18] Scobie, p.244.

[19] John N. Oswalt, *The Book of Isaiah Chapters 1-39, The New International Commentary on the Old Testament* (Grand Rapids, MI: Eerdmans, 1986), p.320.

[20] Daniel I. Block, *The Book of Ezekiel Chapters 25-48, The New International Commentary on the Old Testament* (Grand Rapids MI: Eerdmans, 1998), p.119.

[21] Oswalt, p. 321.

[22] Boyd, p. 164.

[23] Scobie, p. 243.

[24] Boyd, p. 165.

[25] Based on unpublished notes from the Theology of Wesley course taught by Victor Shepherd at Tyndale Seminary, Toronto, Canada in 1999.

[26] Boyd, p. 178.

[27] Boyd, p. 178-179.

[28] Boyd, p. 180.

[29] David A. deSilva, *Introducing the Apocrypha: Perhaps, Message, Context and Significance* (Grand Rapids, MI: Baker Book House, 2002), p.79.

[30] deSilva, pp. 83-84.

[31] deSilva, p. 84.

Chapter 3

[1] Boyd, p. 181.

[1a] I'm indebted to Roy Matheson for the imagery in this paragraph and for many other subtle influences on my thinking based on his courses at Tyndale Seminary, Toronto, Canada.

[1b] For a more detailed explanation of this extended passage, see Robert H. Mounce, *The Book of Revelation* (revised): The New International Commentary on the New Testament (Grand Rapids: Wm. Eerdmans Publishers, 1997).

[2] Boyd, p. 184.

[3] George Eldon Ladd, *The Presence of the Future* (Grand Rapids MI: Eerdmans, 1974), p.109.

[4]Scobie, p.128.
[5]Ladd, p.122.
[6] Arthur F. Glasser, et al., *Announcing the Kingdom* (Grand Rapids MI: Baker Book House, 2003), pp. 184-185.
[7]Glasser, p. 185.
[8]Glasser, pp. 190-198.
[9]Glasser, p. 199.
[10]Ladd, p.33.
[11]Scobie, p.129.
[12]Glasser, pp. 187, 206.
[13]Glasser, p. 188.
[14]quoted in Boyd, p.185.

Chapter 4

[1]John R. Donahue, *The Gospel of Mark*. Edited by D. Harrington, J., Sacra Pagina (Collegeville, MN: The Liturgical Press, 2002), p.84.
[2]Alan R. Cole, *Mark*. Edited by L. Morris, *Tyndale New Testament Commentaries* (Grand Rapids MI: Eerdmans Publishing Company, 1993), p.144.
[3]Donahue, p. 80.
[4]Donahue, p. 80.
[5]Donahue, p. 80.
[6]William L. Lane, *The Gospel of Mark*. Edited by G. D. Fee, *The New International Commentary on the New Testament* (Grand Rapids, MI: Eerdmans, Inc., 1975) p. 74.
[7]Donahue, p. 80-81.
[8]Donahue, p. 81.
[9]Lane, p. 75.
[10]Lane, p. 114.
[11]Lane, p. 75.
[12]Lane, pp. 72-76.
[13]Cole, p.116.
[14]Lane, p. 83.
[15]Lane, p. 131.
[16]Donahue, p.162.
[17]Donahue, p.170.
[18]Lane, p.183.
[19]Lane, pp. 183-184.
[20]Donahue, p. 165.
[21]Lane, p. 184.
[22]Donahue, p. 166.

[23]Donahue, p. 166.
[24]Boyd, p. 195.
[25]Boyd, p. 197.
[26]Raymond Brown, *New Testament Essays* (Garden City, NY: Doubleday, 1967) p. 223.
[27]Boyd, p. 202.

Chapter 5

[1]Daniel, J. Harrington, *The Gospel of Matthew*, Edited by D. Harrington, J., (Sacra Pagina, Collegeville, Minnesota: The Liturgical Press, 1991), p. 123.
[2]R.T. France, *Matthew*, Edited by L. Morris, *Tyndale New Testament Commentary* (Downers Grove, IL: InterVarsity Press, 1985), p. 163.
[3]France, p. 1.
[4]Harrington, p. 121.
[5]Harrington, p. 134.
[6]France, p. 173.
[7]William Jackson, *Breakthrough Church Then and Now: Using a Conflict Model to Interpret Acts*, (Pasadena CA: Fuller Seminary, 2011), p. 71.
[8]Harrington, p. 183.
[9]Harrington, p. 183.
[10]France, pp. 208-209.
[11]Harrington, p. 183.
[12]Luke Timothy Johnson, *The Gospel of Luke*, Edited by D. J. Harrington (Collegeville, MN: The Liturgical Press, 1991), p. 181.
[13]Harrington, pp. 183-184.
[14]France, p. 209.
[15]France, pp. 209-210.
[16]Stanley Hauerwas, *Matthew* (Brazos Theological Commentary on the Bible. Grand Rapids MI: Brazos Press, 2006) p. 125.
[17]Hauerwas, p. 124.
[18]Boyd, pp. 195-196.
[19]Morris, Leon, *New Testament Theology* (Grand Rapids, MI: Zondervan Publishing House, 1986), p. 218.
[20]Morris, p. 184.
[21]Joel Green, *The New International Commentary on the New Testament: The Gospel of Saint Luke* (Grand Rapids, MI: Eerdmans, 1997) p. 187.
[22]Green, pp. 195-196.
[23]Green, p. 196.
[24]Green, p. 212.
[25]Green, p. 212.
[26]Morris, pp. 116-117.
[27]Johnson, p. 83.

[28]Johnson, p. 182.
[29]Morris, p. 244.
[30]Johnson, p. 212.
[31]Johnson, p. 214.
[32]Johnson, p. 212.
[33]Green, pp. 525-526.
[34]Clinton Arnold, *3 Crucial Questions About Spiritual Warfare* (Grand Rapids, MI: Baker Book House, 1997), pp. 79-80.
[35]Clinton Arnold, *Exorcism 101, What Can We Learn from the Way Jesus Cast out Demons?* In Christianity Today Magazine, September 3, 2001, p. 58.
[36]I first heard this illustration in a class with Roy Matheson in 2000 while at Tyndale Seminary, Toronto, Canada.

Chapter 6
[1]Morris, p. 185.
[2]C. Peter Wagner and F. Douglas Pennoyer, *Wrestling with Dark Angels* (Ventura, CA: Regal Books, 1990), p. 24.
[2a]This term was used by Roy Matheson in his class on spiritual warfare at Tyndale Seminary, Toronto, Canada in 2000.
[3]William J. Larkin, *Acts,* The IVP New Testament Commentary Series (Downers Grove, IL: InterVarsity Press, 1995), pp. 84-85.
[4]Ajith Fernando, *Acts,* The NIV Application Commentary (Grand Rapids, MI: Zondervan Publishing House, 1998), p. 204.
[5]Boyd, p. 280.
[6]F. F. Bruce, *The Book of Acts*, Edited by G. D. Fee, The New International Commentary on the New Testament. Grand Rapids, MI: Eerdmans Publishing Company, 1998), p. 171.
[7]Bruce, pp. 166-167.
[8]Larkin, pp. 193-196.
[9]I. Howard Marshall, *Acts.* Edited by L. Morris, Tyndale New Testament Commentaries. Downers Grove, IL: InterVarsity Press, 1980), p. 217.
[10]Everett F. Harrison, *Acts: The Expanding Church.* Chicago, IL: Moody Press, 1975), p. 26.
[11]Larkin, p. 244.
[12]Boyd, p. 280.
[13]Fernando, p. 444.
[14]Larkin, p. 238.
[15]Boyd, p. 278.
[16]Bruce, pp. 362-370.
[17]Wagner and Pennoyer, p. 326.

[18]Fernando, p. 515.
[19]Bruce, pp. 367-368.
[20]Quoted in Fernando, pp. 516-517.
[21]Larkin, p. 279.
[22]Larkin, p. 282.
[23]Wayne Grudem, *Systematic Theology, an Introduction to Biblical Doctrine* (Grand Rapids, MI: Zondervan, 1994), pp. 55-103.
[24] Gary S. Greig, etal., *The Kingdom and the Power* (Ventura, CA: Regal Books, 1993).
[25]Grudem, p. 1034.
[26]Grudem, pp. 1031-1042.
[27]Grudem, p. 368.
[28]Greig, p. 75.
[29]Grant R. Osborne, *The Hermeneutical Spiral: A Comprehensive Introduction to Biblical Interpretation* (Downers Grove, IL: InterVarsity Press, 1991), p. 172.
[30]Ben Witherington, *The Acts of the Apostles: A Socio-Rhetorical Commentary.* Grand Rapids, MI: Eerdmans, 1998), p. 100.

Chapter 7

[1]Margaret Y. MacDonald, *Sacra Pagina Series: Colossians and Ephesians* (Collegeville, MN: Liturgical Press, Michael Glazier, 2000), pp. 104-105.
[2]Annang Anumang, "Powers of Darkness: An Evaluation of Three Approaches to the Evil Powers in Ephesians", in Conspectus: Journal of South Africa Theological Seminary #3, 2008.
[3]Robert Moses and Alicia Mosgren, *Practices of Power: Revisiting the Principalities and Powers in the Pauline Epistles* (Minneapolis: Fortress Press, 2004), p.21.
[4]Moses and Mosgren, p. 74.
[5]Moses and Mosgren, p. 5.
[6]C. S. Lewis, *The Screwtape Letters* (New York: Macmillan, 1962), p. 3. Lewis actually wrote: "There are two equal and opposite errors into which our race can fall about the devils. One is to disbelieve in their existence. The other is to believe, and to feel an excessive and unhealthy interest in them. They themselves are equally pleased by both errors, and hail a materialist or a magician with the same delight."
[7]Paul G. Hiebert and R. Daniel Shaw, et. al., *Understanding Folk Religion* (Grand Rapids: Baker Academic, 2000), pp. 48-50.

Chapter 8

[1]David W. Bercot, et al., *A Dictionary of Early Christian Beliefs* (Peabody, MA: Hendrickson Publishers, Inc., 2000).
[2]Bercot, p. 268.
[3]Bercot, p. 268.

[4]Steven McKinion, editor, *Isaiah 1-39 Ancient Christian Commentary on Scripture: Old Testament*, Volume 10 (Downers Grove, IL: InterVarsity Press, 2004), p. 290.

[5]Bercot, p. 268.

[6]Bercot, p. 299-300.

[7]Bercot, p. 268.

[8]McKinion, p. 287.

[9]Bercot, p. 268.

[10]McKinion, p. 287.

[11]Bercot, p. 302.

[12]Bercot, p. 301.

[13]Bercot, p. 301.

[14]Bercot, p. 301.

[15]Bercot, p. 205.

[16]Bercot, p. 269.

[17]Bercot, p. 269.

[18]Bercot, p. 269.

[19]Oscar Skarsaune, *Possession and Exorcism in the Literature of the Ancient Church and the New Testament*, 2000 (Der Incarnatione Verbi, p. 32), (Accessed 3/5/08 from www.lausanne.org/nairobi-2000-overview-1.html).

[20]Skarsaune, (Der Incarnatione Verbi, p. 32).

[21]Skarsaune, (Der Incarnatione Verbi, p. 32).

[22]Skarsaune, (Der Incarnatione Verbi, p. 32).

[23]Skarsaune, (De Spectaculis, p. 26).

[24]Arnold, p. 111, and Oden, p. 282.

[25]Tormod Engelsviken, *Historical Overview Three, 2000* (Accessed 3/5/2008 from www.lausanne.org/nairobi-2000/historical-overview-3.html).

[26]Engelsviken.

[27]Engelsviken.

[27a]Bede, *Ecclesiastical History of the English People* (New York: Penguin Classics, 1991).

[28]Philip Schaff, *The Greek and Latin Creeds* Vol 2. *The Creeds of Christendom* (Grand Rapids, MI: Baker Book House, 1998), pp. 492-493.

[29]Thomas Oden, p.281.

[30]Papademetriou, George C. Greek Orthodox Archdiocese of America. 2007 (Accessed 3/3/08 from http://www.goarch.org).

[31]Engelsviken.

[32]J. P. Toner, *The Catholic Encyclopedia* (Robert Appleton Company, 1909) (Accessed 3/7/08 from http://www.newadvent.org/cathen/05711a.htm).

[33]Joseph Ratzinger, *Catechism of the Catholic Church* (New York, NY: Bantam Doubleday, Dell Publishing Group, Inc., 1995), pp. 465-466.

[34] Cardinal Medina, *Rite for Exorcism*, 1998 (Accessed 3/8/08 from www.trosch.org/chu/exorcism.htm).

Chapter 9

[1]Brian P. Levack, *Oxford Encyclopedia of the Reformation Encyclopedia of Christian Theology, Vol 1.* Edited by J.-Y. Lacoste, (New York: Oxford Press, 1996), pp.319-320.

[2]Levack, p. 319.

[3]Engelsviken.

[4]Levack, pp. 310-320.

[5]Engelsviken.

[6]Engelsviken.

[7]Benjamine Mayes, *Quotes and Paraphrases from Lutheran Pastoral Handbooks of the 16th and 17th Centuries on the Topic of Demon Possession* (Accessed 3/6/08 from http://www.angelfire.com/ny4/djw/lutherantheology.html).

[8]Frederick, S. Leahy, *Satan Cast Out:* A Study in Biblical Demonology (Carlisle, PA: The Banner of Truth Trust, 1975), pp. 113-114.

[9]M. Pesrse, *Biographical Dictionary of Evangelicals,* Edited by T. Larson (Downers Grove, IL: InterVarsity Press, 2003), p. 236.

[10]Kathleen R. Sands, *John Foxe: Exorcist* (Minister-Performed Exorcisms in Sixteenth-Century England) 2001 (Accessed 3/3/08 from http://findarticles.com/p/articles/mi_hb4706/is_200102/ai_n17277198).

[11]Levack, p.319.

[12]Engelsviken.

[13]John Warwick Montgomery, *Demon Possession* (Minneapolis, MN: Bethany Fellowship Inc., 1976).

[14]John Wesley, *Journal of John Wesley* (Chicago: Moody Press 1951) (Accessed 10/15/07 from http://www.ccel.org/ccel/wesley/journal.html).

[15]Gary S. Greig, et.al., *The Kingdom and the Power* (Ventura CA: Regal Books, 1993), p. 300.

[16]Leahy, p. 122.

[17]Leahy, p. 122-124.

[18]Geoff Thomas, *Deliverance from Demon Possession by Jesus Christ* (2008) (Accessed 3/5/08 from http://www.banneroftruth.org/pages/articles/article_detail.php?375). Lloyd-Jones, op cit, p.71.

[19]The following is a limited summary of where to find some accounts, which again are more than praxis or theological writings but actual experiences of seeing Jesus set people free. They are Anglican, Baptist, Brethren, Lutheran, Evangelical Free, working at Dallas, Fuller, Moody, Talbot and Tyndale semi-

naries (Neil T. Anderson: *The Bondage Breaker*, Fred Dickason: *Demon Possession and the Christian*, Michael Green: *I Believe in Satan's Downfall*, The Report of a Commission Convened by the Bishop of Exeter, Chuck Kraft: *Christianity with Power*, Kirk Koch: *Christian Counseling and Occultism*, Roy Matheson: *Spiritual Warfare* (unpublished lecture notes) Chuck Swindoll: *Demonism: How To Win Against the Devil*, Merrill Unger: *What Demons Can Do To Saints*, John White: (chapter 18 in *Demon Possession*). (Montgomery 1976; Unger 1976; Swindoll 1981; Matheson 2000; Koch 1978; Kraft 2002; Anderson 2001; Dickason 1987; Green 1981).

[20]Greig, p. 354. (see also *Christianity with Power* and *Confronting Powerless Christianity* (Kraft 1989, 2002).

[21]John R. Nevius, *Demon Possession* (Grand Rapids, MI: Kregel Books, 1968), and *Demon Possession and Alien Themes* (Grand Rapids MI: Kregel Books), 1983. See also Richard F. Lovelace, *Dynamics of Spiritual Life, an Evangelical Theology of Renewal* (Downers Grove, IL: InterVarsity Press, 1979), pp. 135, 139, 142.

[22]Lewis Sperry Chafer, *Demon Experiences in Many Lands* (Chicago: Moody Press, 1960).

[23]C. Peter Wagner, and F. Douglas Pennoyer, *Wrestling with Dark Angels* (Ventura, CA: Regal Books, 1990).

[24]Scarsaune.

[25]Philip Jenkins, *The Next Christendom, the Coming of Global Christianity* (New York: Oxford University Press, 2002), p.8.

[26]Wagner and Pennoyer, p. 211.

[27]Wagner and Pennoyer, p. 2.

[28]Jenkins, pp. 124-131.

[29]Jenkins, pp. 134-135.

[30]Charles Hummel, *Fire in the Fireplace: Contemporary Charismatic Renewal* (Downers Grove, IL: InterVarsity Press, 1980).

Chapter 10

[1]Graham Twelftree, *In the Name of Jesus: Exorcism among Early Christians* (Grand Rapids MI: Baker Book House, 2007) p.295.

[2]Twelftree, p.290.

[3]Gerald L. Bray, *We Believe in One God*, Edited by T. Oden. 5 vols. Vol. 1, (*Ancient Christian Doctrine*). Downers Grove, IL: IVP Academic, 2009), p.xxxiii.

[4]Paul G. Hiebert, *Spiritual Warfare and Worldview*, 2000 Accessed 10/10/2008 from http://www.lausanne.org/nairobi-2000/contemporary-trends.html.

[5]Gerry Breshears, *Three Models of Deliverance* Accessed 10/10/2008 from http://www.westernseminary.edu/papers/Faculty/gerry2.html.

⁵ᵃDavid Powlison, *Understanding Spiritual Warfare: Four Views,* Beilby and Eddy, editors (Grand Rapids, MI: Baker Academic, 2012), p.92.
⁶Millard J. Erickson, *Christian Theology* (Grand Rapids, MI: Baker Publishing Group, 1988) p. 968.
⁷Erickson, p. 968.
⁸Clinton Arnold, *The Christian and Demonization,* Accessed 10/10/2008 from http://www.westernseminary.edu/Papers/Faculty/Breshears/Arnold.doc., 2002.
⁹Sent to me in private correspondence by Charles H. Kraft.

Chapter 11
¹Neil T. Anderson, *The Bondage Breaker* 2nd ed. (Eugene, OR: Harvest House, 2000) (see also Wagner and Pennoyer).
²Anderson, p.255.
³Anderson, p.255.
⁴Anderson, pp. 255-256.
⁵Anderson, p. 256.
⁶Anderson, p. 256.
⁷Neil T. Anderson, *The Bondage Breaker* (Eugene, OR: Harvest House, 1993), p. 218.
⁸Anderson, (2000), p. 258.
⁹Anderson, pp. 259-260.
¹⁰Anderson, pp. 19-24, 31-35,187-192.
¹¹Anderson, pp. 187-192.
¹²Anderson, pp. 199-252 (see also Wagner and Pennoyer).
¹³Anderson, p. 261.
¹⁴ Anderson, (1993), p. 218.
¹⁵Anderson, p. 227.
¹⁶Anderson, pp. 226-229.
¹⁷Anderson, (2000), pp. 201-251.
¹⁸Anderson, (1993), p. 231.
¹⁹Wagner and Pennoyer, pp. 161-162.
²⁰Wagner and Pennoyer, p. 162.
²¹Wagner and Pennoyer, p. 164.
²²Charles H. Kraft, *Appropriate Christianity* (Pasadena, CA: William Carey Library, 2005), p. 100.
²³Kraft, pp. 104-106.
²⁴Charles H. Kraft, *Confronting Powerless Christianity* (Grand Rapids, MI: Baker Book House, 2002), pp. 121-122.
²⁵Kraft, p. 103.
²⁶Kraft, (2005), p. 108.
²⁷Wagner and Pennoyer, p. 165.

[28]Wagner and Pennoyer, p. 166.
[29]Derek Prince, *They Shall Expel Demons* (Grand Rapids, MI: Chosen Books, 1998), pp. 203-204.
[30]Prince, p. 205.
[31]Prince, p. 206.
[32]Prince, p. 207.
[33]Prince, p. 207.
[34]Prince, p. 207-208.
[35]Prince, p. 208-209.
[36]Prince, p. 209-210.
[37]Prince, p. 210.
[38]Prince, p. 210-211.
[39]Prince, p. 211.
[40]Prince, p. 212.
[41]Prince, p. 214.
[42]Prince, p. 213-214.
[43]Prince, p. 213-216.

Chapter 12
[1]Joseph Ratzinger, *Catechism of the Catholic Church* (New York, NY: Bantam Doubleday, Dell Publishing Group, Inc., 1995), pp. 465-466.
[2]Ratzinger, p. 255.
[3]Cardinal Medina, *Rite for Exorcism*, 1998 (Accessed 3/8/08 from www.trosch.org/chu/exorcism.htm), pp. 266-287.
[4]Medina.
[5]Peter Kreeft, *Catholic Christianity* (San Francisco: Ignatius Press, 2001), pp. 286-287.
[6]Medina.
[7]Medina. Note that the signs of cross are printed throughout the document, placed to tell the priest when to cross himself or the subject.
[8]Medina.
[9]Medina.
[10]Medina.
[11]Medina.
[12]Kreeft, pp. 289-290.
[13]Francis MacNutt, *Deliverance from Evil Spirits* (Grand Rapids, MI: Chosen Books, 1995), pp. 241-247.
[14]Charles H. Kraft, *Appropriate Christianity* (Pasadena: William Carey Library, 2005), p. 258.

Chapter 13
[1]Kraft, pp. 139-142.
[2]Kraft, p. 141.
[3]Kraft, p. 141.
[4]Kraft, pp. 141-142.
[5]Kraft, p. 142.
[6]Kraft, p. 145.
[7]Kraft, p. 150.
[8]Kraft, p. 154.
[9]Kraft, pp. 150-153.
[10]Kraft, p. 183.
[11]Kraft, pp. 185-187.
[12]Kraft, pp. 184-185.
[13]Kraft, p. 185.
[14]Kraft, p. 186.
[15]Kraft, p. 187.
[16]Kraft, p. 188.
[17]Kraft, pp. 188-189.
[18]Kraft, pp. 190-191.
[19]Kraft, p. 195.
[20]Kraft, pp. 195-196.
[21]Kraft, p. 160.
[22]Kraft, p. 167.
[23]Kraft, p. 167-168.
[24]Kraft, p. 172.
[25]Kraft, pp. 132-135.
[26]Kraft, pp. 197-198.
[27]Kraft, p. 156.
[28]Charles H. Kraft, *I Give You Authority* (Grand Rapids, MI: Chosen Books, 1997), p. 51.

Chapter 14
[1]Karl Barth, *Church Dogmatics* (Peabody, Mass.: Hendrickson Publishers, 2010), Vol 1, page 301.
[2]Marshall Shelley, *Christian Theology in Plain Language*, (Waco, Tx.: Word Books, 1985), p. 143.
[3]Gordon Fee, *Philippians*, IV New Testament Commentaries (Downers Grove: InterVarsity Press, 1999), p.95.
[4]Eugene Peterson, *The Message*, (Colorado Springs: NavPress).
[5]N.T. Wright, *Climax of the Covenant*: Christ and the Law in Pauline Theology (Minneapolis: Fortress Press, 1993), p. 84.

[6]R.T. France, *Matthew:* An Introduction and Commentary, (Grand Rapids: Wm. B. Eerdmans Pub. Co., 2007), p.99.

[7]Alan Cole, *The Gospel According to Mark: Introduction and Commentary* (Grand Rapids: Wm. B. Eerdmans Publishing Co. 1961) p. 109.

[8]Charles H. Kraft, *Appropriate Christianity* (Pasadena: William Carey Library, 2005) pp.108-109.

Chapter 15

[1]I'm indebted to J. Robert Clinton for this helpful classification of the gifts into Love, Word, and Power gifts. While other classifications have been used, these groupings seem to make practical sense as I watch the gifts in operation.

[2]J. Robert Clinton, *Spiritual Gifts*, (Camp Hill, PA: Horizon Books, 1985), pp. 88-89; Thompson, pp. 107-111

[3]Clinton, pp. 67-68; Thompson, pp. 185-196.

[4]Clinton, pp. 60-62; Thompson, pp. 203-211.

[5]Clinton, pp. 60-62; Thompson, pp. 203-211.

[6]Thompson, pp. 175-178.

[7]Clinton, pp. 69-70; Thompson, pp. 179-185.

[8]Clinton, p. 81; Thompson, pp. 218-223.

[9]Clinton, pp. 52-53; Thompson, pp. 159-161.

[10]Clinton, pp. 65-66; Thompson, pp. 162-178.

Chapter 16

[1]This outline was used by Roy Matheson in his class on spiritual warfare at Tyndale Seminary, Toronto, Canada in 2000. From unpublished notes.

[2]Clinton Arnold, *Three Crucial Questions about Spiritual Warfare* (Grand Rapids: Baker Academic, 1997), pp. 180-185.

[3]See https://www.redeemercitytocity.com/blog/2017/3/24/new-york-city-a-lab-for-the-global-church.

[4]This conversation was started for me by David Gushee, *Preparing for Christian Ministry: An Evangelical Approach* (Wheaton, IL: Victor Books, 1996), p. 275.

Chapter 17

[1]See Neil T. Anderson, *The Bondage Breaker* 2nd ed. (Eugene, OR: Harvest House, 2000), Roy Matheson, Spiritual Warfare (unpublished lecture notes, 2000), Toronto: Tyndale Seminary, and Alfred C.W. Davis, *A Theory and Practice for Christian Counseling and Inner Healing*, Oakville, Ontario Unpublished Training Course (no date).

[2]These emphases and the following ones come primarily from Alfred Davis reinforced by our growing experiences.

[3]This insight from Alfred Davis has led to our practice of seeking permission in almost all ministry-related actions. This affirms the person's participation in the process—we're not doing something *to* them, particularly against their will; we're inviting Jesus to do something *with* them.

[4]MacNutt, p. 280.

Conclusion

[1]Bill Hybels, *Courageous Leadership* (Grand Rapids, MI: Zondervan Publishing House, 2002), p. 81. Some may note that there have been concerns raised regarding Hybels' own character. However, those concerns don't change the truth of what he says here, but actually underscore how crucial character is for us as leaders.

REFERENCES CITED

Anderson, Neil T. 1991. *Winning Spiritual Warfare*. Eugene, OR: Harvest House.
———. 1993. *The Bondage Breaker*. Eugene, OR: Harvest House.
———. 2000. *The Bondage Breaker*. 2nd ed. Eugene, OR: Harvest House.
———. 2001. *Victory over the Darkness*. Ventura, CA: Regal Books.

Arnold, Clinton. 1997. *3 Crucial Questions About Spiritual Warfare*. Grand Rapids, MI: Baker Book House
———. 2001. Exorcism 101, What Can We Learn from the Way Jesus Cast out Demons? In *Christianity Today*.
———. 2002. *The Christian and Demonization*. Accessed 10/10/2008 from http://www.westernseminary.edu/Papers/Faculty/Breshears/Arnold .doc.

Becking, Bob. 1999. *Dictionary of Deities and Demons in the Bible*. Edited by B. B. et al. Grand Rapids, MI: Eerdmans.

Bercot, David W et al. 2000. *A Dictionary of Early Christian Beliefs*. Peabody, MA: Hendrickson Publishers, Inc.

Block, Daniel I. 1998. *The Book of Ezekiel Chapters 25-48, The New International Commentary on the Old Testament*. Grand Rapids MI: Eerdmans.

Bloesch, Donald G. 1988. *The Struggle of Prayer*. Colorado Springs, CO: Helmers & Howard.

Bosch, David J. 2006. *Transforming Mission, Paradigm Shifts in Theology of Mission* Maryknoll, NY: Orbis Books.

Boyd, Gregory A. 1997. *God at War*. Downers Grove, IL: InterVarsity Press.

Bray, Gerald L. 2009. *We Believe in One God*. Edited by T. Oden. 5 vols. Vol. 1, *(Ancient Christian Doctrine)*. Downers Grove, IL: IVP Academic.

Breshears, Gerry. *Three Models of Deliverance*. Accessed 10/10/2008 from http://www.westernseminary.edu/papers/Faculty/gerry2.html.

Brown, Raymond. 1967. *New Testament Essays*. Garden City, NY: Doubleday.

Bruce, F. F. 1998. *The Book of Acts*. Edited by G. D. Fee, *The New International Commentary on the New Testament*. Grand Rapids, MI: Eerdmans Publishing Company.

Bugbee, Bruce. 2005. *What You Do Best in the Body of Christ : Discover Your Spiritual Gifts, Personal Style, and God-Given Passion*. Revised and expanded ed. Grand Rapids, MI: (Barrington, IL): Zondervan ; Willow Creek Resources.

Chafer, Lewis Sperry. 1960. *Demon Experiences in Many Lands*. Chicago: Moody Press.

Clinton, J. Robert. 1993. *Unlocking Your Giftedness*. Altadena, CA: Barnabas Publishers.

Cole, Alan R. 1993. *Mark*. Edited by L. Morris, *Tyndale New Testament Commentaries*. Grand Rapids MI: Eerdmans Publishing Company.

Constantindes, Evagoras. 2003. *The Priest's Service Book*. Greece: Melissa Printing Company.

Dahood, Mitchell. 1965. *Psalms Vol 3 (1-50), The Anchor Bible*. Granden City; NY: Doubleday and Company.

Davis, Alfred C.W. n.d. *A Theory and Practice for Christian Counseling and Inner Healing*. Oakville Ontario Unpublished Training Course.

deSilva, David A. 2002. *Introducing the Apocrypha: Perhaps, Message, Context and Significance*. Grand Rapids, MI: Baker Book House.

Dickason, C. Fred 1987. *Demon Possession and the Christian*. Chicago, IL: Moody Press.

Donahue, John R. 2002. *The Gospel of Mark*. Edited by D. Harrington, J., *Sacra Pagina*. Collegeville, MN: The Liturgical Press.

Engelsviken, Tormod. *Historical Overview Three* 2000. Accessed1 3/5/2008 from www.lausanne.org/nairobi-2000/historical-overview-3.html.

Erickson, Millard J. 1988. *Christian Theology*. Grand Rapids MI: Baker Publishing Group.

Fernando, Ajith. 1998. *Acts, The Niv Application Commentary*. Grand Rapids, MI: Zondervan Publishing House.
———. 2002. *Jesus Driven Ministry*. Wheaton, IL: Crossway Books.

Flynn, Leslie B. 1974. *19 Gifts of the Spirit: Which Do You Have? Are You Using Them?* Wheaton, IL: Victor Books.

Foster, Richard J. 1992. *Prayer: Finding the Heart's True Home*. 1st ed (San Francisco): HarperSanFrancisco.

France, R.T. 1985. *Matthew*. Edited by L. Morris, *Tyndale New Testament Commentary*. Downers Grove, IL: InterVarsity Press.

Glasser, Arthur F. et al. 2003. *Announcing the Kingdom*. Grand Rapids MI: Baker Book House.

Green, Joel. 1997. *The Gospel of John*. Edited by G. D. Fee, *The New International Commentary on the New Testament*. Grand Rapids, MI: Eerdmans.

Green, Michael. 1981. *I Believe in Satan's Downfall*. Grand Rapids, MI: Eerdmans.

Greig, Gary S etal. 1993. *The Kingdom and the Power*. Ventura CA: Regal Books.

Grudem, Wayne. 1994. *Systematic Theology, an Introduction to Biblical Doctrine*. Grand Rapids MI: Zondervan.

Gushee, David. 1996. *Preparing for Christian Ministry: An Evangelical Approach* Wheaton, IL: Victor Books.

Hamilton, Victor P. 1990. *The Book of Genesis Chapters 1-17, The New International Commentary on the Old Testament*. Grand Rapids, MI: Eerdmans.

Harrington, Daniel, J. 1991. *The Gospel of Matthew*. Edited by D. Harrington, J., *Sacra Pagina*. Collegeville, Minnesota: The Liturgical Press.

Harrison, Everett F. . 1975. *Acts. The Expanding Church*. Chicago, IL: Moody Press.

Hauerwus, Stanley. 2006. *Matthew, Brazos Theological Commentary on the Bible*. Grand Rapids MI: Brazos Press.

Hiebert, Paul G. *Spiritual Warfare and Worldview*. 2000 Accessed 10/10/2008 from http://www.lausanne.org/nairobi-2000/contemporary-trends.html.

Hummel, Charles. 1980. *Fire in the Fireplace: Contemporary Charismatic Renewal*. Downers Grove, IL: InterVarsity Press.

Hybels, Bill. 2002. *Courageous Leadership*. Grand Rapids, MI: Zondervan.

Jackson, William. 2011. Breakthrough Church Then and Now Using a Conflict Model to Interpret Acts. Pasadena CA: Fuller Seminary.

Jenkins, Philip. 2002. *The Next Christendom, the Coming of Global Christianity*. New York: Oxford University Press.

Johnson, Luke Timothy. 1991. *The Gospel of Luke*. Edited by D. J. Harrington. Collegeville, MN: The Liturgical Press.

Koch, Kurt E. and Alfred Lechler 1978. *Occult Bondage and Deliverance*. Grand Rapids, MI: Kregal Publications.

Kraft, Charles H. 1989. *Christianity with Power*. Ann Arbor MI: Servant Publications.
———. 1992. *Defeating Dark Angels*. Ventura: Regal Books.
———. 1997 . *I Give You Authority*. Grand Rapids, MI: Chosen Books.
———. *Contemporary Trends in the Treatment of Spiritual Conflict in the Mission of the Church*. 2000 (Accessed 10/10/2008 from http://www.lausanne.org/nairobi-2000/contemporary-trends.html).
———. 2002. *Confronting Powerless Christianity*. Grand Rapids, MI: Baker Book. House
———. 2005. *Appropriate Christianity*. Pasadena, CA: William Carey Library.

Kreeft, Peter. 2001. *Catholic Christianity*. San Francisco: Ignatius Press.

Ladd, George Eldon. 1974. *The Presence of the Future*. Grand Rapids MI: Eerdmans.

Lane, William L. 1975. *The Gospel of Mark.* Edited by G. D. Fee, *The New International Commentary on the New Testament* Grand Rapids, MI: Eerdmans.

Larkin, William J. 1995. *Acts, The IVP New Testament Commentary Series.* Downers Grove, IL: InterVarsity Press.

Leahy, Frederick, S. 1975. *Satan Cast Out.* Carlisle, PA: The Banner of Truth Trust .

Levack, Brian P. 1996. *Oxford Encyclopedia of the Reformation Encyclopedia of Christian Theology Vol 1.* Edited by J.-Y. Lacoste, *Oxford Encyclopedia of the Reformation Encyclopedia of Christian Theology.* New York: Oxford Press.

Lovelace, Richard F. 1979. *Dynamics of Spiritual Life, an Evangelical Theology of Renewal.* Downers Grove, IL: InterVarsity Press.

MacNutt, Francis. 1995. *Deliverance from Evil Spirits.* Grand Rapids, MI: Chosen Books.

Marshall, Howard I. 1980. *Acts.* Edited by L. Morris, *Tyndale New Testament Commentaries.* Downers Grove, IL: InterVarsity Press.

Matheson, Roy. 2000. Spiritual Warfare (unpublished lecture notes). Toronto: Tyndale Seminary.

Mayes, Benjamine. *Quotes and Paraphrases from Lutheran Pastoral Handbooks of the 16th and 17th Centuries on the Topic of Demon Possession (*Accessed 3/6/08 from http://www.angelfire.com/ny4/djw/lutherantheology.html).

McKinion, Steven, editor, *Isaiah 1-39 Ancient Christian Commentary on Scripture:* Old Testament, Volume 10. Downers Grove, IL: InterVarsity Press, 2004.

Medina, Cardinal. *Rite for Exorcism.* 1998 (Accessed 3/8/08 from www.trosch.org/chu/exorcism.htm).

Montgomery, John Warwick. 1976. *Demon Possession.* Minneapolis, MN: Bethany Fellowship Inc.

Morris, Leon. 1986. *New Testament Theology.* Grand Rapids, MI: Zondervan Publishing House.

Nevius, John R. 1968. *Demon Possession*. Grand Rapids, MI: Kregel Books.
————. 1983. *Demon Possession and Alien Themes*. Grand Rapids MI: Kregel Books.

Osborne, Grant R. 1991. *The Hermeneutical Spiral: A Comprehensive Introduction to Biblical Interpretation*. Downers Grove, IL: InterVarsity Press.

Oswalt, John N. 1986. *The Book of Isaiah Chapters 1-39, The New International Commentary on the Old Testament.* Grand Rapids, MI: Eerdmans.

Papademetriou, George C. *Greek Orthodox Archdiocese of America.* 2007 (Accessed 3/3/08 from http://www.goarch.org).

Pesrse, M. 2003. *Biographical Dictionary of Evangelicals.* Edited by T. Larson. Downers Grove, IL: InterVaristy Press.

Prince, Derek 1998. *They Shall Expel Demons*. Grand Rapids, MI: Choosen Books.

Ratzinger, Joseph. 1995. *Catechism of the Catholic Church*. New York, NY: Bantam Doubleday, Dell Publishing Group, Inc.

Reid, Daniel G. 1995. *God as Warrior.* Grand Rapids, MI: Zondervan Publishing.

Sands, Kathleen R. *John Foxe: Exorcist (Minister-Performed Exorcisms in Sixteenth-Century England)* 2001 (Accessed 3/3/08 from http://findarticles.com/p/articles/mi_hb4706/is_200102/ai_n17277198).

Schaff, Philp. 1998. *The Greek and Latin Creeds Vol 2. The Creeds of Christendom.* Grand Rapids, MI: Baker Book House.

Scobie, Charles H.H. 2003. *The Ways of Our God.* Grand Rapids, MI: Eerdmans.

Skarsaune, Oscar. *Possession and Exorcism in the Literature of the Ancient Church and the New Testament.* 2000 (Accessed 3/5/08 from www.lausanne.org/nairobi-2000-overview-1.html).

Swindoll, Charles R. 1981. *Demonism: How to Win against the Devil.* Portland, OR: Multnomah Press.

Thomas, Geoff. *Deliverance from Demon Possession by Jesus Christ.* 2008 (Accessed 3/5/08 from http://www.banneroftruth.org/pages/articles/article_detail.php?375)
.

Toner, J.P. *The Catholic Encyclopedia.* Robert Appleton Company 1909 (Accessed 3/7/08 from http://www.newadvent.org/cathen/05711a.htm).

Toorn, K. Van Der. 1999. *Dictionary of Deities and Demons in the Bible.* Edited by B. B. Etal. Grand Rapids, MI: Eerdmans.

Twelftree, Graham. 2007. *In the Name of Jesus: Exorcism among Early Christians.* Grand Rapids MI: Baker Book House .

Unger, Merrill F. . 1976 *What Demons Can Do to Saints.* Chicago, IL: Moody Press.

Wagner, C. Peter. 1992. *Prayer Shield : How to Intercede for Pastors, Christian Leaders, and Others on the Spiritual Frontlines, The Prayer Warrior Series.* Ventura, CA: Regal Books.
———. 1994. *Your Spiritual Gifts Can Help Your Church Grow.* 15th anniversary ed. Ventura, CA: Regal Books.
———. 1995. *Wagner Houts Inventory of Spiritual Gifts.* Winfield, BC: The International Centre for Leadership Development and Evangelism.

Wagner, C. Peter and F. Douglas Pennoyer. 1990. *Wrestling with Dark Angels.* Ventura, CA: Regal Books.

Wesley, John *Journal of John Wesley.* Moody Press 1951 (Accessed 10/15/07 from http://www.ccel.org/ccel/wesley/journal.html).

Westermann, Claus 1980. *The Psalms, Structure, Content and Message.* Minneapolis: Ausburg Publishing House.

Witherington, Ben. 1998. *The Acts of the Apostles: A Socio-Rhetorical Commentary.* Grand Rapids, MI: Eerdmans.

Jon Thompson

ABOUT THE AUTHOR

Jon Thompson serves as the Senior Pastor at Sanctus Church (formerly C4 Church), just outside of Toronto, Canada. He has been on staff for more than 20 years. Sanctus is a regional church with a community of over 3,000 people that gather in multiple locations in the Greater Toronto area. Under Jon's leadership, Sanctus is characterized by dynamic Biblical teaching, vibrant community groups, compelling media, and powerful times in worship.

Jon has a Master of Theological Studies from Tyndale Seminary, Toronto and a Doctorate of Missiology from Fuller Seminary, California. Jon is husband to his wife Joanna and father to three kids—Hannah, Emma, and Noah.

ALSO AVAILABLE FROM
JON THOMPSON

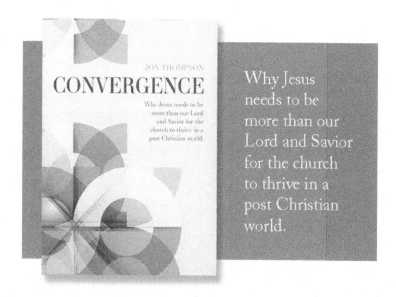

Convergence is when three unexpected things come together. Spiritual gifts, spiritual disciplines and unusual works of the Spirit (revival) converge to form the authentic Christian life. What we will explore in this book is how Jesus modeled these three factors in convergence. Jesus Christ is not just Savior and Lord but also our Model, and that truth changes everything for you personally, your church and the area God has placed you.

Available on amazon.com

Made in the USA
Monee, IL
23 September 2021